The Ideal Life: 50 and Over

by
Gordon Elliott
and
Mary Elliott

We wish to thank the following persons who have made this book possible: Gay Gervin for the help on finance, Thomas Smallwood for assistance with the legal chapter, all who participated in our mini-survey and to our editors, especially Patricia Pingry, who aided us so skillfully.

ISBN 0-89542-081-3 595

Copyright © MCMLXXX by Mary and Gordon Elliott
All rights reserved
Printed in the United States of America

Published by Ideals Publishing Corporation
11315 Watertown Plank Road
Milwaukee, Wisconsin 53226
Published simultaneously in Canada

Contents

Preface 7
Introduction 9
Your Health Is What You Make of It 13
Medicare, Medicaid, and Private Insurance 49
Ways to Have Money 67
The Ideal Home for You 115
How the Law Can Serve You 135
Second Careers 153
Getting a Job 169
Families 193
Retirement: The Best Time 211

For Janet and Stephen.

Preface

We join over fifty million other Americans who are indebted to Dr. Ethel Percy Andrus, founder of the American Association of Retired Persons and the National Retired Teachers Association. Her pronouncement, "Age is not a defeat, but a victory," is the rallying point for these dynamic associations. It is doubtful that any of the country's fifty-and-over group have not been touched in some way by the associations' accomplishments on behalf of mature persons.

My appreciation is more personal, for it was my good fortune to work closely with Dr. Andrus for several enlightening years as editorial consultant on her four magazines, *Modern Maturity, NRTA Journal, AARP International,* and *Dynamic Maturity.* For me it was a learning experience. Out of such a stimulating background comes this book's wide selection of

The Ideal Life

tips and ideas on how to head into an ideal life once you have accumulated fifty years' worth of living.

The first tip to be passed along is that you maintain a good sense of humor and positive attitude throughout your next fifty years. Dr. Andrus was fond of recalling the story about the old Yankee captain who encouraged his men, "Now, my hearties, you've got a tough battle ahead of you. You must dig in and fight like the heroes you are until your powder runs out, and then run for it. Because I'm a bit lame, I'll get started now." If your planning for the years ahead has been a little lame, the second tip is to get started now.

Introduction

And therefore, if a man lives many years, let him enjoy all of them.

   Sometime around the age of fifty when you have shooed the last child from the family door with his degree in hand and probably rice in his shoes, you call out happily to him, "Write when you find work!" and close the door firmly, very firmly. From here on in, you are free, emancipated, and almost a member of a new leisure class. But not quite. In order to join those ranks who have second careers, comfortable incomes and happy lives in the twenty-five or thirty years ahead, you have some serious planning to do. And right now is not a moment too soon.

   You have arrived at a time when your place in the work force is stable, and there is still opportunity to evaluate, review, predict, and possibly change your

The Ideal Life

financial planning. Because of confidence in your ability to make appropriate decisions, you will want to answer a number of questions now: Do we have enough money to retire in the next ten or fifteen years? Where will we live? And, what on earth will we do to fill all of those years in the future? And what can be so "ideal" about all that?

Life after fifty really can be an ideal life, but preparation now is essential. In our investigation for the writing of this book, we decided to conduct a mini-survey of persons fifty and over as to what they considered to be the ideal life after fifty. Throughout this book, we try to share their answers with you, for we believe our own views and plans can benefit from the thoughts and experiences of others. For instance, the response of Rosalie Fladoos seems to sum up an ideal life for all of us.

"From a practical point of view, the ideal life on this good earth, after crossing the half-century threshold, is to remain active in mind and body, to thrive on being busy and involved. Live each day to its fullest, realizing it can never be relived, and that each morning we awaken to a miracle.

"After fifty, life opens a myriad of new interests at a time when one's ability is at its most excellent and experienced state, and a person is at a period of highest prosperity. What better criteria and setting to make things happen? The challenge is for the young at heart, you and me!

Introduction

"Retirement arrives at a prophetic interim in our lives. It presents us an abundance of new free time—not that we've asked for it, but because of the law of nature. The precious child-rearing years and family life responsibilities are over. The children are grown and recently married; home seems stark and quiet. Suddenly Mom and Dad realize they need one another more than ever. Their love deepens as they pick up where they were decades ago—as a couple alone—determined to conquer the world! This honeymoon is destined to last an eternity.

"New interests and activities bolster and elevate the heart and soul. The options available are limitless, and now is the time to fulfill your life's dreams. If working is your bag, but you are tired of the same old routine, start a *new* career—at the bottom if you prefer. Listen to your own impulses, and do what makes you happy. You've learned to see things as they are by now, not as you'd like them to be. Decide what rouses you into activity and then take pursuit—be it golfing, swimming, fishing, dancing, hiking, camping, flying, culture, science, reading, handicrafts, traveling, etc. The four corners of the earth and the sky are the limit. If your own beloved America and even your home state are foreign to you, start now to explore them a day or weekend at a time via motorbike, bicycle, bus or buffalo.

"If you aren't the type to venture far from home, look to your own community. Become involved. You may enjoy a part-time job. Babysitting is a joy, and

The Ideal Life

assuredly it's a challenge. Volunteer work is rewarding—at the church, hospitals, schools, for civic or group organizations. You are sorely needed in so many ways, and you will brighten the lives of so many people—the elderly and ill, the young, the handicapped. In bringing sunshine to their lives, you bring it to your own.

"Enjoy your lifelong hobbies, and begin new ones. Keep in top physical condition through exercise and participation in sports . . . take lessons in your favorites, or practice and strive to improve the ones you like best. Take long walks and study the birds, flowers, shrubs and trees. Go to auctions, concerts, plays. Take adult education courses in subjects that interest you most and see how mentally stimulating they are.

"Grandchildren are the crowning glory of one's life. They are ever radiating love, joy, trust, and priceless memories and chuckles to mull over time and time again. We have the world in our hands, and God's love in our hearts. The moment to live and to share is now. What are we waiting for?"

Any successful retirement must be framed with a state of good mental and physical health and financial security. Within this framework, all things are possible. It is the intention of this book to pass along helpful information as well as new ideas and experiences of others which we hope will aid you in establishing the retirement lifestyle that pleases you most: the lifestyle for your own ideal life after fifty.

Your Health Is What You Make of It

"If we can keep people from withdrawing into seclusion with their aches and pains by helping them stretch their health maintenance dollars, we will have saved them for an active, useful life with dignity, independence and purpose." That was the motivation of Dr. Ethel Percy Andrus in founding the National Retired Teachers Association and the American Association of Retired Persons. Through these associations, Dr. Andrus devised plans for members to buy medications under generic names, obtain full-line insurance policies, and created a worldwide travel program to help retired persons remain active. Remaining active at any age is dependent on remaining healthy, and this qualification was voiced by many respondents to our personal survey. One of those surveyed was Casey Corrigan of Des Moines who wrote:

"The ideal life after fifty for a simple country boy from Hannibal, Missouri, would have to include,

The Ideal Life

above all else, having good health. This, of course, includes good health for both man and wife, since there is no ideal life anywhere if one has no loving wife with whom to bicker.

"So, having good health, where do we settle down for the second fifty years? Hawaii? The Ozarks? Vermont? Paris? None of these. We stay right here where all our old friends and enemies are. At my age, shy lad that I am, I do not make friends easily, so I take to heart the advice of Polonius to Laertes: 'The friends thou hast, and their adoption tried, Grapple them to thy soul with hoops of steel . . . '

"Now, having reached fifty, being in good health and having a loving wife, what else do I need? Perhaps a few grandchildren within a few blocks, or even a few miles. The ideal life after fifty would include the frequent companionship of grandchildren, which means, of course, a son or daughter or two in the vicinity.

"Oh, yes, a dollop or two of money would also be nice. Not necessarily a barrel of money, just enough to eat, drink and be merry and provide your companion with enough credit at the local shops.

"That's about it. Health, old friends, new grandchildren, a modest roof over one's head, a loaf of bread and a jug of wine on the table, a modicum of money for such necessities as a season ticket to the ballpark and the bowling lanes. What more could one ask? I checked with my companion, Mary, who is also on

Your Health

this side of fifty, and she agrees."

We also agree with Casey that health is the most important consideration for any time in life. Optimum physical and mental health have many facets: exercise, adequate rest, sound nutrition, calorie counting, wise use of drugs, and control over unhealthful habits. The years stretching from the forties through the sixties are the prime years of life. These are the years in which to evaluate your health habits, cultivating new ones, such as healthy diets, and eliminating or controlling unhealthy ones, such as smoking; these are the years also in which to develop a daily disciplined physical fitness program. One physician says that if you will take care of your body in the fifties, the cost of your medical care in the sixties will be sharply reduced. What holds us back from getting into a good fitness program is largely plain old inertia.

With the exception of heredity, most of the factors that contribute to longevity are within our control. *Healthy People,* the Surgeon General's Report on Health Promotion and Disease Prevention, states: "While not yet definitely proven, the role of exercise in preventing heart disease is attractive and plausible. An example of the growing evidence supporting the association between exercise and reduced cardiovascular risk comes from a study of 17,000 Harvard alumni. The physically active among them had significantly fewer heart attacks than the more sedentary. Those who expended less than 500 calories a week in exer-

The Ideal Life

cise were found to develop heart disease at about twice the rate of those expending 2,000 or more calories a week (approximately 100 calories are used for each mile run or walked). Regular, vigorous exercise was found to reduce risk of heart disease independently of other risk factors, such as cigarette smoking or high blood pressure."

Within the past twelve years, Americans have become more interested in good health and physical fitness. A survey taken in 1977 reported that half of American adults said they exercised regularly to keep fit. Millions participate in tennis, swimming, skiing, bicycling, calisthenics, or other forms of exercise.

Before embarking on any exercise program, however, have a complete physical checkup, including a treadmill stress check. Depending on the results of your test, vigorous sports may or may not be ruled out for you, particularly if you (1) had a recent heart attack, (2) are an uncontrollable diabetic, (3) have a history of internal bleeding, or (4) are fifty pounds or more overweight.

If, however, the doctor gives you a clean bill of health and you have been physically active throughout your first fifty years, by all means continue with your tennis, jogging, racquet-ball, or whatever sport you enjoy. If you have led a more sedentary life, consult with your physician about an exercise program best for you.

Your Health

What Kind of Exercise Is Best?

Many exercise programs are available, but not all condition you in the same way. Body changes occur only with specific types of exercise and when certain conditions are met. Isometrics and calisthenics can improve strength, flexibility, and muscle tone; but they will not increase heart and lung capacity. Many popular sports are not taxing enough for the heart, because they are punctuated by long pauses or rest periods. The best exercises are rhythmic, continuous, and vigorous.

If exercise is to be truly beneficial to your circulatory system, it must meet the following standards; if one of them is missing, little conditioning will occur:

1) Exercise should be gradual and progressive. Start by pushing the body just beyond the point of comfort, but not to the point of fatigue. When you are just beginning, experts recommend periods of rest. Don't strain your body suddenly. By building up gradually, your cardiovascular system is challenged to handle increased physical demands more efficiently.
2) The duration of exercise should be for at least twenty to thirty minutes, exclusive of warm-up and cool-down periods.
3) Exercise at least three times weekly, on alternate days. This allows the body time to recover between bouts of exercise. Exercising only on week-

The Ideal Life

ends could be dangerous and isn't enough to be beneficial.

4) Endurance exercise is needed to elevate the pulse rate, force deep breathing, and promote perspiration. This is the application of the "overload" principle which states that exercise must be strenuous enough to use sixty to seventy-five percent of the lungs' maximum oxygen capacity.

5) Ongoing exercise is cumulative and gains are quickly lost. If you tire of or become bored with one program, don't stop exercising. Change to a different type of exercise. After seven months of exercising, you'll have a fifteen to twenty percent increase in cardiovascular fitness.

6) Choose a program tailored to you. Don't force yourself into the water if you hate to swim. A lot of costly equipment or membership in a health spa is not necessary either.

7) Include a warm-up and a cooling-down period. Five to ten minutes before and after strenuous exercise are essential to allow the body to prepare for and then recover from exercise bouts. Try light calisthenics, stretching exercises, or slow walking or light jogging.

Some Fun Exercises

Walking is probably the easiest way to begin a physical fitness program. Begin by walking around the block, perhaps, if you think that's as far as you can

Your Health

make it; but increase the distance gradually until a daily brisk walk equals at least two miles. Walking not only improves muscle tone, breathing, and the circulatory system, but provides for mental and emotional peace of mind. When walking, we are able to see the natural world at leisure and close up. The same route walked daily is as ever-changing as the seasons.

Running has become a national obsession. Ten percent of American men between the ages of twenty to forty-four run and many are joined by wives and girl friends. Some people jog a specified one-and-a-half to two miles daily. Others have graduated to long distance running, gradually entering the marathon distance. More and more of the over-fifty age group are even finding the competition of races fun. Most organized runs are divided into age groups.

The thought of running even two miles may be overwhelming to some people who have scarcely moved from their easy chair for years. But if brisk walking suddenly seems tame, venture out into the world of jogging, beginning by running part way and walking the rest.

Swimming is probably the most perfect exercise and one many people enjoy all of their lives. Swimming uses every muscle of the body and is a great way to slim down and tighten sagging muscles. Lake swimming is invigorating, but the local YMCA offers swimming year-round—an advantage running does not have in the northern climates. Competition is also

The Ideal Life

available in this sport, as the AAU (American Athletic Union) offers a masters program for various ages.

Bicycling is a good exercise for legs and ankles. Like walking, it also affords a delightful view of nature at close range. With the three-wheelers available, bicycling makes a great exercise for the older person who might combine a trip to the market with exercise.

Square Dancing is a sociable, fun type of exercise. Many community and church groups offer square dancing; and this not only provides exercise, but a way to meet new people with similar interests.

Sustained exercise improves the efficiency of the heart and increases the amount of oxygen the body can utilize in a given period of time. The type of physical activity probably most beneficial to the cardiovascular system is sometimes called aerobic exercise which requires large amounts of oxygen for energy production. Examples include brisk walking, climbing stairs, running, cross-country skiing, and swimming. A reasonable goal for any individual ought to be fifteen or thirty minutes of exercise at least three times a week. A beginner should start slowly. Such activity may cause the blood pressure of a hypertensive individual to fall an average of ten points and may also lower serum cholesterol. Vigorous exercise can also reduce weight. Walking or running a mile a day or swimming a quarter of a mile daily can lead to a weight reduction of more than ten pounds a year.

Your Health

Most older people, however, do not exercise regularly. Yet suitable exercise programs can help in many ways: by replacing fat with muscle; in maintaining good posture and muscular strength required for efficient movement in daily activities; by improving joint mobility for the better balance skills needed for safety; and in stimulating cardiovascular endurance. But how does the individual find a program? If you are not the type who likes to do things alone, or if you simply lack motivation, look into fitness programs in your community. Hospitals, clinics, or your local YMCA may offer low-cost or free exercise programs staffed by trained specialists. If you'd rather join a health spa, be sure it is a reputable one and only sign a short-term contract.

A Few Words of Encouragement

A common mistake people make in the early weeks of an exercise program is to expect startling results right away. Experts stress that at least six weeks are needed for you to notice a real increase in your stamina; it takes longer for exercise to become enjoyable. Sounds like a lot of work? It is, but it can also be a lot of fun, and may be the tonic you need.

To give you some help in beginning, two government booklets published by the President's Council on Physical Fitness include a series of graded programs, charts, and lists of exercise. For *Adult Physical Fitness* (#040-000-00026-7), 70¢, and *An Introduction to Physical Fitness* (#017-000-00122-1), 60¢, send check

The Ideal Life

or money order to Superintendent of Documents, U.S. Government Printing Office, Washington, D.C. 20402.

Most Worn Parts Can Be Fixed Up

Be on the lookout for certain health conditions that go hand in hand with the middle years. The good news is that many of these complaints aren't serious if they are caught and treated in time.

Eyes after age forty don't function as well for near vision, because eye lenses become less able to focus. This condition, called *presbyopia,* can easily be corrected with reading glasses or bifocals.

Cataracts, a cloudiness in the eye lens that interferes with vision, may develop quickly or over a number of years. Usual signs are hazy vision, double vision, or difficulty seeing at night. Special eyeglasses may help initially, but surgery is usually needed in one or both eyes. Once, cataract surgery involved a lengthy and painful recuperation period; but today, with the advent of new techniques for lens removal, the patient can be fitted with glasses or contact lenses and resume most usual activities soon after surgery. A recently developed technique, lens implantation, eliminates the need for special glasses or contact lenses.

Glaucoma, loss of vision associated with increased pressure on the eye, can lead to blindness if left untreated. Caught and treated promptly, however, it needn't cause serious vision loss. Because "open-angle" glaucoma, the most common form, is usually

Your Health

painless, tests to detect the condition are most important. Vision that is lost can't be restored. Treatment involves medication and, in some cases, surgery.

For diagnosis and treatment of these and other eye conditions before they become advanced, visit your ophthalmologist regularly.

Ears. Look for these signs of gradual hearing loss: Do you ask people to repeat what they say? Do you turn up the volume of the radio or TV? Do you withdraw from conversation at social occasions? If any or all of these signs are present, visit an otologist. Even if you aren't experiencing hearing loss, a hearing checkup once every two years is recommended.

Before visiting a hearing aid dealer, consult your doctor first. These dealers usually aren't qualified to diagnose. If you buy a hearing aid, ask for a thirty-day trial period: Aids take getting used to and often need readjustment.

Teeth, in the middle years as gums recede, become more susceptible to surface decay. The following practices help counteract decay: using a flouride mouthwash if flouride is not in your drinking water supply; brushing and using dental floss at least once a day, preferably before bedtime; and limiting foods with high sugar content.

Periodontal (gum) disease, affecting two in three middle-aged Americans, is easy to control if detected early. Pyorrhea, the most common form, starts with

The Ideal Life

inflamed gums and occasional bleeding. Gums then begin to recede and roots are exposed. Eventually, teeth loosen and are lost. To help prevent pyorrhea, use dental floss daily and have hardened plaque (tartar) removed by your dentist every four to six months. If periodontal disease becomes advanced, surgery may be needed.

The procedures outlined above *can* save your teeth. The alternative is a full set of dentures.

Feet. Aching feet are no laughing matter. They can bring on fatigue, leg and back pain, and generally make us feel miserable. But foot problems are frequently ignored until they become unbearable.

Corns, calluses, plantar warts, excessive sweating, and itching may all be signs of foot problems. Feet are also indicators of disease. Arthritis, diabetes, kidney disease, or heart trouble are sometimes diagnosed first in the feet. Signs to look for are dry skin, brittle nails, numbness, and discoloration.

To keep your feet in good working order, use them as much as possible, bathe and powder them daily, buy well-fitted shoes, and, if you notice any signs listed in the above paragraph, see your podiatrist. Most foot problems can be corrected.

We Are What We Eat

The American Medical Association believes that a great deal of illness can be prevented by individual

Your Health

eating habits. One medical authority even went further than the AMA when he flatly stated that thirty percent of Americans die because of overeating. Small wonder that food news seems to bombard us on all sides: claims praising a new "miracle" diet, headlines frightening us of cancer-causing agents in certain foods, and the glad tidings of the benefits of fiber in the diet. There is no other topic so full of fallacies and so dominated by fads.

It doesn't require a genius to figure out how much harder the heart must work with every excess pound of weight, because each pound has many miles of blood vessels. Recent research has shown that each man, woman and child in the United States consumes 125 pounds of fat and 100 pounds of sugar annually! I well remember my first visit to a new doctor. The nurse put me on the scale, adjusted the weights, looked at the chart and said, "Let's see, with your weight, you should be nine feet, seven inches tall." Perhaps I came by this weight by parental example. I remember my mother sizing up my dad and admonishing, "Lem, it's about time you start keeping an eye on your beltline." Dad, patting his protrusion with both hands, responded, "I agree, Dot, and I am. I'm keeping it right out here where I can see it."

To the overweight person, however, obesity is no laughing matter. And our weight is one thing we can control through exercise and sensible diet. We are all interested in avoiding weight gain and will agree that

The Ideal Life

"it takes a lean horse to run a long race." Experiments with laboratory animals who have been fed a sharply reduced caloric diet during their early lives have shown an increased lifespan of from thirty to fifty percent. Whether this would also be true of humans has not been proven; but it is known that overeating has become a dominant public health burden with about twenty percent of all adults in the United States seriously overweight and preventing their own optimal health and longevity.

The Department of Agriculture's nutritionists report that "men and women fifty-five to seventy-five years old need 150 to 200 fewer calories per day than when they were thirty-five to fifty-five, but their needs for essential nutrition remain the same and so does the need for minerals and vitamins. It is more important than ever for each food to do double duty; there is not much room for low-nutrient, high-caloric food."

Yet many Americans do not eat well balanced diets. Why? Often they live alone, dislike cooking, snack on the empty calories of sugar products, or consume too much alcohol. Good diets, for those who eat alone or prefer not to cook, take some conscious effort; those who drink the empty calories in alcohol, too, must take steps to eat nutritious meals. Those who eat between meals might make certain that they snack on nutritious raisins or fresh, crunchy vegetables.

Diet is one of the things we can change if we want to, and good nutrition need not be more expensive.

Your Health

The Department of Agriculture estimates that a couple on a moderate income spends about thirty percent of their budget on food. This percentage could be reduced with a home garden or freezing and canning fruits and vegetables purchased from farms and orchards. This is not only a more economical diet, but the U.S. Committee on Nutrition and Human Needs advises that foods from the garden have a greater nutrient content than their processed counterparts. "Garden foods" differ from the fresh vegetables and fruit purchased from the supermarket. The same government committee has determined that quick-frozen foods may be more nutritious than the fresh ones from the local grocery store, due to inefficient marketing, shipping, and storage procedures.

As long as a balanced diet is maintained, there need to be few changes in eating habits as we age. There will be changes in the amount of food consumed and the frequency of eating because of metabolic changes which occur in the aging process and the fact that caloric intake should be consistent with the decrease of activity.

Just what is a balanced diet? The foods necessary in our daily diets for good fitness and health are the following four groups:

1) *Milk, cheese, and other dairy products.* The milk group is the daily source of calcium, especially important as a person ages. Milk products with their calcium are needed to keep bones and teeth strong. Approxi-

The Ideal Life

mately two or more servings a day are required.

2) *Meat, fowl, seafood, eggs, and protein alternatives,* such as beans and peanut butter. These foods are the primary sources of protein, iron, thiamin, riboflavin, and niacin. At least two servings a day are recommended, but care should be taken to balance the need for protein against the growing evidence of an unhealthy fatty diet.

The over-consumption of fat, along with sugar, salt, cholesterol, and alcohol has been related to six of the ten leading causes of death: heart disease, cancer, cerebrovascular disease, diabetes, arteriosclerosis, and cirrhosis of the liver. There is also a strong relationship between fat intake and the incidence of breast and colon cancer. The latter has a high correlation to the consumption of meat. According to the National Cancer Institute, it is not clear whether the meat itself or its fat content is the real contributing factor.

High levels of fat, saturated fat, and cholesterol most often enter our diets through the consumption of red meat in our pursuit of protein. People from countries such as Japan, where the meat intake is low, or who, for reasons of religion, do not eat meat have considerably less breast and colon cancer. One gerontologist is of the opinion that cream, fat bacon and fat meats of all kinds should not appear on the menu. He also would not have his patients eat more than two eggs a week.

At least two servings a day from this group are

Your Health

recommended; but care and good sense should be taken to balance the need for protein against the growing evidence of an unhealthy fatty diet. Choose lean meats, supplementing them with fat-free legumes.

3) *Bread, cereal, and other grain products.* These foods are high in the B vitamin complex and provide energy in the form of carbohydrates; and the bulk of whole grain foods satisfies the appetite quickly without excessive calories, making them great for dieters.

When choosing from this group, keep in mind that refined grain and cereals have less nutritive value than do the unrefined ones. Rice is probably the most nutritious of the grain products. Of the many types of rice available, brown rice retains the most value, then parboiled or converted rice, and last of all the common white "enriched" rice and instant rice. The old-fashioned hot cereals have excellent nutritional value, although instant and quick hot cereals have fewer nutrients than the longer cooking variety. Choose from wheat (not cream of wheat), rye, and oat whole-grain cereals. The popular granola really offers a high caloric intake for the amount of nutrients that it provides. Choose it only if you do not need to watch your weight. At least four servings a day are recommended from this group.

4) *Vegetables and fruits.* These are excellent sources of vitamins and minerals; it is especially important to eat those that are high in vitamin C and vitamin A. Citrus fruits and juices, strawberries, persimmons, tomatoes,

The Ideal Life

and even guavas are excellent sources of vitamin C. For vitamin A, the red and yellow vegetables are best, that is, carrots, tomatoes, squash, and sweet potatoes.

If fruits and vegetables are overcooked, vitamins can be lost. And for snacks or for those watching their weight, raw fruits and vegetables are ideal. The high water content of fruit and vegetables satisfies the appetite more quickly than do foods high in sugar. Vegetables also provide the fiber so necessary for the gastrointestinal tract; and recent studies indicate they may also lower blood cholesterol. Include at least four servings a day of this group in your daily diet.

Other Considerations

Special diets may be necessary for persons with diabetes, heart disease or hypertension. Diets of older persons are likely to be deficient in calcium, iron, and fiber; so the law of percentages indicates that most people over the age of fifty should pay special attention to the diet in regard to these needs.

Taste and smell change with age and may diminish the enjoyment of food, creating problems in maintaining a well-balanced diet. Absence of teeth (sixty percent of the over sixty-five group have this problem), difficulties with dentures, and gum disease can affect good diet.

Salt has been found to cause and increase blood pressure, creating hypertension in some individuals; whereas others do not seem to be genetically suscep-

Your Health

tible. Forty percent of older persons are hypertensive. To avoid unintentional salt intake, read all labels on food to determine the additives.

Recently, so-called "health foods" have been touted as the ultimate in nutrition. The U.S. Agricultural Research Service disagrees: "There is no scientific evidence that plants grown with only organic fertilizers or meat from animals raised on only organically fertilized feed have greater nutritive value than our regular food produced by the usual agricultural methods." There is evidence, however, that most "health food" is more expensive than other foods.

Tips That Take a Swipe at Inflation

Health care costs are rising alarmingly. To keep medical expenses under control and still be sure you receive the best available care, act upon some of the following money-saving tips:

Doctor bills. The once sacrosanct complete annual physical has come under fire lately as being expensive and unnecessary. One leading health clinic advocates a complete annual physical for those over sixty, five exams between fifty-one and sixty, and four exams between forty-one and fifty. In between, of course, seek medical attention, if necessary, and see that procedures like blood pressure checks and Pap smears are performed yearly.

Comparison shop for doctors' fees and services. If you think you're being overcharged, find out

The Ideal Life

what other doctors in your area charge for the same procedure.

Get a second opinion for some kinds of nonemergency surgery. Every year many unnecessary operations, such as hysterectomy, are performed. Remember that while you'll pay for these opinions, the cost of needless surgery would probably be more.

Take advantage of free community clinics. If there's a medical or dental school in your area, see if it provides low-cost treatment. In addition, avail yourself of free procedures like blood pressure and diabetes tests given by your employer or community.

Do-it-yourself medicine. It is estimated that as many as half of all visits to a doctor's office are needless, because a patient can treat many minor ailments himself or herself. Complaints like simple headaches are "self-limiting": they cure themselves with or without medical intervention. Take, for example, the common cold. Although some doctors prescribe antibiotics for viral infections like colds and flu, these medicines are often ineffective. Bed rest and aspirin will probably do the job.

Medical procedures you can do at home include taking your blood pressure and examining your breasts. If you're interested in a course on drug use or diagnosis and treatment of simple ailments, check with local universities and hospitals.

Hospital charges. In 1950 the average one-day hospital

Your Health

stay cost about $16. In 1976 it cost $175. Today the cost is outrageous! This trend toward higher hospital costs shows no signs of abating. There are, however, ways in which you can save. For nonemergency procedures, choose a weekday rather than a weekend stay. If the operation is uncomplicated, ask if you can have it as an outpatient.

Hospitalized patients are now entitled access to their medical records. This provision is part of the "Patient's Bill of Rights," enacted in 1973 by the American Hospital Association. Other provisions include confidentiality of patients' records and the right to have clear explanations of procedures.

Income taxes. Keep receipts of all medical expenses; transportation to and from doctors' offices and hospitals, drugs a doctor prescribes, eyeglasses, orthopedic shoes, etc., for tax deductions.

Prescription drugs. Before having a prescription filled, unless it's an emergency, shop around for the best price. Costs vary greatly from one pharmacy to the next. Try to get price quotations by phone. Although many pharmacies don't like to quote over the phone, there's no law prohibiting the practice.

When your doctor prescribes a medicine, ask for the "generic" (scientific) name rather than the brand name. Generic drugs are generally as good and can cost less.

Health insurance. Take a long, hard look at your

The Ideal Life

health insurance coverage. You might be underinsured, be carrying overlapping coverage, or need supplemental benefits. If you don't feel qualified to read your insurance policy, seek outside advice from an independent authority.

Use, Misuse and Abuse of Drugs

Drugs are big business. Every year the average American spends $30 on prescription drugs and $20 on over-the-counter remedies. And that figure rises the older we get.

Prescription (Rx) drugs, which doctors prescribe and pharmacists fill, are usually more expensive, more powerful, and more capable of producing side effects than those bought without prescriptions. If a patient receives the appropriate prescription, follows directions, and continues taking the medicine long enough, all well and good.

But a drug, for many reasons, may end up doing no good. It is estimated that twenty to fifty percent of patients do not take the medicines prescribed for them, and that one-fourth take drugs prescribed for someone else.

Over-the-counter (OTC) remedies, bought without prescription, include sleeping pills, cough medicines, laxatives, and aspirin. Though usually safe if taken as directed, all OTC drugs have potential risks. For example, aspirin can lead to stomach irritation if too many are consumed.

Your Health

In spite of advertising claims, OTC sleeping pills have been shown to be ineffective in combating insomnia. Instead, these pills interfere with natural sleep and dream patterns so a person winds up more fatigued.

Laxatives are greatly overused. According to the FDA, laxatives, when used repeatedly, can impair normal bowel functions and, ironically, lead to chronic constipation.

For headaches, insomnia, or constipation, try changing eating habits, and more exercise before reaching for an aspirin, sleeping pill, or laxative.

Tobacco

Cigarette smoking contributes to deaths from heart disease and lung cancer. It is also linked with increased risk of cancer of the mouth, pharynx, larynx, esophagus, and bladder, as well as with emphysema and chronic bronchitis.

For those who'd like to try to stop smoking, a "Smoker's Self-Testing Kit" is available for 45¢ from the National Clearinghouse for Smoking and Health. (Send for DHEW publication #0.7-001-00180-5 to Superintendent of Documents, Government Printing Office, Washington, D.C. 20402. Or contact your local chapter of the American Cancer Society for methods of quitting.

Alcohol

Ten million men and women suffer from alcoho-

The Ideal Life

lism. Alcohol taken in excess over a period of time can damage the liver, brain, and heart. Malnutrition is often a byproduct, since alcohol contains no nutrients and the alcoholic often skimps on food. Several studies support moderate drinking as being a factor in a longer life expectancy. "Moderate" is usually defined as two glasses of wine or beer per day or one drink per day containing hard liquor.

Many people can drink moderately; the alcoholic can't. Once an alcoholic is "cured," he or she should steer clear of alcohol for the rest of his or her life. For free information about alcohol abuse, write to the National Clearinghouse on Alcohol Information, Box 2345, Rockville, MD 20852.

Mental and Emotional Health

Mental illnesses of the older segment of our population are either functional, organic, or a combination of both. Functional illnesses, such as most depressions, are caused by emotional stress. Organic illnesses are caused by physical impairment, such as arteriosclerosis or drug intoxication. It is estimated that fifteen percent of older Americans have mental disorders (about three million people) and approximately five percent have severe disorders. Most of the functional disorders are curable; and some fifteen percent of the organic disorders are. The longer the duration of the disorder, however, the less likely the patient is to improve.

The National Institute of Mental Health esti-

Your Health

mates that there are between six and eight million persons who suffer, to some degree, from depression. Treating depression in the elderly is of urgent importance, for they account for twenty-five percent of all suicides in the U.S.

Depression is most often brought on by the stress of the losses of income, jobs, spouse, or friends, or by divorce or the impairment or diminishing of physical abilities. Sometimes it's a result of too many changes occurring in one's life in too short a time. Some symptoms of depression are the individual's feelings of sadness, hopelessness, helplessness, loneliness, and worthlessness.

There is a direct relationship between mental and physical health. Depressed feelings seem to disturb the neuroendocrine system which regulates blood pressure. High blood pressure (hypertension) is a possible result, as are increased susceptibility to strokes (cerebrovascular accidents), myocardial diseases, and kidney failures. (For some older individuals, changes in the brain circulatory system or endocrine system can interfere with adaptive responses, leading to changes in behavior or mood.)

Studies show that a person's immunity system is less effective than usual during depression; and depression can lead to inactivity, nutritional deficiencies and excessive and inappropriate use of drugs and alcohol. On the other hand, the sudden appearance of certain mental symptoms, not only depression but confusion

The Ideal Life

and disorientation, may be indicative of physical illness.

Certain changes in behavior, decreased learning capacity, some types of senility, and depression may well be caused in part by nutritional deficiencies. The aging brain seems more vulnerable to anoxia (lack of oxygen), low blood pressure, and low blood sugar. Arteriosclerotic patients sometimes suffer from lack of blood supply to the brain, and hypertension and other illnesses may lessen the ability to think.

The depression that afflicts too many retired persons is the result of stress, which in itself can be either beneficial or harmful, and which warrants a closer look.

What is stress? Stress is the effect of the wear and tear of daily living. It may be constant, as with a job; moderate, as with a mild upset in plans; or severe, as with a major life change like the death of a loved one, divorce, or loss of a job.

Is stress always harmful? If stress produces something welcome, such as writing a best seller or winning a race, it's beneficial. When chronic and unrelieved, however, it may lead to ulcers, migraine headaches, emotional breakdown and even cancer, heart attack or stroke.

How do our bodies react to stress? Acute, short-term stress causes a basic "fight or flight" response in everyone. The pulse rate quickens, blood pressure rises, we

Your Health

perspire and the hormone adrenaline is released. These reactions are natural. But stress can also produce more insidious body responses, such as the inability to concentrate, irritability, fatigue, loss of appetite, chronic anxiety, or depression.

Do people differ in their reactions to stress? Some people become angry and let off steam; others adjust well by adapting to and balancing extremes of stress; still others bottle up, or repress, emotions. Some doctors designate these responses as three distinct personality types: A, B, and C. The aggressive, hard-driving "A" personality is thought more likely to suffer heart attack. The "C," who turns feelings inward, may be more cancer prone; research has not been concluded. The lucky one is "B," who compromises and accepts the things he can't change.

Do responses to stress, then, actually "cause" disease? Chronic, severe emotional stress is undoubtedly a factor in many illnesses. It's estimated that eighty percent of the physical complaints for which we seek medical attention are psychosomatic in origin, that is, bound up with our emotions.

What's the best way to cope with stress? Experts recommend the following:

Withdraw for awhile. Set aside a ten to fifteen-minute period daily when you have a talk with yourself about the day's problems and goals.

Exercise. Take a walk, play a set of tennis; exercise in

The Ideal Life

your home or office. You'll be both invigorated and relaxed.

Take a trip. Stressful situations won't disappear just because you're away, but when you return, you'll often have a new perspective.

Rest. Fatigue makes even small problems loom large and appear worse than they are.

Seek outside advice. Sharing problems with others, individually or in a group setting, can help you find new ways of coping. Seek guidance from a person with whom you can talk honestly: a trusted friend, family member, clergyman, or other lay counselor. If you feel your stress symptoms warrant medical attention, don't delay in getting professional help.

Take action. When you're in a muddle, do something positive to break the deadlock. Indecision is one of the worst stress producers.

Decide whether that which is causing the stress is worth it. Are you driving yourself to achieve an impossible goal? Stop for a moment and examine that goal. Maybe it's not worth all the worry.

Laugh more. The ability to laugh at yourself can go a long way toward relieving stress.

Stress and depression are often the results of loneliness, insufficient money, malnutrition, and feelings of worthlessness after retirement. The time to combat the possibilities of these feelings is prior to retirement, with good exercise, sensible nutrition, a sound savings

Your Health

plan, and a conscious effort to initiate new and worthwhile activities in life.

In addition to depression, boredom can also be a problem for some people. Boredom is often cumulative over a period of time. It doesn't become particularly noticeable until its acuteness is felt. If the symptoms are recognized early enough, the problem can sometimes be headed off with a change of lifestyle. Although boredom can happen almost anytime, it is particularly noticeable when the children are grown, all of the daily excitement disappears, and there is always a quiet house. The age of fifty is the time to begin a recycling program. Chances are Dad is still finding sufficient excitement on the job to keep him geared up mentally, but the time will come when retirement might turn into a complete bore for him.

So before you get trapped in the dingy world of boredom, turn up your creativity wick and light up your life. A former colleague developed her own stimulant with the simple question, "Why not?" Even though she was an administrative executive in a responsible position, she was, from time to time, able to respond to this simple self-directed question. Such was the case when a friend invited her to join in a month-long tour of Southeast Asia. Her first response was, "I'd love to but . . . ." And then she asked herself, "Why not?" It took some creative thinking to get the workload organized to permit an unplanned month away from the job, but everything worked out fine.

There are so many possibilities for activities after retirement offers the extra time, but the person easily bored must make an extra effort to become involved in life.

Everyone can read, certainly daily newspapers or the newest magazine; and many new interests evolve from reading. Through reading, we can pursue a subject of interest, such as antiques, a historical period, a philosophy, or a sport until the foremost expert lives in our home. There are a growing number of people tracing their family tree, reading history books, county, and state records, and family records. This hobby can involve a great deal of travel also, from trips to state archives to treks to country graveyards.

Others find a new dimension in life when they actively pursue a dormant idea for a collection or hobby. Some begin collections of antique tools, pitchers, records from their teenage years, even stickpins. To others, the collection might be an outgrowth of a skill, such as needlepoint (not for women only) or indoor gardening. The collection or hobby expands in interest as one seeks more knowledge through reading or discussions with others of a like interest. Travel is the opportunity to add a piece or book on the subject, and even a trip to the local shopping center becomes special when one's eye is searching for a new item or information to add to the collection.

An avocation which many frustrated authors adopt is writing letters. This is beneficial both for parents

Your Health

and children if several hundred miles separate them and there are few opportunities to get together. Letter writing can become an art, and one's creativity can run free when the writer uses it as an opportunity to say those things he never said in person. Often, it is through written words that people are brought closer, for that which is put in writing is often our private thoughts and can be reread—cherished anew as no verbal conversation can be. For grandparents, there is a special benefit in writing grandchildren. It is a way to keep in touch with busy children, telling them about the lives of the parents when they were younger and the experiences of their grandparents. Grandchildren may never voluntarily return a letter, yet when grown will recall the words and, thus, the lives which Grandpa and Grandma let them enter through weekly letters.

Letter writing can take on a different dimension if one adopts a cause. Perhaps you have strong views on energy programs, Social Security legislation, capital punishment, or any of a number of timely and controversial topics. The "Letters to the Editor" column in the local newspaper is a good place to start a letter writing campaign. Then pursue your cause through county and state officials, right up to your Congressman and Senator, digging out facts to support your case.

Retirement-age people often find they miss the sociability of fellow workers. If entertaining has never

The Ideal Life

been something you liked to do or took the time for, try it now. A barbecue or a snack after the theater is an easy way to begin and, when continued, guarantees prolonged social contact after daily trips to the office cease.

Perhaps you don't care to keep business contacts, but we all still need friends. Take a new look at your neighbors down the block whom you may not have had the time to see much of. Or check with your church, university, or community center for students here temporarily from other countries who might enjoy celebrating Thanksgiving or a birthday at your table. Social interaction is not only necessary for all of us, but it is the quickest way to relieve depression or boredom. And if your social contacts have disappeared over the busy career years, the pre-retirement years are a good time to seek new friends and acquaintances.

Another great way to defeat anyone's boredom or depression is travel. What a way to recycle and beat the blahs. Traveling is not only enjoyable and stimulating, it, too, is a demand upon your creative output if you do it on a budget. A longtime friend of ours who has put together tours in all parts of the world has a common complaint: "Americans want to see every place in the world but always expect the same comforts and conveniences they have at home."

Traveling is a much more enriching experience when a tourist can get backstage—behind the tourist attractions to see how the people live, what they do,

Your Health

and how they go about their daily lives. And talk about demands on imagination. Get lost in a foreign land and try to communicate.

However and wherever you travel, it is amazing how much slips out of your memory in but a short time. To aid your memory, photography will reward over and over again, especially if you catch unusual glimpses and exciting compositions in your photographs. Your local library, no doubt, has a wide variety of photographic books to help you learn how to take sensational photos. Today's cameras are so automated one no longer needs to be a mechanical genius to take a technically good photograph. Now most all of your efforts can be directed to getting the type of pictures that you'll love and will also get exclamations from your friends.

In addition to a camera, our friend Richard Davids also carried a sound recorder on his travels. When he returned from his trip, he said, "Listen to the street sounds of downtown Seoul, Korea, at four A.M." Out of the silence came the musical chanting of a man hawking eel while wheeling his cart down the street. Isn't that a great way of bringing back part of another country?

Davids had another great idea on his five-month world tour. He collected men's headgear from the various countries. He can now pose as an Arab Shiek, a high priest from Korea, or any number of interesting persons.

The Ideal Life

Keeping a daily diary helps relive your travels over and over. Here, too, your library can be helpful in giving you a preview of the country you plan to visit. This is especially helpful if traveling on a budget; you can see more and do more for less cost, because you know what you are about.

We know a person who, in his travels in Europe, ran across a round jigsaw puzzle. It was just an ordinary jigsaw puzzle, but it was round instead of having square corners. He introduced the round puzzle into the U.S. with his own designs and became a millionaire. So the other dimension to being creative is to recognize a new idea when you bump into it.

Some people combine travel and schooling, as demonstrated by my youngest sister, who did not have the opportunity for college when she was younger. Through her interests and accomplishments in music, she became interested in sculpture and painting. From there her interests broadened to history. Now she goes to school during the academic year and tramps around Europe in the summer, both learning experiences.

The opportunities for mind-broadening with more schooling appear almost endless. A few years ago someone came up with the idea for commuters into New York to enroll and participate in college courses while commuting. Many colleges offer reduced tuition to retirement-age individuals. The wife of a lawyer friend went back to school a few years after her sons graduated from college. She not only got her degree,

Your Health

but was named a member of Phi Beta Kappa and is now teaching at the university.

If you are near a college or university, you may know or can easily learn of all the educational opportunities offered by the institutions. If you are not nearby, there are still opportunities. Your local high school very likely conducts adult education classes. There are other opportunities, such as using cassettes, television or correspondence courses. Also, there are many local trade schools and community college extension programs.

Probably the greatest relief from boredom or depression comes from peace of mind. In our survey seeking opinions as to what constituted the ideal life over fifty, some replies indicated that many persons had found answers to their problems in a belief in God. They and others had come to terms with their lives as they are now, accepting and enjoying each day. One such reply came from Darlene Johnson of Aurora, Colorado. She had recently become a widow but gives an optimistic view of her life and includes a formula for life we'd like to share:

"Say to yourself, 'Today I am living enthusiastically, joyfully!' Don't wish your life away. Thank God for the beautiful morning and keep your mind open and your sense of humor close at hand. Expect only the *best* from life, and that is what each day will bring.

"The only moment we live is this very moment, so don't spoil it by what happened yesterday or by what

The Ideal Life

may never be. Most of our problems are only temporary. Celebrate them; the burdens will lessen.

"The only thing certain in life is change. Accept it as an exciting challenge, adjust to it with courage, and cling to a faith in yourself; for you are important and you can survive."

Medicare, Medicaid and Private Insurance

One of the greatest concerns of the twenty-four million Americans over the age of sixty-five is having adequate protection against the high costs of health care. Over eleven percent of the retirement budget is spent on health care, so it is essential to have a comprehensive medical insurance program to cover the ever-rising health care expenses that threaten many older Americans. Pre-retirement is the time to learn about public programs and private health insurance for the over sixty-five group. Armed with this knowledge, you can estimate the need for private insurance for you and your family, including parents who might require your assistance with complicated Medicare procedures.

Medicare

In 1965 Congress passed the Medicare law. Medicare, a health insurance program for Americans sixty-

The Ideal Life

five and over and a part of the Social Security System, is designed to protect workers and their families against the increased costs of medical care in old age. Medicare is considered the greatest single contribution by Social Security since its inception in 1935. The Medicare program is run by the Health Care Financing Administration and funded through Social Security taxes. Payments are handled by private insurance organizations which are under contract with the Federal Government.

Medicare coverage is divided into two parts—hospital insurance, which is paid for by contributions during working years, and medical insurance, which is paid for by small monthly premiums after age sixty-five. Medicare, however, does not provide total health care coverage. Many private insurance companies sell medical insurance to supplement Medicare.

Although almost everyone is eligible for Medicare, coverage does not come automatically to a person approaching his sixty-fifth birthday. You will be notified by Social Security that you are nearing entitlement to Medicare coverage, and that you should apply for it at your local Social Security Office three months before your sixty-fifth birthday. You do not have to retire to receive Medicare insurance; in fact, your employer's group policy may ask Medicare to cover the primary cost of your medical expenses. You may want to discuss this option with your employer to determine company policy.

Medicare, Medicaid

Even if they have not reached sixty-five, two categories of people qualify for Medicare: disabled persons who have been entitled to Social Security or railroad disability benefits for at least two continuous years; persons insured under Social Security or railroad retirement who need dialysis treatment for kidney disease or kidney transplants because of permanent kidney failure.

Medicare Hospital Insurance (Part A)

Eligibility: Medicare hospital insurance, the basic plan, covers hospital and directly related health care expenses. This plan is financed through Social Security contributions withheld from income earned during years of employment. Everyone aged sixty-five and over and entitled to Social Security or railroad retirement benefits automatically receives hospital insurance without paying monthly premiums. Persons ineligible for Social Security or railroad retirement benefits may purchase hospital insurance for a monthly premium based on the cost of living index. However, they must also enroll in the medical insurance program at the regular premium. Application can be made at your local Social Security Office.

Hospitalization Coverage: For each benefit period you are covered a maximum of ninety days after an initial deductible is paid. Co-payments on a sum-per-day basis are required after the first sixty days. A benefit period begins when you are admitted to a hospital and ends sixty-days after you are discharged

The Ideal Life

as an inpatient from the hospital or extended-care facility. There is a lifetime reserve of sixty additional inpatient hospital days that can be used should you need more than ninety days of hospital care in any benefit period. Each reserve day you use permanently reduces the total number of reserve days you have left. This reserve-day benefit is a one-time-only arrangement—once used, it will not be available again.

Deductibles and co-payments for the various benefits change about once a year, so it is wise to keep informed regarding them. For benefit periods starting in 1980, your share of costs of covered care are as follows: (1) deductible for the first sixty days in the hospital, $180; (2) for the sixty-first through the ninetieth day in the hospital, $45 per day; (3) for the sixty reserve days, $90 per day. After you pay the initial $180 deductible for the year, Medicare will pay for sixty days of full hospital care for each period of illness, charges that include semiprivate room, meals, regular nursing services, laboratory and x-ray fees, intensive care costs, operating and recovery room, drugs, casts, dressings, splints and in-hospital therapy. For the sixty-first through the ninetieth day, you will co-pay $45 per day on your hospital bill.

Benefits not covered by Medicare hospital insurance include doctor's services, private-duty nurses, extra charges for a private room unless specified by the doctor for medical reasons, room convenience items (telephone, radio or television, etc.) the first three

Medicare, Medicaid

pints of blood you receive in a benefit period, unnecessary services and supplies used in the diagnosis and treatment of an illness or injury, and homemaker services (meal delivery, custodial care, etc.).

Extended Care Coverage: Medicare hospital insurance also pays for up to twenty days of care for each benefit period in a skilled nursing facility, a specially qualified facility which is staffed and equipped to furnish skilled nursing care, skilled rehabilitative care, and many related services. Medicare will also pay all but $22.50 per day for an additional eighty days if all of the following conditions are met: (1) you have been in the hospital at least three days before your transfer to the nursing facility; (2) you are being transferred because you require care for a condition that was treated in the hospital; (3) you are being admitted within fourteen days after leaving the hospital; (4) a doctor certifies your need and you actually obtain skilled nursing or rehabilitative care on a daily basis; (5) and the facility's Utilization Review Committee does not disapprove your stay.

Extended care in a skilled nursing facility includes a bed in a semiprivate room, customary nursing services, medical social services, meals, drugs and other medical supplies provided by the facility for therapy. Benefits not covered are the same as those not covered by hospitalization coverage.

Home Health Care Coverage: If you are confined to your home, you may also receive a lifetime total of

The Ideal Life

up to one hundred home health "visits" from a home health agency approved by Medicare, providing the home health care is further treatment for a condition that had been treated in a qualifying hospital or nursing facility. You must have been in the hospital three consecutive days, and the doctor must have set up a home health plan within fourteen days after your discharge from the hospital or nursing facility. Patients who need part-time skilled nursing care, physical therapy or speech therapy are candidates for this type of care. Payment for these visits can be made for up to twelve months after your most recent discharge from a participating hospital or skilled nursing facility.

Medicare Medical Insurance (Part B)

Eligibility: Disabled persons eligible for Medicare and almost anyone reaching the age of sixty-five after June 1973 are automatically enrolled in Medicare medical insurance. This plan however, is voluntary, so you can elect not to have it. If you decide to retain your enrollment, you must pay for the insurance. The basic premium you pay each month is matched by a payment from the Federal government. Beginning July 1, 1980, the basic premium you will pay is $9.60. The premium is deducted from your Social Security check. Since Medicare medical insurance is voluntary, it can be cancelled at any time by notifying your Social Security Office. Once you elect to cancel, however, you will have only one opportunity to re-enroll. To re-enroll you must apply within the first three months of the calendar year. Premiums will be ten percent higher

Medicare, Medicaid

for each twelve-month period that has passed since the time of cancellation. Your protection will not start until the following July.

Coverage of Doctor's Services: After you pay an initial deductible each calendar year, Medicare medical insurance will pay eighty percent of the expenses for physician and surgeon services rendered in a hospital, the doctor's office, an extended-care facility, or at home. Such expenses must be reasonable and necessary. If your doctor will accept "assignment"—that is, if he will accept what Medicare pays for your care—you will not have to pay as much. If your doctor will not accept these terms, your expenses will include all the following: (1) the initial deductible, (2) the twenty percent co-insurance features, (3) and that part of the doctor's charges in excess of Medicare's definition of a "reasonable" charge. A working knowledge of Medicare can sometimes reduce your expenses. Consult with your doctor early if you anticipate that your illness will last a long time. He can advise you as to whether the latter part of your treatment could be managed in a skilled nursing facility instead of a hospital. If so, the transfer should be made before you start co-payments. If you could manage your recovery at home, using the one hundred home health care visits from Part A and an additional one hundred visits from Part B, you can cut costs.

Medical insurance covers the following services by medical doctors and osteopaths: medical and surgical services, office nursing services, medical supplies

The Ideal Life

furnished by the doctor in his office, diagnostic tests, and drugs that cannot be self-administered. The insurance does not cover routine physical examinations, immunizations and prescription drugs.

Certain limited services by chiropractors and dentists are covered. Dentists may be paid for surgery on the jaw, including repair of fractured facial bones, medical supplies administered in the dentist's office, and diagnostic tests and procedures related to surgery. Replacement and general care of the teeth and gums are not covered. Medicare does not cover eye examinations or hearing tests.

Coverage of Other Services: On an outpatient basis, Medicare covers services in an emergency room or outpatient clinic, laboratory tests billed by the hospital, x-rays and other radiology services billed by the hospital, medical supplies such as splints and casts, and drugs and biologicals that cannot be self-administered. Physical therapy under the doctor's personal supervision is also covered.

Medicare medical insurance covers some home health services. There are, however, several eligibility requirements that must be met. The home health agency must participate in the Medicare program. You must be homebound and in need of part-time skilled nursing care. Your doctor must prescribe, supervise, and review the service. Other home health care benefits are the same as those of Medicare hospital insurance. Emergency ambulance service is also cov-

Medicare, Medicaid

ered. The ambulance must be approved for Medicare and can be used only to transport you to the nearest facility that can provide the necessary care.

Medicare does not pay for any of the following: acupuncture, Christian Science practioners' services, custodial care, drugs and medicines you buy yourself, with or without a doctor's prescription, eye examinations for prescribing eye glasses or the glasses themselves, hearing aids, homemaker services, injections which can be self-administered, nursing care on a full-time basis in your home, physical examinations and tests that are routine, private-duty nurses. Also, it will not pay your family to take care of you. It will not pay for services that are payable by workmen's compensation or another government program. Neither will it pay for services that the patient or another party, on his or her behalf, has a legal obligation to pay.

If an older family member requires psychiatric help, Medicare is of little help. Medicare covers care only by a psychiatrist which can be office, clinic or institute visits, but only up to $250 *a year*. Hospitalization is covered but for no more than 190 days in a *lifetime*.

If you believe you will be unable to pay for Medicare costs for which you are liable, find out if you are eligible for Medicaid or other special assistance plans, or try to find a supplemental insurance plan that will cover some of the expenses not covered by

The Ideal Life

Medicare. If you need additional help with your Medicare benefits, contact your Social Security Office.

Private Insurance

Since Medicare does not provide comprehensive coverage, many persons purchase supplemental policies which are designed to reduce the deductibles and co-payments they are liable for under Medicare. The Senate Special Committee on Aging says Medicare covers only about thirty-eight percent of the total medical expenses for those eligible for Medicare. Supplemental policies are considerably cheaper than total coverage policies. They generally pay twenty percent of Medicare's "reasonable charge," but will not pay for the services Medicare defines as unnecessary. Several types of supplemental insurance are available.

In addition to comparing return on the premium dollar and checking for duplication of Medicare coverage, several other steps should be taken before purchasing supplemental insurance. Make certain the company offering the policy is licensed by the state. Check deductible, premium, and co-insurance rates and watch for escalator clauses which can raise them. Determine which expenses will not be paid by the policy, the daily payments the company will make to you, as well as the benefit periods they cover. Check the terms of cancellation and conditions for renewal.

The Department of Health, Education and Welfare provides a free informational booklet entitled *Guide*

Medicare, Medicaid

to Health Insurance for People with Medicare (HCFA booklet No. 02110), which is available at Social Security Offices, state insurance departments, and many senior citizen centers. This booklet explains what Medicare covers, describes kinds of private insurance supplements available, and provides useful information to beneficiaries concerning the purchase of supplemental insurance. No private company or agent selling Medicare supplemental insurance is connected with the federal government.

Catastrophic or Major Medical Expense policies help cover the high cost of serious illness or injury. These policies usually have deductibles and co-insurance features. If such a policy is included in your employer's group plan, check to see if it can be continued in retirement. Employer group insurance may be an excellent form of coverage if it can be continued or converted to a suitable individual Medicare supplement policy. Check price and benefits for both you and your spouse. If a continuation can be arranged, you will have no waiting periods or refusals of coverage because of preexisting conditions.

Health Maintenance Organizations (HMO's) may provide the most complete service for your health care dollar. An HMO is a community organization of doctors, hospitals and others that offers members a wide range of health and medical services for an annual enrollment fee paid in advance. The annual fee entitles you to inpatient and outpatient hospital

The Ideal Life

services, physician services, emergency health services, limited mental health care services, diagnostic laboratory and radiology services, medical supplies, and preventative health services. HMO's promote and emphasize early detection and continuity of essential preventative care.

The annual cost to enroll in an HMO is low because doctors and hospitals maximize the efficient use of facilities and personnel. In addition, most problems are handled on an outpatient basis rather than in a hospital. In an HMO, the incidence of elective surgery is considerably less. The Health Maintenance Organization is a relatively new idea, and not every community has one. Check with your Social Security Office to see if there is an HMO that participates in the Medicare program in your community.

Two other types of policies are available. A Hospital Income Policy is a limited policy but is widely used. Its benefits are paid directly to the insured, which offers some flexibility in meeting other charges not covered by Medicare, such as private-duty nursing, prescriptions at home, or building a personal health-cost savings plan to meet the expense of future illnesses. A "wrap-around" policy also fills in the gaps of Medicare coverage and is available through agents of a number of insurance companies, through Blue Cross-Blue Shield, and through major retirement associations. These policies pay for several health expenditures not covered by Medicare.

Medicare, Medicaid

Medicaid

Medicaid is another government health care program for low-income persons. There is one basic Medicaid program, with each state administering its own version through state, county, and city welfare departments and special agencies. The Federal Government insists on specific minimum standards, and it finances about fifty-five percent of each state's Medicaid program. The rest of the program is financed through state and city grants. Medicaid is free to all eligible recipients and often covers services not covered by Medicare. Without regard to race, color, national origin, or length of residence, the program assists children under Aid to Dependent Children, the aged, the blind and disabled who receive Supplemental Security Income, and persons aged sixty-five or over who are not eligible for Medicare. You can apply for assistance at your local Welfare Department.

Medicaid covers doctor's, hospital and nursing home care and may include dental care, eye glasses, clinical services, prescribed drugs, and diagnostic and rehabilitative service in an intermediate care facility. Unfortunately this program has been abused by both providers and recipients, and has been widely criticized in newspapers with regard to fraudulent practices. There has been a growing trend to develop a program that will be mainly preventative in nature in an effort to keep the aged healthy and out of institutions. Medicaid assists Health Maintenance Organizations

The Ideal Life

in supplying subscribers with most of the medical care they need.

Nursing Homes

It has been estimated that twenty-five to thirty percent of America's nursing home residents could lead partially self-sufficient, independent lives in their own homes or apartments. Communities, families, and neighbors are becoming increasingly concerned with the trend in institutionalizing older persons. To counteract this trend and in an attempt to keep more older persons in their own homes, several outreach programs and services, such as visiting nurses, therapists, homemakers and home health aides, outpatient care, and "Meals on Wheels" have been instituted.

But even with all of this backup help, the need may arise to place an older relative in a nursing home. The problem should be discussed with the person who requires this care in regard to the desires and needs of all those involved. The physician and hospital social workers should also be consulted as to the type of facility chosen.

Nursing homes participating in the Medicaid or Medicare programs are required to meet federal government standards for services, safety and sanitation. Each state must follow these standards when it inspects and certifies facilities which receive money from either Medicaid or Medicare although they follow their own standards in the inspecting and licensing of all other nursing homes. If the patient is eligible for Medicare

Medicare, Medicaid

or Medicaid, make certain that the home is certified for the program.

The two types of certified nursing homes are "skilled nursing facilities" and "intermediate care facilities." Medicare and Medicaid will cover expenses, but the coverage is different under each. Under Medicaid, the state will cover expenses for housing in either facility. Medicare covers expenses for skilled nursing facilities only.

A skilled nursing facility provides the level of care closest to hospital care with twenty-four-hour nursing services. Medical supervision and rehabilitation therapy are also provided. Generally, a skilled nursing facility cares for convalescent patients and those with long-term illnesses. Medicare helps pay for up to one hundred days in a skilled nursing facility; remember, though, that from the twenty-first day through the one-hundredth, you will be paying $22.50 per day. The patient must have had at least three days in a hospital prior to admission, and the attending physican must recommend the continuation of care in the nursing facility. Medicaid usually picks up charges after the one-hundredth day for eligible, low-income persons.

An intermediate care facility provides less extensive health related care and services. It has nursing service, but not around the clock. These facilities serve people not fully capable of living by themselves, yet not ill enough to need twenty-four-hour nursing care. These

The Ideal Life

homes provide rehabilitation programs, but their primary functions are personal care and social services.

Nursing homes are sponsored by one of three groups: nonprofit religious, fraternal, or charitable organizations; federal, state, or local government groups; and private businesses operating for a profit. Denominational nursing homes have proven to be preferable to the profit-making ones. Homes run by religious organizations generally have more volunteers and, because of their tax-exempt status, can put more money back into the home.

Selecting a nursing home can often be painful and difficult, but knowing that the nursing homes are licensed and regulated, with standards of care set by Federal and State authorities, should make the search less traumatic. A patient's physician, hospital Social Service Department, Social Security Office, health department, and clergyman may all be helpful in suggesting possible facilities, but the individual must do the inspecting and selecting. Visit several facilities to compare services and personnel. Visit the facility in late morning or midday to observe the home at mealtime, its atmosphere, standards of cleanliness, safety, rehabilitation and activities programs, the cheerfulness of staff and patients, and the nursing service. Will the patient have privacy and a chance to decorate his room with a few of his own possessions? Talk about charges and determine the expenses insurance will

Medicare, Medicaid

cover. It is wise to compare the cost of several homes. A home that is near a hospital and also close to relatives is advantageous. The Department of Health, Education and Welfare's booklet *Nursing Home Care* provides valuable information regarding the selection of a nursing home.

Help is available through the Hospice program to families who wish to keep a terminally ill person at home. The goal of this program is to help a family function independently as a home care unit, with hospital sponsorship and a team of nurses, doctor, chaplain, and pharmacist coordinating the home care and services and being available for medical, emotional and spiritual support and advice. A Hospice nurse says she is often in a teaching role in that she is available to advise a family on how to administer treatment and what to do to make the patient more comfortable. Volunteers assist the family by stopping in and taking over for a few hours while a family member can shop—or even have someone to visit with.

Hospice volunteers and workers not only assist the patient, but extend their ministry to the whole family. The helpers are most interesting and unusual people; and contrary to what might be expected, they are vital and remarkably well-adjusted people who love life. These are the Mother Teresa's of our world who serve with joy and love.

The Ideal Life

Retirement

These government services are designed to help people, whatever their financial worth, continue to be assured of their personal worth. This idea is best summed up by Harold and Anabel Carlson, who wrote: "Our twenty-five years after fifty have been mainly an extension of those enjoyed before fifty. They have been good years. We cherish each day we can be with each other. We appreciate being able to do meaningful work, to learn, and to enjoy family and friends. These things we crave to the very end.

"Any decline in health and vigor in our remaining years after fifty should ideally be such that we never become a burden to ourselves, to each other, or to anyone else. To this same end we also wish for sufficient expendable income to handle any emergency.

"It would mean a lot to us to be able to contribute more to organizations and people in need. Then, of course, there are places and people we would like to see, some of them more than once, before it is too late.

"Essential, however, to a fulfilling life after fifty, regardless of circumstances, is our continued feeling of personal worth as responsible human beings and children of God, growing from everyone and everything we meet."

Ways to Have Money

Most of us are nearing the peak of our earning years in our fifties. At the same time, the burden on the family paycheck is easing—school costs are winding down and the kids are becoming self-supporting. The costs of food, clothing, transportation and housing are not taking nearly as big a bite out of the family income. Now is the ideal time to plant a "money tree" and get your spare dollars sprouting more dollars for the years ahead.

Tom Columbus and his wife Jon actually did that. "We're planting more than one tree though," says Tom. "We'll have around 1,700 trees on our 53 acres."

Tom has planted a grove of pecan nut trees in southern Arizona near the border of Mexico. Tom still works at his job while Jon looks after the digging, planting, feeding, irrigating and cultivating of the grove.

The Ideal Life

"The trees were five years old when we planted them and about this big," Tom demonstrates, "and when they're ten years old they'll start to produce. A mature tree will produce over a hundred pounds of nuts a year and they're selling for over a dollar a pound now."

Talk about a money tree! Shows what Mom and Dad can do after the kids are out on their own.

The time for us to count our blessings and our assets is about now—before we retire. We know where we've been, but we should also know where we are going. This is the time when Mom and Dad can put their heads together after years of Mom's interests being increasingly focused on the children while the job has practically swallowed up Dad.

Comparing your income with your outgo will give you a quick look at how much money can be put to work. You can then get into the position of the man pointed out by a friend who said, "he's got so much money his money's got money." This position comes from investing (renting out our money) and collecting interest (rent). Where will the investment money come from? Each of us has a different lifestyle and will need to determine where pruning the outgo will be least painful.

Some folks barter—trade their skills of car tune-ups, yard care, tax help, etc. for someone else's skills in areas such as electrical, plumbing and carpentry jobs.

Ways to Have Money

Food is a big ticket item. There are ways to cut back on this item by eating out less often, clipping coupons and buying store brands. Are designer-label clothes a must? How about the clubs? What else?

There is, however, the opposite philosophy: "Don't spend time figuring out how to save but rather figuring out how to earn more." Some folks have kept the big old house after the kids have left and made part of it into income-producing units. Today over fifty percent of married women are working outside the home to supplement the family income. However we manage to get investment funds together, it is well to remember that most people at this point in life wrongfully expect to work for all their money instead of giving their money a chance to work for them. Putting money to work takes some doing but there is plenty of help around.

To determine the amount of money you can comfortably invest during these peak earning years you must first figure out your net worth. Calculating your family's net worth is easy—just list your assets (what you own) such as cash, investments, life insurance, company pension rights, property, etc. The total is your gross assets. Always use current market prices and cash values when estimating assets. Next list your liabilities (what you owe) such as unpaid bills, home mortgage, taxes due, car loan, tuition due, etc. Net worth is determined by subtracting total liabilities from gross assets.

The Ideal Life

The Budget

We all hate this part. How and where are you spending your money? Get out all your receipts, cancelled checks, income tax reports, property taxes, insurance and maintenance costs on home; car expenses including tags, insurance, repairs, gas etc.; entertainment, contributions, education, travel, health and insurance, clothing, refurbishing and replacements, and personal expenses.

After subtracting the outgo from the income, you will get some idea of your financial health. If your balance was distressing, organize and reorganize your expenditures. Go on a trial run and live a year on a retiree's income. Eliminate the losers from your portfolio; spend less and shift investments to areas that will give better and completely safe returns. Invest your surplus in good government securities. This is important, for you are no longer able to take risks.

Other than a two- or three-month emergency fund in passbook savings, the over fifty consistently seek safety and good return. Christmas fund accounts, passbook savings, Series EE and Series HH bonds are not keeping up with the rate of inflation and are self-defeating. Talk with your accountant or stock broker and be informed yourself. Read and ask questions about investments. There's lots of help out there, so make your investigation broad and expert.

Ways to Have Money

The Retirement Budget-Estimating Expenses

Generally, overall expenses are reduced at retirement. Many expenses that currently take a large chunk out of the budget will become less important in retirement and not figure so prominently in the budget. Other expenses will be greater.

Employment related expenses will cease or be greatly reduced. Transportation expenses will be minimized without daily travel to and from work. Fewer lunches away from home will result in lower food bills. Business entertainment and travel expenses will stop. Special clothing, equipment, and tools for work will no longer be needed.

Basic living expenses will also be reduced. By the time you retire your mortgage should be almost paid off. If you retire to a warmer climate, much of the high cost of energy can be avoided. Food cost should be less when it's just the two of you. Raising, educating, and supporting children will be a thing of the past. Life insurance expenses should be sharply reduced because you will need less protection, or your present policy may be paid up.

Federal and State income taxes will be lower. The present tax laws provide retired persons several important money-saving deductions, exemptions, and credits. Ask your local Internal Revenue Service for a free copy of *Tax Benefits for Older Americans*. This

The Ideal Life

booklet points out the major benefits available to the retired.

Some expenses will be greater. Medical expenses increase with age; per capita health care cost for an older person is three times higher than for a younger person. The loss of your employer's contributions to health insurance will increase its cost to you. Although Medicare may offset part of this increase, it does not provide comprehensive protection, and a supplemental policy must be purchased. With more leisure time on your hands, you will probably spend more money on travel and recreation or education.

Many factors influence the amount of income you will need for a comfortable retirement. The age at which you plan to retire will determine the period of time your financial plans must cover. Perhaps you are not interested in complete retirement. You may choose to work part time or pursue a second career to make the transition from the nine to five world more gradual. This will add income and some expenses to your retirement budget. If you opt for the life of leisure, extra finances will be needed.

No matter what retirement lifestyle you decide to lead, always be realistic in estimating expenses. In estimating all expenses, allow for an annual inflation cushion. It is wise to establish an emergency fund in a savings institution during the peak income earning years so cash will be readily available for any unexpected expenses you might incur.

Ways to Have Money

Preparing a chart like the following will give you some idea of the money you will need after retirement.

Expenses	Actual Pre-retirement Expenses	Estimated Expenses After Retirement
Rent, mortgage, etc.	$	$
Food and Beverage		
Clothing and Cleaning		
Entertainment, recreation, and travel		
Automobile and Transportation		
Telephone		
Utilities (Electricity, oil, etc.)		
House repair and maintenance		
Furniture		
Working expenses		
Personal items		
Medical expenses		
Health insurance		
Education, Books, Journals, etc.		
Contributions, Gifts		
Life insurance		
Other insurance		
Income taxes		
Other taxes		
Other items		
Total Expenses	$	$

The Ideal Life

The Past Determines the Future

When determining the lifestyle of the future, and the finances necessary for it, many people seek a continuance of the best parts of their first fifty years of life: "the-best-things-in-life-are-free" type of experiences. It is true that in today's world those "best things" hardly come inexpensively; but when planning for the future, it is wise to review the past, as did Mary Kay Butz when she wrote: "I often think back to my early years. I was born on a sandhill farm in central Wisconsin to city people—both Chicagoans—who tried diligently to scratch out a living among the jack pines and the screech owls. There was no electricity, no indoor plumbing, no dental care in our budget. We were poor; but so was everybody else, so we didn't even know it. My mother's beautiful blue eyes never faded, and my dad knew where every bird's nest was. I shall always remember, almost tearfully, how one hot, humid August day, Pop heaved an extra high load of hay onto the old hay wagon, stood on top of it all and boosted me onto his strong shoulders so that I could see into a fabulous oriole's nest made of horsehair. Could we really have been poor? With all the ups and downs, that was the ideal life for any lucky child.

"College was not in the picture for me, so I worked as a secretary for a time until I was hired by a Chicago radio station as a vocalist—a thrill to be on the air, money or not. After 3½ years of work at Midwest radio stations, I was happy to quit, marry and

Ways to Have Money

start my own home. We have reared and educated our five, and it's been fun.

"We are retired, and soon we shall head for southern Illinois to a beautiful lake deep in the Shawnee National Forest, which is filled with all those hardwoods, whose leaves are turning into a glimpse of heaven—black gums, sassafras, dogwoods, the coral maples, sweet gums, hickory—all against a background of deep green and red cedars. This is where we will build our home—"ideal" for two farm people who have spent all their adult lives in the big city. We loved it all as we went along, but the thought of returning to the freedom of country living was always in our hopes.

"Finally, for me, the ideal life must be lived secure in the loving protection of one's Maker. A staunch faith, preferably inherited from devout parents, just has to be considered the ideal gift of gifts. I could not relish life as I do without that security."

Most of the people we surveyed saw retirement as an opportunity, the chance to do as they wished, as Darwin D. Tucker, a retired corporate executive from Clover, South Carolina, saw his life after fifty: "The ideal life would be doing what you want to do, when and where you want to do it—with good health and an active mind. This would be the recipe for the ideal life, of course, at any age. The ideal life, fifty and over, would be solidly grounded on a state of good physical

The Ideal Life

and mental health, permitting continued pursuit of any remaining professional or occupational goals or objectives, and the structuring of hobbies and other personal interests to sustain an active and stimulating life in the retirement mode. With this enabling umbrella, underpinned with adequate financial security, a person—or a couple—could successfully follow whatever path pleases them most."

Others saw the ideal life after retirement in more specific terms, dependent upon the planning made during the pre-retirement years. This was the case of Loran W. Durlam, who wrote: "I love my kind of retirement: 18 rounds of golf, two fishing trips to Alaska, two to Canada, one to Minnesota, and one in the Pacific Ocean, plus twenty days of pheasant hunting. In the spring, the gardens and mushroom hunting require my services.

"My dad, who is ninety-four years old, retired twenty-four years ago. My two younger brothers are also retired. My dad has to be the only retired man in town who has three retired sons.

"My wife Gracelyn retired last January, and her Social Security check plus mine add up to enough to pay our income tax. It is sort of like being born free."

"Being born free" is the way many retired couples view their new freedom from the confines of a job. There were some, however, who felt that a continuation of their careers was their way of expressing freedom—the freedom to continue working, if they

Ways to Have Money

wish. This was the wish expressed by Barbara Roth, a business executive, who intends to continue working—as long as *she* wants to: "Ideally for me, life after fifty will be a continuation of the life I've lived up to now. It will include family, friends, work and play in about the same proportions they've always had. That is the way it appears to me at age fifty-three; perhaps I shall feel differently about things as I move up the chronological ladder, and I reserve the right to change my mind. I should also point out that I have never been very observant of the popular notions about what one should be doing at any given age. I married later than most, became a mother much later than most, and, in general, have followed my own timetable to my own satisfaction. I dislike the thought of being expected to retire from work when I reach a particular birthday, and hope to march to my own tempo to the end."

The Retirement Budget—Estimating Income

The principal sources of income for retired persons are Social Security benefits, private pensions and income from investments. For aged, blind and disabled people with limited or no resources, a Supplemental Security Income payment program, guaranteeing a minimum monthly income, has been in effect since 1974. Some persons may be eligible for Railroad Retirement, Civil Service, and Veterans benefits.

Retirement income can and should come from many sources; the more sources, the stronger your

The Ideal Life

financial base. If your estimated retirement income will cover your estimated expenses, you are in great financial shape. But if your balance is distressing, some adjustments must be made. There are two methods of adjustment. Decide which expenses in the original retirement plan can be reduced or eliminated and cut accordingly, or take steps now to improve your retirement financial status.

If you choose the first alternative, look more closely at each of your expenses. A smaller home can significantly reduce several expenses. Transportation and recreation are other areas that can usually withstand some trimming. In most cases the food and medical budgets should not be greatly reduced.

If you wish to retain your original plans without sacrificing any of your needs and desires, you will need to generate additional income to cover the current difference between estimated expenses and income. This is achieved by either working part time or by investing spare dollars accumulated during the peak income earning years. Various types of investment are discussed later in this chapter. For now, we will concentrate on the fixed sources of income.

Social Security

Social Security is a complex, often confusing system of retirement insurance programs. Social Security laws have changed so rapidly in recent years

Ways to Have Money

that many persons do not realize that they are eligible for certain benefits. Benefits are not automatic and application must be made at the nearest Social Security Office.

The system consists of three separate programs: it provides a pension when income stops at retirement; it provides survivor benefits (life insurance) and payments to the disabled; and it provides health insurance through the Medicare program discussed in Chapter 2. Social Security is administered by the Federal Government and is financed through taxes withheld from payroll. Each worker and employer contributes equal percentage rates. Tax rates, along with benefits, have increased steadily over the years and will continue to do so in the future.

Eligibility To be eligible for Social Security benefits, the worker must have been under Social Security approximately a quarter of his or her working life, from age twenty-one or from the year 1950, whichever is later, by the time he reaches retirement age or becomes disabled. Generally, to be insured for benefits, a worker needs one quarter for each year since 1950. If he reached sixty-two in 1979, he needed twenty-eight quarters. In no case will more than forty quarters be needed, and quarters need not be consecutive.

If a worker has not acquired enough quarters to qualify for benefits, his employer might allow him to continue working until he has the amount needed. A

The Ideal Life

worker eligible for Social Security can take full benefits at age sixty-five or reduced benefits after reaching age sixty-two. Also a self-employed individual may contribute Social Security tax on earnings to the program at a slightly higher percentage than the employed person. A widow may also be eligible for survivor's benefits, if she has earned a year and a half of work credits, three years before her husband's death. But she must apply. Railroad workers are eligible for Social Security but are jointly covered with their own retirement program. Most federal civilian employees eligible for the civil service retirement program are not eligible for Social Security.

Those wishing to retire may do so at sixty-two (with twenty percent less in monthly checks) or at sixty-five or later. The mandatory retirement age has been raised to seventy, and benefits are increased by one percent per year over sixty-five up to the age of seventy-two, three percent per year for those who reach sixty-five after 1981—up to age seventy years. But along with this there are disadvantages for the worker. Social Security payments will be lost and the worker will be paying Social Security taxes, federal and state income taxes on his salary. The worker will not recover the five years of payment sacrificed to stay on the job.

Application You must apply for Social Security benefits. Three months before your birthday or retirement you should telephone or visit the nearest Social Security Office to advise the government that you are

Ways to Have Money

planning to apply for benefits, and ask what proofs are needed to establish eligibility. A delay may result in a reduction of benefits. Ordinarily, officials will want Social Security cards and birth certificates or baptismal certificates of the wage earner and spouse, the most recent income tax report and W-2 form, and marriage certificate. If you are a widow or divorced spouse, you may need other information as well. To qualify for an ex-spouse's benefits, a divorced spouse must have had a marriage that lasted ten years. (Sometimes more than one divorced spouse may qualify for the same ex-husband's benefits.)

If the family breadwinner dies before retirement, the spouse at eligible age will get one hundred percent of the amount the primary income earner would have received had he/she lived. Benefits could be drawn at age sixty but the payments would be smaller. Remarriage under the age of sixty means forfeiture of benefits from former spouse's entitlement. If, however, the widow or widower is over sixty, he or she can remarry without losing benefits. This 1977 amendment was written into the Social Security law to eliminate situations in which beneficiaries were living together and not marrying out of fear that they would lose benefits.

A widowed disabled homemaker can begin to collect Social Security benefits at age fifty. Vocational factors, such as age, education, and previous work experience cannot be used in deciding whether a

The Ideal Life

widow or widower is disabled, though they may for a disabled worker.

The Amount of your Benefit. The exact dollar value of the benefits you are eligible for will not be determined until your application is processed and your income record checked by the Social Security Office. Benefits are based on average earnings and retirement age. In theory, the more years you have worked under the Social Security program and the higher your income, the greater your benefits will be. But this statement can be misleading. The government is the great equalizer. Under the amended 1977 Social Security law, Congress dealt with the replacement of income lost through retirement—granting to the *minimum* wage earner fifty-two percent of income lost (seventy-eight percent to a couple). The high-wage earner would receive benefits of only about twenty-eight percent; and a couple who earned high wages would be entitled to only forty-two percent.

Recent Social Security law guarantees that benefits will keep pace with increases in the cost of living. If the cost of living increases by three percent or more in a year, benefits will automatically increase by the same percentage the following July. If there is a benefit increase, you will be notified by your Social Security Office.

Ways to Have Money

Estimating Your Social Security Check

If you wish to estimate the amount you will receive from Social Security, write to the Social Security Administration, P.O. Box 57, Baltimore, Maryland, 21203. Give name of the wage earner, Social Security number, address, and ask for a report on the earnings record of the wage earner on file with the administration. The wage earner must sign the request because this information is confidential. The report may not be complete for the calendar year because of the time needed to receive and process data. If the wage earner disagrees with the report, he should advise the Social Security Administration in writing immediately or visit the local Social Security Office, bringing W-2 forms, periods of employment, employer's names and addresses, pay slips and other proof of unreported wages. If he has been self-employed, he should bring income tax returns, indicating Social Security contributions for the years in question.

Your check should arrive about the same time each month, usually around the third. The check can be directly deposited in the financial organization of your choice. Contact your Social Security Office or financial institution to arrange for direct deposit of your checks.

Employment after Retirement

As mentioned earlier, Social Security benefits alone will not adequately support any retired person comfortably. Additional income is essential. It is not

The Ideal Life

necessary to stop working completely to be eligible for Social Security benefits, but wages and salaries earned after retirement are limited by law. If earnings exceed these strict limits, benefits will be reduced and federal taxes will be paid on all excess income. The limits change periodically, so check with your Social Security Office to stay updated. Retirees are encouraged to save and develop income-producing investments to supplement Social Security benefits because investment income is not subject to these limits. Social Security insures only against the loss of earnings from employment. There would be little incentive for people to establish wise savings plans and sound investments if Social Security benefits would be significantly reduced for retirees with good incomes from stocks, real estate, bonds, etc.

If you plan to work after you begin receiving benefits, there are limits to the amount you can earn without penalty. In 1979, you could have earned $4,500; in 1980, $5,000; in 1981, $5,500; and in 1982, $6,000, and so on. In 1982, after age seventy, there will be no limits on what a person can earn without penalty. But, for persons age sixty-five to seventy, of every two dollars earned above the annual exempt amount, Social Security will deduct one dollar in retirement benefits. The Congressional Amendment of 1977 brought about changes in the earnings test. It is complicated, and careful planning with Social Security on the age of retirement might be wise. For example, even applying for Medicare hospital coverage

Ways to Have Money

before retirement might be interpreted as the first year of retirement—even though no Social Security benefits were paid.

A widow is also entitled to earn the limit, such as $5,000 in 1980, and still receive her Social Security check as a dependent. Also, if she earns over the amount specified, her benefits will be reduced one dollar for every two dollars earned.

If you are self-employed after retirement, your Social Security benefit is determined on the basis of your involvement with the company rather than total earnings. In general, if you are self-employed and work more than forty-five hours per month, your services will be considered substantial. If you are self-employed in an occupation that requires a high level of skill or you are managing a large business, your services or involvement may be considered substantial even though you work less than forty-five hours a month. If you work less than fifteen hours a month, your services are not considered substantial under any circumstances. Check with your Social Security Office for a ruling on your self-employment status.

If you earn or expect to earn more than the limit, you must report your earnings to your Social Security Office each year unless you are age seventy-two or older. The Social Security Office will send you a form for reporting estimated earnings in February. You must complete the form and return it by April 15.

The Ideal Life

Women's and Survivors' Benefits

Women who work and pay Social Security taxes qualify for their own benefits. Women who have not worked or who interrupted their careers for several years to raise children will probably not have enough quarters to qualify for their own benefit. When a dependent woman (or a husband that depends on his wife for at least half of his support) reaches age sixty-five, she is entitled to receive a benefit one-half that of her husband's, whether he is working or retired. A woman can choose to receive dependent benefits at age sixty-two, but the amount will be permanently reduced.

Almost sixty percent of the women in the United States work outside the home and qualify for Social Security benefits on their own record. But women generally receive lower salaries, and the burden of raising children most often lies on their shoulders, forcing them to quit work or to work part time for a number of years. At retirement age their own benefits often do not equal the benefit they would receive as a dependent. A woman is entitled to the larger benefit but never both.

If a worker dies, the eligible widow or widower and any dependent children will receive survivors' benefits equaling three-quarters of that worker's Social Security benefits. A widow or widower over sixty-five receives one hundred percent of all benefits but can elect to receive permanently reduced benefits as early

Ways to Have Money

as age sixty. A divorced person can collect survivors' benefits at age sixty only if the marriage lasted twenty years or longer. A widow or widower should check with the nearest Social Security Office to see if his or her own benefit would be larger than the survivors' benefits. In addition to monthly benefit checks, survivors receive a lump-sum death benefit payment equal to three times the monthly benefit up to a certain limit. This is most often used to cover funeral expenses.

Disability

A worker who becomes severely disabled before sixty-five can receive disability checks. Under Social Security regulations, a worker is considered disabled if he has a severe physical or mental condition which prevents him/her from earning a living, if the condition is expected to or has lasted at least a year, or if the condition is expected to result in death. Checks can start after the sixth full month of disability and will continue as long as the worker is disabled, even though he may work a small amount. He receives the same amount as he would be eligible for at retirement, and when he reaches age sixty-five, the disability payments are converted to a retirement pension without influencing the amount.

Certain members of a disabled worker's family are eligible for monthly disability payments. Dependents receiving disability benefits must meet the same eligibility requirements as for a retired person.

The Ideal Life

The amount of the disability payment is the same amount as if the worker had retired at age sixty-five. For an estimate of your disability payments, contact your local Social Security Office.

Medical evidence from a physician or other sources will indicate the severity of the condition and the extent to which it prevents a person from doing substantial, gainful work. Age, education, training and work experience also may be considered in deciding whether an individual is able to work. If the worker can perform some substantial, gainful work, he will not be considered disabled.

When a worker applies for disability assistance, he/she will be afforded an opportunity for rehabilitation training and special employment services. This is financed by state and federal funds. State Departments of Public Assistance are often interested in these programs both from the point of view of reducing the state's welfare expense and also to providing a more meaningful life for the recipient.

There's a movement afoot to reduce the rolls of disability beneficiaries, the current complaint being that the recipients get more from insurance benefits than they did from working. Eighteen percent get eighty percent of pre-disability earnings. If they are paid only fifty percent, they tend to return to work.

Ways to Have Money

Supplemental Social Security Income For Older Persons

Social Security income is administered by the Social Security Administration but is funded by the Federal Government with supplements from state governments and general revenues. The purpose of the program is to provide a minimum monthly income to needy people of limited or no financial resources, sixty-five or older, to the disabled or blind, or to veterans without service-connected disability who cannot manage on their veterans pensions.

To be eligible for this program, a single person cannot have cash or cashable assets of more than $1,500 and a couple cannot have cash or cashable assets of more than $2,250. This does not include the value of a home, furnishings, and personal goods. A person will not be eligible if he owns a car valued over $1,200, unless it is necessary for trips to the doctor, etc.

Income from Social Security benefits, veteran's compensation, workmen's compensation and personal income producing investments will reduce Social Security income payments if they exceed certain limits. A single person who qualifies will receive checks of $177.80 to $208.20 per month and a couple who qualifies will receive checks of $266.70 to $323.30 per month. "Spend down to a legitimate need and qualify" say advisors.

Proposals for New Social Security Legislation

Congress has been considering the following pro-

The Ideal Life

posals: (1) freezing rates for 1981 at the 1980 level; (2) making one-half of Social Security benefits subject to Federal income tax; (3) raising the retirement age from sixty-five to sixty-eight; (4) tightening the program and reducing disability payments by fifteen percent, so that payments would not be more than the worker earned in regular employment and (5) bringing to the Social Security program all federal, state and local employees, thereby increasing money in the system and preventing such employees from collecting federal pension benefits and Social Security benefits; (6) cutting benefits; (7) turning Medicare and health costs over to general treasury revenues and giving income tax credit. Contact your Social Security Office to keep abreast of all law revisions.

Your Right to Question a Social Security Administration Decision

If you are in disagreement with the Social Security Administration regarding a claim for retirement, survivors' or disability insurance benefits, you must do the following:

(1) First ask, within sixty days of the date you received notice of initial decision, that the decision be reconsidered.
(2) Next, if you disagree with the results of that reconsideration, ask for a hearing before an administrative law judge; the judge may be an officer of the Bureau of Hearings and Appeals of the Social Security Administration, but must be a judge who took no part in the initial

Ways to Have Money

or reconsidered decision. Your request must be made within sixty days from the date you receive notice of the reconsidered decision.

(3) If you disagree with the decision of the administrative law judge, you may then ask for a review of that decision by the Appeals Council, again within sixty days of receiving hearing decision.

(4) If you disagree with the Appeals Council decision or if the Appeals Council denies your request, you may bring a civil action in a Federal Court. Your complaint must be filed in a district court of the U.S. within sixty days of the date of mailing of the notice of the Appeals Council's decision or denial of review.

The Social Security Administration agrees that you have a right to be represented by a qualified person of your choice at any stage of your claim. See the pamphlet from the Social Security Administration, *Your Right to Question the Decision Made on Your Social Security Claim*.

Other Government Services

For you who are concerned about the welfare of parents or other relatives, there are many government and private programs designed to assist and fill the needs of older persons. And as one government handbook says, "Unless you know about them and how to reach them, it can be like trying to find your way out of a forest." Many people will not avail themselves of services to which they

The Ideal Life

are entitled if they are unable to cope with new and often changing bureaucratic requirements. They may feel they are evidently not qualified for benefits that are too bureaucratically difficult to attain. Realizing how essential it is to secure information on such matters, Congress passed a law which requires that all older people, no matter where they live, must have "reasonable access" to information and referral services linking them to opportunities in the community.

The Area Agency on Aging, listed in your telephone directory, will be helpful. Every state has a State Agency on Aging at the state capitol. The Federal government has an Administration on Aging in the U.S. Department of Health, Education and Welfare. Together with the local Agency on Aging, these public agencies dispense tax funds for many programs and serve as advocates for older workers, inspiring Congress, state legislators and local officials to act responsibly in meeting the needs of older citizens.

Senior Centers expand and improve social services to the older persons. They assist in providing housing for the elderly, either in their own or rented homes, hot meals, personal care, health clinics, outreach, counseling, education programs, food stamps, and transportation to grocery stores.

The Amended Older American Act, Title III, 1978 brought these programs about by specifically encouraging state and local Agencies on Aging to

Ways to Have Money

concentrate resources in developing comprehensive social service systems. The purpose of these programs is to assist older individuals in maintaining their independence and dignity in their homes and aiding in their economic and personal independence while providing a continuum of care.

In April 1979 nearly 4,226,600 persons were receiving federally administered supplemental security aid, costing $433.9 million. State supplementation was $127.5 million for 257,800 persons. Each state is involved in the implementation of the program; and many states, Pennsylvania for example, give assistance to the elderly for energy bills if their annual income does not exceed $5,600. Today, the poor pay about twenty-five percent of their income for fuel according to the U.S. Senate Labor and Human Relations Committee. Help, also, may be given on automobile tags in Pennsylvania if the family's income is $7,500 or less, reducing the cost from eighteen dollars to ten dollars.

Pensions

The growth of the private pension system has been phenomenal. Pension funds have grown from $12 billion in 1950 to over $200 billion in 1980. In 1950 approximately twenty-two percent of the labor force was covered by some form of pension program and today over half of the nation's workers are participating in private pension plans. Virtually all major U.S. corporations and unions have instituted pension programs.

The Ideal Life

This tremendous history of growth has caused monumental problems and a multitude of misconceptions. In 1974 the government attempted to eliminate many of the unfair pension practices, guarantee employee pension rights and regulate the management of pension programs by passing the Employee Retirement Income Security Act (ERISA). The reform laws were passed after an investigation by the Senate Committee on Labor and Public Work revealed that millions of Americans were being cheated out of their hard-earned pensions. Workers were dismissed just prior to becoming eligible to collect their pensions or employers simply refused to pay any pension benefits.

ERISA eliminated most major problems, but several injustices still remain. Most private pension plans only provide fifteen to twenty-five percent of pre-retirement income, hardly satisfactory to maintain a comfortable standard of living. Most plans do not provide survivor's benefits. Executives usually receive disproportionately higher benefits. Part-time and temporary employees are not covered by most pension plans. Federal pensions are protected against inflation, but private pensions are not.

Our good friends, Frank and Genevieve Gollon from St. Paul, Minnesota, who "are pushing seventy-five years," have recently celebrated their fiftieth wedding anniversary and give the pre-retirement group a bit of advice concerning money. Frank writes, "Having been born and raised in the northern states, our 'Ideal Life' is a home on a lake, near the city and

Ways to Have Money

shopping centers; with space for flowers and vegetable gardens during nine months of the year. We spend the other three months down south or traveling, but always returning to our 'anchor spot' where our children, grandchildren and old friends can always visit us.

"Oh yes, a small detail. A good pension helps which, added to Social Security benefits, enables us to enjoy our life together. We always keep in mind that we did not do all these things by ourselves. There has been Someone looking over our shoulder, so we thank Him for the gifts He has bestowed."

Your Rights

The recent regulations ensure that pensions earned during employment will be available upon retirement. But the reform established several other important pension rights. Ignorance and apathy have resulted in millions of dollars of benefits that have been needlessly uncollected. One of the rights guaranteed by this reform is the accessibility of comprehensive information regarding company pensions. The company's pension plan administrator must provide details and conditions of the plan and rules for eligibility. The plans also must spell out how the pensions are financed, and what circumstances would cause the worker to be ineligible. ERISA protects benefits against bankruptcy. An employee no longer loses pension rights if he/she changes jobs. In most cases, employees are guaranteed a percentage of their benefits after just one year of service.

The Ideal Life

The Labor Department and Internal Revenue Service determine whether the plans are in harmony with the law. Each year the employer must furnish a detailed financial report to the Labor Department on the amount of money every worker has accrued. Employers must make this information available to employees upon request. If an employee has a complaint against the plan, he may bring suit against the administrators in federal court.

To further assist the worker, Congress passed the 1978 Amendment, in effect since January 1, 1979, which said a worker could continue to work until he was seventy and he could not be denied a job or a promotion because of age, alone. A worker who is sixty-two and a new employee can legally be denied a place in the pension plan.

Vesting

ERISA established miniumum vesting standards that ensure pension rights in the event a worker is dismissed, layed off or changes jobs.

There are three types of vesting plans employers can choose between:

(1) A fully vested employee is entitled to one hundred percent of pension benefits after ten years of service.
(2) Graded vesting permits employees to receive twenty-five percent vesting after five years of work plus five percent for each additional year of service up to ten years. At that point,

Ways to Have Money

the worker is eligible for fifty percent vesting with an additional ten percent for every year thereafter.

(3) Rule of forty-five is based on age plus years of service. An employee who has worked for a company for at least five years and whose age and years worked total forty-five is eligible for fifty percent vesting. Thereafter, ten percent vestment is awarded yearly.

These pensions are government insured by Pension Benefit Guaranty Corporation to protect the worker from a company bankruptcy or a dislocating merger.

Even with ERISA, a worker can lose all his pension credits if for some reason his work is interrupted. The law does not see anything less than a year as an interruption. If pension funds have already been completely vested and then there is a stoppage of work, regardless of how long, this interruption cannot threaten benefits. If a worker is not vested, however, it is possible that pension rights could be eliminated, depending upon when he returned to the job and the kind of a plan in effect.

Because of the wide variance between pension plans, especially between private industry and government agencies, there is growing discussion about a universal pension system. Municipal workers and military personnel can retire after twenty years and draw benefits for forty or forty-five years. The auto industry encourages early retirement by offering an

The Ideal Life

excellent pension program after thirty years of service. But many persons must work until age sixty-two or sixty-five to be eligible for complete pension benefits. ERISA is the framework for a unified system, but it will be many years before this law is fully in effect, and several amendments will be necessary to eliminate existing and future problems.

For now it is up to the employee to know all he or she can about the pension program. ERISA requires all employers to provide an accurate description of their pension plan. Examine it and ask questions if you don't understand something. You should know the following points about your pension plan:

* What are the various eligibility requirements and how are they influenced by early retirement?
* Does all compensation count toward benefits; are benefits based on a fixed sum, salary or length of service?
* When do benefits begin and how are they paid, are they protected against inflation in any way?
* What are the vesting provisions?
* Does previous employment count toward benefits?
* How much does the employer contribute; how are contributions figured; can benefits be increased through mandatory or voluntary employee contributions to the plan?
* What happens to contributions and benefits in the event of merger, bankruptcy, layoff, change of profession, or termination of employment?

Ways to Have Money

* How many employees receive pensions; are benefits commensurate with length of service and salary.
* What type of survivor's benefits or options are available through the plan; are the benefits reduced with this option?

Retirement Funds

Half the labor force is employed by companies offering pension plans. The other half of American workers are either self-employed or work for companies that do not provide pension benefits. These individuals have only Social Security for retirement, and Social Security alone cannot possibly provide an adequate retirement income. Other sources of income are essential for these individuals.

Individual Retirement Accounts: An IRA is a retirement plan for persons not participating in a tax-qualified pension plan. An IRA allows them to set aside fifteen percent of their salaries or $1,500 a year, whichever is less, and not pay taxes on it until they retire. This money immediately begins earning interest at rates higher than conventional savings accounts. Since these funds are intended for retirement, they cannot be withdrawn before age 59½. Nor can they be borrowed against or used as collateral. In both situations, to violate the rules would result in a ten percent penalty and additional income tax. The money must be withdrawn, starting at age 70½. If less is taken out than the schedule states, a fifty percent tax is charged on what has not been withdrawn, unless the IRS can

The Ideal Life

be convinced that a reasonable error was made but corrected as soon as possible.

Money can be moved from one IRA plan to another, as from a mutual fund to a certificate of deposit, but the withdrawal check from one institution must be made out to the institution that is next going to have custody of the money; thus tax penalties are avoided. Funds may be withdrawn and held tax-free, once, for 60 days, while it is decided how to "roll over" the money. After the first time, no tax-free roll-over is permitted for one year. Any violation of the rules by a person not 59½ or disabled may result in the IRS determining that there has been a "distribution," which will be taxed as ordinary income with an additional ten percent penalty.

IRA funds can be invested in a number of different ways: flexible annuity contracts, savings accounts, certificates of deposit, credit union shares, mutual fund shares, stocks and special government retirement bonds. On interest-bearing accounts, find out what the effective rate of interest is. A rate of seven and three-quarter percent compounded daily from the day of deposit to day of withdrawal may yield more than a simple eight percent account. If you have questions regarding IRA's it might be advisable to secure advice from your CPA, or lawyer or the financial institution you are considering.

Keogh Plans: These plans are for the self-employed businessmen, professionals and moonlighters, and are similar to IRA's. The primary difference is the

Ways to Have Money

amount a person may contribute. He may contribute fifteen percent of his annual income up to $7,500; and if he earns only $500, he can place it in the fund, tax free. Keogh accounts can be of great advantage to a husband and wife team. By employing a spouse in the business you can open an account for the spouse as well as yourself and contribute up to $15,000 a year, tax free. All Keogh plans must be set up as retirement funds with some kind of financial institution such as a bank, insurance company, mutual fund, etc. Employer pension funds may not be rolled over into a Keogh as they can be into an IRA.

Withdrawals cannot be made until age 59½ and must be withdrawn at 70½. Taxes are assessed at time of withdrawal and if rules are violated, stiff penalties must be paid.

The IRS determines how much can be withdrawn in monthly installments. There is no need to establish an annuity. Taxes on the monthly payments are based on the basic regulations that govern annuities.

Investing for Retirement

Earlier in this chapter you calculated how much money you can reasonably afford to put in various types of income-producing investments and savings plans for retirement. This figure can and should be revised occasionally to accommodate increases and decreases of present income. Investing this capital now for retirement is very important for it is the third resource, after Social Security and private pensions,

The Ideal Life

for developing a strong financial base for the rest of your life.

Careful planning is essential. Social Security benefits, private pensions, and cash resources decrease in purchasing power as inflation worsens. But investing resources in a diversified portfolio that concentrates on reduced risks can protect your retirement income against inflation and provide a secure financial future.

An investment program should be begun prior to retirement. The composition of the investment portfolio will vary according to a number of factors: 1) the years remaining to retirement; 2) the current adequacy of a family's income from other sources; and 3) the amount of investable cash. For instance, a young man with a salary adequate to his needs might invest in growth stocks in anticipation of building up his investments through capital gains. The result would be sacrificing income in the interim, but saving taxes, due to the fact that by law a capital gains deduction would lower his effective tax rate more than had he received an equal amount of interest or dividend income. On the other hand, a middle-aged individual in a relatively high tax bracket might shelter his income by buying medium-term tax-exempt bonds. At retirement, both individuals may want to switch into taxable bonds, depending on their tax bracket and their need for taxable income. The maturity of these bonds purchased should then not only reflect the expected lifespan of the parties involved, but also

Ways to Have Money

market conditions and the effect of mounting inflation to erode the value of these securities. A continuous and moderate investment in stocks coupled with bond holdings could be considered prudent depending on income requirements.

Stocks

Stocks represent a share of ownership in a corporation and offer the opportunity to participate in the long-term capital appreciation. If the corporation prospers so does the shareholder, but if the company does not do well or fails, there is little chance of recouping the cost of the stock.

Between 1926 and 1976 stocks provided a total return (dividends plus appreciation) of 9.2 percent. But risk is a major factor.

Selecting stocks in stable companies with long histories of increased dividends and capital appreciation may protect your investment. Natural resource companies have kept pace with inflation and have steadily increased capital because they have assets that rise in value with inflation. Another area of relatively "safe" stock is companies that offer preferred stock. These stocks produce a steady cash income through dividends that rarely fluctuate. If profits decrease and dividends must be cut, the dividends of the common stock shareholders are cut first. Preference is given to holders of preferred stock; if profits rise sharply, preferred dividends remain the same.

The Ideal Life

You should keep capital in stocks only if you do not depend on that capital for retirement income. Most of us cannot afford this luxury. If a person facing retirement in a few years invests his or her capital in a corporation that experiences a downtrend for several years in the midst of continuing inflation, that investment will depreciate greatly leaving the retiree with little income.

Bonds

Bonds represent corporation debt. When you buy a bond you are lending a corporation or municipality money for a specified period of time for which you are paid a consistent rate of interest. Between 1926 and 1980 the return on corporate bonds was 4.2 percent. At maturity, bonds pay off at face value (price at which they were purchased). Therefore, bonds are considered a more secure investment than the stock market although not foolproof.

Bonds have several disadvantages. They must be purchased for minimum denominations of $1,000 and generally mature in twenty or more years. Bonds can be sold at any time, but prices fluctuate with current interest rates. If prices decline, you may be forced to wait until the bond matures to recoup your entire investment. Bonds could tie up capital for long periods of time. However, most high-quality bonds are good, safe investments that provide a steady rate of return.

Ways to Have Money

The bond market is divided into three categories: government bonds, corporates and municipals.

Government Bonds: There are two types of government bonds, U.S. Treasury securities, which are marketable, and U.S. Savings Bonds which are nonmarketable. U.S. Treasury issues afford a wide range of maturities and a steady flow of new issues. The return on these securities far exceeds those on savings bonds because they reflect the going market rates acceptable to private financial institutions.

Treasury securities can be purchased through a stockbroker or banker for the principal plus a commission or service charge. Commissions and service charges can be avoided by purchasing the securities directly from the Federal Reserve Bank. When the security reaches maturity it can be sold back to the institution from which it was purchased, or it can be "rolled over" at the prevailing interest rates.

There are three kinds of treasury securities. U.S. Treasury bills have maturities of three, six, nine and twelve months. They can be purchased for a minimum of $10,000, which is returned with accrued interest at maturity. They can be sold on the open market at the prevailing rates before maturity.

U.S. Treasury notes are securities with maturities from one to ten years requiring a minimum purchase of $1,000. Specific issues may have higher minimums. These securities pay interest semiannually.

The Ideal Life

U.S. Treasury bonds mature in ten years or more with a minimum purchase of $1,000. These securities offer the highest rate of return for Treasury securities.

Corporate Bonds: Individual investors began investing aggressively in the corporate bond market in the seventies when the interest rates were at their highest level. Industrial corporations, utilities, financial institutions and real estate firms borrowed billions of dollars by offering bonds. Several types of bonds are available on the market today, but only a couple are suitable for persons investing for retirement income. Before purchasing any bond it is wise to seek advice from a major, reputable brokerage house capable of standing behind its recommendations and personnel. Never give a salesman total discretion in handling your account.

Before considering any corporate bond, check its quality in one of the principal rating services, either Moody's or Standard and Poor. The highest quality is AAA, the poorest is C. A person investing for retirement can minimize risk by selecting bonds rated A, AA, or AAA and by avoiding inexpensive bonds. Most dealers quote ratings as well as prices. Ratings indicate overall company strength and predict, to a degree, the likelihood that the corporation may "call" the bond once issued.

If interest rates decline below the level at the time they were issued, a corporation may call in the bond

Ways to Have Money

and replace it with a bond paying the lower interest rate. Most bonds offer a call provision to protect investments against redemption. Call provisions are in effect for a specified period, but the length of the period varies with individual bonds.

Corporate bonds can be divided into two primary categories: utilities and industrials. Utility bonds generally mature in thirty years and industrials in twenty-five. Some intermediate term bonds are available. Utility bonds traditionally have offered five years of call protection, and industrials offer ten years. Bonds can only be called when interest rates have decreased rapidly and reinvestment potential is poor, so longer call-protection provisions are desirable. Highly rated corporate bonds with noncall provisions are expensive but offer the retirees a very safe investment.

Municipal Bonds: Municipal bonds are offered by states, cities and villages, local port authorities and housing authorities and many other local government agencies. These bonds are an excellent investment for the retiree because, with the tax exemptions, the rate of return is somewhat higher than other investments. Municipal bonds are exempt from federal taxes and exempt from state and local taxes if the investor lives in the state of issuance. The rating services rate municipals in a manner similar to corporate bonds. Highly rated municipals are extremely safe and, therefore, very attractive as a retirement investment. The bonds

The Ideal Life

are easy to sell and the prices are recorded in the financial pages of major newspapers every day.

There are several types of municipal bonds available, offering a selection of maturities ranging from one to thirty years with minimums ranging from $1,000 and up. Longer maturities are more readily available. Shorter maturities have higher minimums.

The best time to invest in long-term municipal bonds is when the demand for short-term credit increases and investors anticipate declining interest rates. Municipal bonds must be safeguarded, because the owner's name is not printed anywhere on the bond. The person who possesses the bond is considered the legal owner.

Short-term Investments

At the moment, high short-term rates have generated considerable interest in new short-term instruments:

Banks and savings and loans can offer $10,000 certificates geared to the six-month treasury bill rate. Advantages are the absence of any bank service charge and $40,000 Federal insurance. Disadvantages are the fact the interest is subject to state taxes, unlike that on bills, and bills are bought at a discount which increases the effective return. Premature redemption of the certificates would result in a penalty while proceeds from the sale of bills would be dependent on market conditions.

Ways to Have Money

Money market funds are composed of various short-term instruments. The rate they pay relative to prevailing market levels depends on how well they anticipate market trends as well as the quality mix. There are credit risks related to this mix and a degree of market risk dependent on whether a fund could meet substantial outflows without having to liquidate assets at a loss. Some funds are also rumored to have operational problems which could impair their ability to afford customers twenty-four hour liquidity as promised.

Other Retirement Investment Possibilities

Life insurance policies may offer investment opportunities. The primary reason for purchasing life insurance is to protect your family against financial loss from death or disability. As you near retirement this protection is not as important as when the family was young and dependent. It would be foolish to use the limited income of retirement to pay insurance premiums for continued protection. Only enough insurance will be needed to cover final expenses.

If you anticipate the need for continued life insurance protection during the retirement years, convert your present policy to a paid-up policy. This would allow you to maintain the policy's value at the time of retirement without paying additional premiums, which avoids some of the financial drain on your retirement income.

The Ideal Life

For investment purposes, you may be able to convert all or part of your life insurance into an annuity plan. An annuity guarantees a fixed monthly payment at retirement for a sum paid in advance. Converting life insurance essentially reinvests the cash value of the policy into an annuity. Prices for annuity plans vary considerably among insurance companies and hefty sales commissions are common. Shop around to find the best deal.

There is a primary disadvantage to annuities as retirement investments. Annuity payments are fixed, which means that, as inflation increases, the purchasing power of each fixed payment decreases. Since annuities offer no anti-inflation features, it would be wiser for a person approaching retirement to invest the cash value of the life insurance policy in income-producing investments that also provide a hedge against inflation.

Real Estate

Traditionally, real estate has been considered a good investment and a fine hedge against inflation. Anyone who owns a home knows how it has appreciated in value over the past decade. That home is still of value and is still appreciating. Sometimes retirees are told that they should "get rid of that house and rent an apartment." "Don't do it," say financial counselors. In times of inflation, your money will erode and the rent you will be paying for the apartment will continue to increase substantially without building any equity.

Ways to Have Money

Real estate is an excellent retirement investment. It is stable and offers a very high rate of return. Your home should be the focal point of retirement investment plans. Real estate offers many tax advantages to the investor holding a mortgage during the peak income earning years. You are able to pay housing expenses and invest at the same time and you can deduct mortgage interest and property taxes from your federal income taxes. Try to arrange to pay off your mortgage a few years prior to retirement. You will then be able to live with minimum housing expenses and can put the extra cash in other income-producing investments for retirement.

Real estate does have some drawbacks. It is not a liquid form of investment, and purchasing property or land can tie up money for as long as twenty-five or thirty years. There are few bargains on the market and financing has become more difficult with soaring interest rates. Inflation is expected to remain high, and house prices probably won't drop. Luxury houses are not for the small investor because of costly mortgage payments, taxes, insurance and other expenses.

There are several other ways to make money in real estate. Income-producing real estate, such as multiple-living dwellings and business property, can be very lucrative but often requires a great deal of work. A good sense of the market is a must. Seek growing areas that will increase in value as improvements are made and development begins. Timing is

The Ideal Life

extremely important. The best time to buy investment real estate is when real estate buying in general is at a low. Real estate, like most businesses, follows a cycle of ups and downs. Properties bought when the market is at a low can be sold for good profit at a peak buying time. Be prepared to spend several hours a week managing and maintaining the properties, more time if you are inexperienced.

In recent years many investors have purchased and renovated houses in the inner city or nearby suburbs to sell or rent to persons returning to the city because of the energy crisis and the increasing cost of transportation. These people buy a home, live in it for a couple of years while the improvements are made and then sell the property for a good profit or rent it for steady income.

Some people buy a choice lot and build a home on it to increase the value. They live in the home for a couple of years, furnish it, and sell it for a profit. There are several good real estate investments available, but before buying or selling any property, seek the services of a reputable realtor.

Real estate investing, carefully and thoughtfully done, can result in a life such as that of our friends, Don and Carmel Peacock from California, who write:

"In 1957 we decided we could never send our kids through college or retire comfortably unless we increased our income. I went back to work full time. In

Ways to Have Money

1968, as our youngest started to college, we looked at our economic situation and decided we needed to recoup some of the money we had spent on college educations if we were going to retire with 'anything but the shirts on our backs.' Since the only way we could obtain a sizeable amount of money was in the real estate market, we decided to build a house for speculation. We did, and we sold it. We then bought a 127-acre farm which was improved and sold at a profit.

"In 1976 we moved to California, bought a duplex house and have found the 'ideal life after fifty.' The weather is pleasant and we exercise daily. We are able to live comfortably on our income. We have the companionship of each other, our children and our neighbors. We are enjoying our happiest years experiencing freedom and leisure and the abolition of 'deadlines.' We anticipate that the future will bring adjustments in physical health and social adaptation which we hope to manage as successfully as possible."

The Peacocks make an important summation, "We worked for fifteen years in preparation for retirement, and although these were chaotic years, with our children being teenagers and college students in the 'sixties', the years were also fun and the very foundation of what we are now enjoying."

Retirement is an individual concept. Each of us has his own set of definitions, expectations and needs

The Ideal Life

that will govern his retirement lifestyle. Your retirement financial need will depend primarily upon your expected lifestyle and the inflation rate in years to come. Decisions should be based on fact. Analyze the retirement situations and plans of friends, relatives and associates, and never hesitate to revise your plans if your original ideas and dreams cannot be realized. Only careful planning and a positive attitude can make a successful retirement happen.

The Ideal Home for You

Chances are that when you bought your home your main concern was having a place to live. But with recent skyrocketing real estate values, that home has become much more than a shelter. Homes are excellent investments that have proved to be good hedges against inflation.

As you approach retirement, housing needs change. The family is probably getting smaller, so your present house may be too large. A job no longer restricts you to living in the community. On the other hand, the grandchildren may be nearby and you are really comfortable with your little castle. There are many housing alternatives based on a great number of factors. No decision comes easily. Careful thought and planning must go into your decision if future years are to be comfortable and filled with contentment.

The Ideal Life

The options are numerous. Remain in your present home and neighborhood, continuing to let the value appreciate. Sell or rent the home and move to a different part of town. Move to a new climate or region. Buy a condominium, existing home, or trailer home. Build a new house. Rent an apartment, house, or farm. Seek housing in a retirement village, community, or residence club.

When considering the best choice of housing options for your family, it is helpful to list the advantages and disadvantages of the possibilities on separate sheets of paper and compare them. The following financial considerations are important to list in each case.

Determine how much it costs you to live in your present home. Add up the mortgage payments, if any, property taxes, insurance, utility bills, and maintenance and repair costs. Include any possible replacements of large appliances, water heater, or furnace.

If you're considering renting out your home, estimate how much rental income your home might bring. This can be based on rents being charged for similar homes in your area, or a real estate broker can give you an estimate. In figuring return, consider that the property may be vacant at times during change of tenants, but as a landlord, your costs continue for mortgage payments, insurance maintenance, and management costs. List these. If you rent, your cash profit

The Ideal Home for You

will benefit from tax considerations, such as depreciation, and the rising value of the house and land.

If you hope to buy or build a new home, estimate the down payment, monthly mortgage payments, new appliances necessary and maintenance of the home.

Estimate what it would cost you to live in an apartment or a smaller rented house. Include utility costs and lawn care or snow removal.

Investigate the costs of a condominium in your area. In this case, include upkeep, utilities, and fees for recreational facilities, which may be assessed, as well as taxes.

These calculations should help you compare the advantages and disadvantages of the basic options open to you. You may find it's best for you to sell your home, buy a smaller, less expensive one, and invest part of the proceeds to produce additional retirement income.

The ideal place to settle down should fit your retirement lifestyle, so take time now to determine what you want most from the coming years. Most agree that there is only so much fishing, golfing, traveling, etc. to fill all that free time. You may want your home to be the central point of a new business or perhaps a hobby shop or a conference center. These considerations should be taken into account when you think of a smaller house in a new location.

If your retirement housing plans are too drasti-

The Ideal Life

cally opposed to the kind of life to which you have been accustomed you may be overreaching your level of tolerance. This was the case of some friends of ours.

Some years ago our friends carefully planned their retirement away from the hubbub of the city and, for reasons of health, far away from industrial pollution. They sold their city home and invested all of the money in a plot of land by a river bank a few miles from a small town, and built a new home on the site. "We're going to relax and just let the rest of the world go by," they proclaimed. After a year of relaxing, they were the two most bored people we have ever seen. The "For Sale" sign was up for five years or so before they were able to get back to the stimulating city life so essential to their happiness. Before you commit your money and life to a new lifestyle, think the possibility through carefully; and then think it through again.

The first step in deciding whether to stay or move is to evaluate your present home and neighborhood. Here are several reasons why you may want to stay in your present home and neighborhood. You have an emotional attachment to the house. It's home. You've built a lot of yourselves into the house, which you'd never recoup if you sold. You have great neighbors, really more like an extended family. Perhaps more important, you are near other members of your family.

You know the structure of the house, how it's built, how to maintain it, and at present, you have no problems with maintenance costs. You know the age

The Ideal Home for You

and what to expect from all the appliances. You know the condition of the plumbing. Your lot is large enough for lawn and gardening, but not a burden.

The house is in a good neighborhood and will continue to be a solid investment as prices climb. The community is established, so drastic tax increases don't seem likely.

You are close to public transportation, shopping centers, churches, hospital, recreation areas and facilities. You are well established in the community and like your doctor, dentist, and lawyer. The main traffic arteries are far enough removed to avoid noise day and night. The fire and police protection are good, as are the community services, such as street cleaning and upkeep, trash and garbage pickup, and sidewalk repairs.

If, after a thorough search of all the possibilities available, you decide there's no place like home, you may find it advisable to check out all of the money-making prospects of staying in the same house.

Will the zoning ordinances permit you to turn the house into a multiple dwelling? There is an opportunity to produce enough income to pay property taxes and some, if not all, the maintenance.

Often a two-story home can accommodate outside stairs to the second floor. It is possible to convert the upstairs to an apartment. It calls for some remodeling which you can do yourself with the help of a handyman carpenter or architect. Perhaps it's a job to look

The Ideal Life

forward to after retirement. If, however, you would like supplemental income upon retirement, you can get started in time to be in business when you drop out of the work force.

If you need help in financing, you can get a low-interest home improvement loan. Keep in mind that income from rent will not be deducted from your Social Security when you become eligible.

The other outstanding advantage is one-floor living for yourself. As the years go by, the stairs seem to get steeper and the risk of tripping is greater. While remodeling for yourself, don't overlook some of the conveniences and accommodations designed into housing for older persons. Plan rails to hang onto, storage space that doesn't require climbing, and easy operating doors, drawers and windows.

Even if you don't remodel but stay on in a big house you will find it's dollar wise to condense your living space to reduce heating and air conditioning costs.

Owning property is an investment and your investment will usually ride the crest of inflation. The only negative consideration is the possibility that property values in the neighborhood may decline because of freeways, encroachment of commercial zoning, lack of upkeep of surrounding property, etc. As a rule a person's home is the single largest investment he has and deserves careful attention. During periods of mounting inflation it isn't usually wise to sell a home

The Ideal Home for You

and rent an apartment, because rents will continue to go up. Without ownership of property you don't have a hedge against increasing costs of living.

Selling Your Home and Moving

For some individuals, selling a home is indeed a wise move. Even if the mortgage is paid up, property taxes and utilities continue to soar each year. Many elderly persons must scrape to pay gas and heating oil bills. Retirement-age persons can claim a one time tax exemption on the profits of a home sale, up to $100,000, if the person has owned and lived in the house for three of the last five years. With this excellent provision, a couple can sell their large home, buy a smaller home, and have extra capital to invest in other income-producing areas.

There is also another alternative. A couple sells its home for $50,000 and invests the capital in a two-and-one-half-year money market certificate that yields eight percent or $333 a month. Now, if that couple can rent an apartment, including utilities, for $300, quite a savings is realized, since the couple will not be paying property tax and high utility bills. And the initial $50,000 investment never erodes.

Selling your house can be complicated. Should you attempt to sell your property and pocket what would otherwise be paid out in commissions? Many home owners do just that, but, to avoid hitches in the complex transaction, it is wise to employ legal help.

The Ideal Life

Whether you sell it or contract with a broker, you should familiarize yourself with the current market. Find out from your township or county real estate office what similar properties in your area are selling for. The important thing is to get the top dollar for your property.

Timing is most important when you put your house on the market. One of the primary considerations is not interrupting the school year of a prospect's children. Corporations usually move people around soon after the beginning of a new budget year. Late spring or early summer is usually the best time to sell.

After you check out all of the complicated details of selling a home yourself, you may decide the broker truly earns his commission. You will, no doubt, want to visit with three, four, or more licensed organizations before deciding with whom to contract the sale of your property. It is essential to have someone who is local and is familiar with taxes, the ordinances, and facilities of the community. Certainly you want an honest, reputable realtor who knows property values in your community and won't build up false hopes only to get your listing. You may want to examine the various types of contracts with a realty company and go over them with your lawyer.

Types of listings vary from realtor to realtor. With exclusive listings one organization receives all the sales commissions. Multiple listing, on the other hand, allows a realtor the original listing with the

The Ideal Home for You

provision that he will share the sales opportunity with other sales agencies. If the agent with the listing sells the property, he receives all of the sales commission. If one of the cooperating agents makes the sale, the commission is shared. An open listing doesn't give any single broker exclusivity. A number of brokers receive your listing, and the one that makes the sale receives the commission.

Your initial agreement should be for the minimum length of time. The agreement can always be extended or renewed if you are happy with the performance of the realtor or agent.

Pricing is an important factor in how quickly a property sells, so it must be closely checked with the going rate in your particular community. If it is overpriced, it may stay on the market for months, or a year or more. Remember that you can always come down in price, but it's hard to go up.

Once your house is listed on the market, something just short of bedlam may set in. Be sure to require that all brokers who want to show the house give you sufficient advance notice so you can get the house in order. Apologies for an untidy house won't impress a prospective buyer.

It's possible that you can come out ahead by renting your house instead of selling it. The home remains your asset and may continue to appreciate in value and provide a hedge against inflation. You may then rent a smaller place to live. The rent you collect

The Ideal Life

may be more than you pay out, but you still have the obligation of property tax, income tax, and maintenance of your home.

If you're thinking of moving

Most people want to retire in the same general area in which they live; but if you hope to move to a new area, there are several factors you'll need to consider before making a final decision. Your new housing and locale should come as close as possible to satisfying the four basic needs:

1) Health—a climate and housing suited to your physical condition.

2) Economic security—what you can afford for your way of life.

3) Status—a position or voice in the community.

4) Friendship—where you already have friends or an opportunity to make them.

As you grow older, you may pass through three stages of activity—active, slowdown and convalescent. In the middle years you are still in the active stage; you're still working and able to care for yourself and your home. In the slowdown stage, you may no longer be working full time, but you can still take care of yourself. At this stage, you'll need to be close to public transportation and shopping facilities; and you'll want some people your own age nearby. The convalescent stage covers that time in your life when you might

The Ideal Home for You

need regular medical care, so medical facilities should be nearby. At this time, you will want your home to be on one level in case you are in a wheelchair or need a walking aid. Most people think only of their current, or active, stage when they are selecting housing; but thinking ahead to the slowdown and convalescent stages of life is also important as you make plans.

If you're looking for a location with a better climate, it's a good idea to know for sure just what you can expect in your target area. Every part of the country has both agreeable and disagreeable weather at times. You should research the climate and living conditions thoroughly by visiting the locale long enough to experience the whole range of weather; or better yet, try to live there for a short time in an apartment or with friends or family. Many retired couples have found themselves unhappily locked into a climate that proved unsuitable on a year-round basis, simply because they judged living conditions during the most pleasant season.

Myths abound about the relative health-giving qualities of various climates. The Southwest, Southern California, Florida, and the Gulf Coast may be touted as places for the relief of arthritis, respiratory ailments, and heart disease. Yet all of these areas have vast climatic variations within their boundaries. Before you decide to move for health reasons, check with your doctor.

The Ideal Life

If you're looking for an area with lower living costs, you'll need to do some investigating. The Bureau of Labor Statistics is a dependable source to compare costs in different areas of the country. Chances are your local library will have this information. Before you pack up your belongings and venture off to your "retirement Eden," subscribe to the daily or weekly newspaper in the town or city you are considering and read it carefully for information on taxes, business activity, food prices, and real estate prices. And while you're at it, look for items that might give you a "feel" for the community—social activities, the crime rate, recreational opportunities, and if you will be able to have a voice in the community, a chance to participate in civic groups or other organizations. Once you have this information, it should help you decide whether the community will provide the kind of life you enjoy.

One couple, at least three or four years before retirement, made trips to various parts of the country to investigate sites for their new retirement home. They knew exactly what they were seeking: a moderate-size academic community located in a wooded, hilly terrain, where intellectual pursuits found nourishment and there was access to excellent medical care at the university. They also sought a moderate climate where energy costs would not beat them into poverty. The matter of taxation did not escape their investigation, and they found to their satisfaction that the state,

The Ideal Home for You

sales, and property taxes of this new community were considerably less than the national average. It was important for them to shelter their income, and they chose a state that would not drain a surviving spouse of his or her last funds.

As a couple, they were confident, self-reliant, intelligent and capable of problem solving. Their investigation was thorough and extended; they sought and received legal advice, as well as exchange of ideas from members of their family. This counsel confirmed what they had already known and they went ahead to make the decisions they thought prudent.

They had all the necessary ingredients for a successful transfer: proceeds from the sale of a substantial house supplemented by income from good investments, pension, and other comfortable retirement benefits. Although they separated themselves from their immediate families by moving to a new state, the separation is only geographical, for emotionally their relationships are very much intact.

And how did all this work out? The way our super-planners thought it would—right on target! They have gained adventure and a new experience. They have built a new home in a new community and are involved in literary, cultural, and educational experiences. Their retirement plans are working out.

The Alternatives

Don't hesitate to look at all the housing alternatives. You may be in a rut and challenging new expe-

The Ideal Life

riences may be stimulating. Once you bail out from the job and join the ranks who are free to choose how they'll use their time, a number of options open up. No longer do you need to maintain a proximity to your job or live near a school to accommodate the children. Now you can accommodate yourself.

Why should you consider moving? Wouldn't it be nice to get into a smaller house and cut in half the housecleaning, the maintenance, heating, taxes, and all the rest? Instead of being a slave to a place to live, how about making your home work for you?

If you decide to move into another house, should you buy or rent an older house or build a new one? Location may help make this decision. You may want to run a small business (ordinances permitting) out of your home, and the type of business may very well determine where you will live in relation to your market for services or merchandise. When buying an older house you probably won't find the design to your complete satisfaction. Shop around until you find a house that will provide safety, convenience, and a comfortable environment. Privacy is the greatest, single, nonfinancial advantage offered by your own home. To many, this is all-important.

Whether you buy an old or new house or build a house, keep resale value in mind. You need to measure what will be the ideal house for you and still have sales appeal when the time comes to sell it.

The Ideal Home for You

When planning to rent an apartment or purchase a condominium, you should go over the dwelling in much the same way you would a house. In all cases you will want to check out structure, garage and parking facilities, appliances, mail delivery, and nearness to recreation areas, shopping centers, hospitals, entertainment, and transportation.

A condominium may be a series of single units, double units, four, six or more units, or it may resemble an apartment complex. Owning a condominium home is much like owning a house. You have a deed to your condominium home and you can have a mortgage on it. You also pay property taxes and are responsible for the upkeep and the utilities. Because it is your property, you build equity in it the same as in a house, and you may sell it when and to whom you wish. You may also rent it.

When you buy a condominium home, you automatically buy some of the grounds and facilities, such as swimming pools, recreation centers, garage or parking areas, golf course, laundry area, etc. All of these areas and facilities require maintenance, of course, so you will pay a monthly fee to provide for upkeep. As costs for maintenance increases, your monthly fee will increase. As a rule, a condominium owner will get a lot for his money. But shop around before making a decision.

You will want to be sure that the sales price is realistic and includes all of the facilities and main-

The Ideal Life

tenance promised. Sometimes a developer skimps to keep the sales price low, and once units are sold, the quality goes up along with the monthly maintenance fees paid by the owners.

The alternative to a condominium is a cooperative apartment. The living accommodations can be much the same, but the ownership arrangements are different. With a co-op you are part-owner of a corporation and share in the responsibilities of the organization. You have a voice in the operation, of course. The shareowners elect a board of directors and officers much the same as any corporation. The elected officers determine policy for the corporation and its management. More often than not, an experienced manager is employed to carry out the day-to-day managerial jobs.

Similar to a condominium arrangement each shareholder pays a monthly fee to cover maintenance, property taxes, and in this case, mortgage on the building. Because a co-op is a nonprofit organization, efficiency of management can reduce the monthly cost to the shareholders. In many instances the cost of living in a cooperative is less than renting an apartment.

There are ways to reduce your personal risks whether you buy a house, a condominium, or a cooperative apartment. There are homeowner warranties available to protect against poor workmanship in such areas as plumbing, electrical installation, inferior building material, etc. It is an insurance and, like most all insurance, there are variations in costs and coverage.

The Ideal Home for You

You will need to check it out. Most any building association can direct you on whom to see in your area.

A few years ago Pat and Paul Geiger made what many consider a wise decision for the ideal life after fifty. They bought a condominium far enough out from the expanding city to get away from the hubbub but near shopping centers, churches, hospitals and entertainment. They leased it and stayed on in their house.

Even though the income from the condominium didn't quite match the mortgage and upkeep costs, the Geigers profited from the appreciation of the property.

A year ago the Geigers sold their house and some of their accumulated furnishings and moved into their condominium with elevators to the top floor living quarters where they can look out at Colorado's beautiful Rocky Mountains. And speaking of ideal, there is a golf course, swimming inside and out, garden plots, jogging and bicycle runs, beautiful grounds maintenance, underground garage and tight security. No more housing worries—just lock the door and take off for a trip or a couple of winter months of sun in Arizona.

Mobile homes offer an alternative to the usual stationary structures and can be more economical. Federal Housing Authority or Veterans' Administration loans are available with a modest down payment to

The Ideal Life

buy a mobile home. You will then need to shop for the best loan rate to buy land. Rates vary. Before buying the home, determine the location. Some people live in mobile home parks and others on single sites. At any rate, a check on zoning restrictions is important; also be sure of the availability of water, electricity, sewage outlets, and gas lines for heating, if necessary.

Whatever type of housing you decide upon and wherever you move, there is a good deal of checking-up that should be done before the moving van enters your driveway. There may be areas of the country that are more ideal, but most areas have considerable climate variations.

If you want to find a more economical place to live, one of the best sources of information is the U.S. Bureau of Labor Statistics. Also, while checking this source, you can find which area offers the best opportunities for part-time work.

When it comes to moving, even though it is of relatively short duration, there is no part of it that can be considered the ideal life before fifty or after fifty. It's one of those experiences which you find it necessary "to make the best of" if you are to survive.

Finding a reliable mover isn't easy. It is important to check out a number of companies with the Better Business Bureau, local consumer protection organizations, and also with a few companies who move employees around the country. You would be wise to get bids from three or four companies for the best

The Ideal Home for You

price. During the slack season you may be able to get a price break—minimum rate instead of maximum. The costs of moving are packing and unpacking, loading and unloading, and the actual moving or hauling. You may save some money by doing the packing and unpacking, but you will be responsible for damages and losses. Before your move, read all the fine print on your household property insurance coverage.

Where you live will have a direct bearing on what your financial needs will be. Moving is expensive, but the adventure of a new home in a different climate may be very appealing. The cost of living varies considerably among regions of the United States. Although most people facing retirement dream of moving to a new climate or region at one time or another, only eight percent actually move from their home state. The type of living arrangement you decide on will affect your finances. A new or smaller home, an apartment, a condominium, a retirement village or community—each of these alternatives has its own financial requirements. You must consider and evaluate all of the possibilities well before retirement.

To some people, retirement means moving to the country and away from the city. To others, such as Florence and Jim Bloor, it means just the opposite. The Bloors, upon his retirement as president of a New York bank, sold their large home in the country and settled into carefree apartment living in the city. They

The Ideal Life

love New York and find it a stimulating place to live. But as Charlie Hughes says, "What constitutes an ideal life for one person can be a complete bore to another." Successful retirement housing, whether or not a move is involved, requires careful thought and planning, or one may find himself in a boring or unsatisfactory situation. HEW reports, "All too often the older person has little choice about where he will live. For many who would like to move because of deterioration of their homes, the decline of the neighborhoods, or a failure of the personal energy required to maintain a home built for an entire family, there is no housing alternative available within economic reach; and they are forced to remain in a less-than-ideal situation." So plan ahead. Plan now.

How the Law Can Serve You

Many of the changes encountered during preparation for retirement usually involve some form of legal transaction; and many people have never dealt with wills, estate planning and some of the other considerations that go into planning retirement. Legal matters should never be handled on your own. Only a good lawyer can offer expertise on the legal aspects of the many important decisions that must be made prior to retirement.

A friend of ours, attorney Lumund Wilcox, advises those in the fifty and over group; "You must *not* be protected from the cruel world. You must make decisions. I have had older clients to whom the decision of what clothes to wear caused them great distress. You must have confidence in the future and a belief that life is good, or no one will want to be around you."

Perhaps the most difficult decisions are those which involve the law, and we shy away from legal

The Ideal Life

counsel because of the unscrupulous practices and exorbitant fees we all have heard about. Fortunately, most lawyers are well-meaning people who are in business to make an honest living. As in the medical profession, some lawyers are generalists and others are specialists, in corporate law, taxes, criminal law, communications, divorce, inheritance, and so on. As for fees, most lawyers sell their time by the hour. The more highly specialized a lawyer becomes, the higher the hourly rate. Sometimes a flat rate is charged for preparing a contract, drawing up a will, handling simple business transactions, etc., whereas lawsuits may be based on cost plus a percentage of the recovered amount. These arrangements should be worked out between the attorney and his client. In many legal cases, what appears simple becomes complex as we learn more about it through legal help. Things come up that would never have occurred to us. Everything is more complicated today, and complete knowledge of your legal rights and responsibilities becomes increasingly important as you near the time to exchange the working world for the life of leisure, a second career, or a combination of both.

You may be a peaceable, law-abiding person living a very structured, exemplary life, but it is highly unlikely that you can avoid the services of an attorney for your whole life. If we ignore the need for legal advice, a plea of ignorance of the law is not going to evoke any sympathy or resolve the difficulty. There are many laws on the books. Our legislators are constantly

How the Law Can Serve You

adding, cancelling, changing, and revising laws. It is a lawyer's responsibility to keep abreast of all the changes.

Some of the important events you will experience in retirement that may require legal assistance are the purchase or sale of a home or other real estate, moving to another state, estate planning, wills, trusts, taxes, deaths, business transactions, bankruptcy and others.

Selecting a Lawyer

A person should conduct the same type of intelligent investigation in selecting a counselor as he or she would do in trying to find a good family physician. In January 1973 the minimum fee schedule was declared illegal by a federal court, making it possible for the average citizen to negotiate his fee or to shop around for a fee he felt was more reasonable. Attorneys are free to advertise their services and specialities and this may further open the door for the public to know what kind of service is available in a community. Approximately eighty percent of the lawyers in the United States are in private practice. Corporations hire another ten percent for their legal work, and another ten percent are attorneys connected with federal, state, and local governments.

Trying to find an attorney best suited for your needs can be a challenge. If you wait until an emergency or crisis before you select a lawyer, you may wind up in a panic thumbing the Yellow Pages. There is not much chance you will find the best lawyer for your situation by randomly searching through the long list

The Ideal Life

of names in the telephone directory. There are several directories in your public library that provide background information and qualifications of practicing attorneys in the community. Probably the most widely used one is the *Martindale-Hubbell Law Directory* which lists age, rating, education, specialty, and background. The rating which is indicated has been decided by other attorneys, not by clients of the attorney. Other guides are: *Best Recommended Insurance Lawyers, Sullivan's Probate Directory,* and *Markham's Negligence Counsel.* Your local bar association may sponsor and supervise a lawyer referral office. The service can provide the name of a reliable prospect for your legal advisor. The problem with this service is that the referral may be done on a rotation basis without regard to the qualifications and specialties of their members. Find out if the referral service will match the problem you have with an attorney specializing in your problem. The service will set up an interview with the lawyer for you. There will be a modest fee, but you are under no obligation to continue with the lawyer at any time.

The corporate lawyer where you work might very well be the right person to give you responsible advice, or he may be able to provide the name of an attorney who would be right for you. Corporate executives may have good legal contacts, but it is highly doubtful that their legal problems have much in common with your own. To help you to decide, inquire around. Your friends may have had a similar problem and may have found good legal help.

How the Law Can Serve You

Attorneys connected with small firms or who are practicing alone, may be better able to handle personal problems, such as wills, real estate, and estates, rather than commercial transactions of substantial magnitude. Group practitioners include thirty percent of all lawyers. One firm may contain from three or four up to over a hundred lawyers and associates. These large firms offer a wide range of services, but tend to specialize. They may handle commercial or complicated problems better than simple, personal ones. The larger firm may not be able to give as much personal attention to the small client, and the attorney who conducts the initial interview may not be the person who will actually handle your case. In a law firm a case is generally assigned to the person who has the most expertise in the problem area that you are presenting. It might be beneficial for you to know whether the firm's work load might preclude your receiving proper service.

When you do secure the name of a possible attorney, make an appointment for an interview to make sure the client-attorney relationship could work for both of you. Ask in advance specifically how much he charges. You are seeking a reasonable fee, but be realistic about charges. Where the overhead is high, the fee may be also. Your charge will eventually be determined by the complexity of your problem, the amount of time that it will take to resolve, and the office and paper work, phone calls, conferences, research, etc. If the attorney is charging by the hour, the

The Ideal Life

amount may be considerably lower in rural communities. The city lawyer's fees could be $75 to $100 per hour and the small-town lawyer might be charging only $35 to $45 per hour. Sometimes the attorney may decide to charge a "flat fee." Often wills, uncontested divorces, and routine legal work are billed in this manner.

Payment for an attorney's services varies in cost and a method of reimbursement. In any event, at the outset ask for an itemized bill so you know exactly what you are paying for; and ask that all facts regarding charges be put in writing.

There are various ways attorneys figure fees. Contingency fees are used in most negligence cases in which a person seeks monetary damages for personal injury received, for example, in a motor vehicle accident. In such actions, the attorney may agree to handle your case for a percentage of the settlement, which may range from twenty-five to sixty percent, usually about a third. In this type of agreement, ask your attorney to take court costs and expenses off the top of the settlement. Frequently, these settlements are reached through an out-of-court agreement; and this should be kept in mind in deciding the appropriate charge. Another common form of reimbursement is the bonus plan that attorneys seem to prefer in cases involving a great deal of money. The fee in this case is frequently twenty-five percent of the settlement in addition to the hourly charge.

How the Law Can Serve You

When regular legal work is required, there is usually a retainer arrangement which may range from $11 to $1,000 a month, depending on the amount of work involved. Even in a once-in-a-lifetime legal matter, an attorney will probably ask for a retainer from a client, which is really a down payment advanced in the beginning but which will be deducted from the final bill.

Before hiring an attorney, ask if there might be any conflict of interests in taking your case, what type of clients he has, and what his specialty is. Also ask him to fully explain the position of the opposition so that you clearly understand the ramifications of your actions; and if he loses, will he appeal? Your attorney may tell you some facts that you find unpleasant to hear. Keep in mind, however, that if you have chosen him carefully and wisely, his intent is to arm you with all facts and possibilities of the case, no matter how unpleasant they are.

In meetings, *always* be honest. He cannot help you if you withhold information or slant it in your favor. Honesty also involves complete and organized records and keeping the attorney up to date on all developing correspondence and documents.

There are other avenues for seeking out legal assistance. Public Legal Assistance is available for low income persons. The court may appoint a Public Defender for you in a criminal case. Legal Aid and Community Legal Services handle civil matters free or

The Ideal Life

for a small fee. Eligibility for this service is determined by income, family size, and where you live. The taxpayers pay for hundreds of government lawyers serving local, state, and federal governments.

Retirement Matters Requiring Legal Assistance

You will save time, money, and anxiety if you discuss with your attorney matters pertaining to (1) the buying and selling of a home and other types of property. He should be with you on the date of settlement. Zoning laws and the history of land and community are other areas of expertise of the real estate attorney. His expertise is well worth the money. (2) Prenuptial contracts, particularly for two individuals who have estates and grown children. (3) Business transactions, such as forming an individual proprietorship, a partnership, or a corporation. (4) Forming an estate, drafting a will, arranging for an executor, federal estate taxes, and establishing trust funds.

There are some cases in which an attorney is not needed. If you are having difficulty over a bill you are being charged for and all efforts to effect a settlement are fruitless, you can go to a Small Claims Court. You may file suit in District Justice Court or in Municipal Court in the proper jurisdiction and within the limits set down by each District Justice or Municipal Court. The justice and his assistants will help you present your case. After filing, the case is heard within two months, and the justice has five days to make a decision. Either side may appeal the case in the

How the Law Can Serve You

Common Pleas Court where an attorney's services are needed. Procedures of Small Claims Courts differ from state to state. When considering this possibility for redress, seek assistance from law officials or County Courthouse employees for the procedure to follow.

Marriage and Family Arrangements

Prenuptial contracts are particularly important in the lives of two individuals who have estates and grown children. When Vivian Olson, age sixty-three and widow and mother of a grown daughter, and Bob Edwards, age sixty-five and father of three grown children, decided to marry and establish a home together, they did just that. Vivian sold her condominium and Bob sold his home. They bought a new home to spend their remaining years together. The best pieces of furniture from their former homes were moved into the new home. A year after the marriage, Vivian died, but her divorced, emotionally disturbed daughter had been provided for by a trust and a carefully selected executor.

An attorney is necessary in other marital situations, such as separate maintenance suits, child custody situations, collecting back alimony, and divorce. In divorce suits where a minor child is involved, there is also the need for a will naming a guardian should the custodial parent die.

Occasionally the need arises to have a Conservator or Guardian appointed to take care of the affairs of an ill or incompetent relative or friend. The individual

The Ideal Life

may be incapable of handling everyday matters or may be ill, and in a hospital or nursing home. The designation of Conservator does not carry the stigma of incompetency. The appointment of a Guardian is done only after proof that an individual is incompetent and needs the protection and help of a "guardian." A lawyer will be needed in appointing such a person.

The grant of a power of attorney is not a substitute for either of the above. A power of attorney is a document that gives a specified person the right to act in your behalf. It can be limited to certain acts or it can authorize the other person to act for you in all matters. In drawing up such a document, specify just how far you wish the power to extend.

Personal Injury Cases

Such cases as being hit by a shopping cart in the grocery store, stumbling on broken sidewalk in front of the hardware store, being bitten by that mean dog up the street, or being involved in a traffic accident are all in the personal injury category (or your attorney will tell you why not in some cases). If you are in an automobile accident, you will get the name and address of the driver and the car's occupants, any injured person, as well as licenses, registration, insurance company, date and hour of the accident and its location, name and address of the attending physician, a statement of how the accident occurred, names and addresses of witnesses and any bystanders. Call the police immediately and ask for medical help if neces-

How the Law Can Serve You

sary. Do not move the vehicles or injured parties until the police and ambulance arrive and permission is given.

Take all the information to your insurance company and attorney as promptly as possible; but otherwise do not say anything that might be interpreted as your admission of fault.

Generally, the lawsuit, if there is to be one, must be filed within the time set by the statute of limitations which varies from state to state. If you have been injured, an insurance representative for the other party may offer you a settlement (for a nominal sum) and ask you to sign release papers. You, of course, do nothing of the sort without the advice of counsel; nor do you give the insurance representative your version of the accident. It may be used against you.

What Would Happen If You Were Ever Arrested?

What a question! But maybe you were protesting some serious matter, such as nuclear energy use or the tearing down of a historic building, and your crowd got a little carried away and landed in jail. If arrested, give only your name and address to the police, maintain a dignified silence, and use your one telephone call to your attorney to give him the news, "I'm in jail!" You do not have to consent to tests for drunken driving, but refusal may cause suspension of your driver's license in some states. You are not required to take a lie-detector test or answer any questions beyond your name and address. Sometimes you can escape the

The Ideal Life

confines of the jail by posting bail, which is the procedure of putting up money or security to secure your freedom until you come to trial. Your check will not be accepted for this (nor will American Express or charge plates). All they will accept is cash or a bail bond. When you consider the person of limited resources or indigent who cannot put up the funds essential to secure release, you realize that all persons are not equal under the law.

Business Transactions

Many retired persons decide to go into business for themselves to earn extra income and stay active in a profession. Before you take any steps, discuss your plans with your lawyer. Retain him for consultation once your business is under operation. If you close out your enterprise, a lawyer is equally necessary. Sound advice will permit you to take advantage of all the legal provisions that favor the small businessman. As noted earlier, partnerships can be very tricky. Never enter into such an agreement without advice from your lawyer.

Half the businesses that are started fail. In this situation a debtor cannot meet his bills and the only solution is bankruptcy. Declaring bankruptcy discharges debts by making the debtor's assets available to his creditors. Certain debts cannot be discharged: taxes, liability for injury damages, liability for fraud, child support or alimony, and wages earned three months before bankruptcy. There are two types of

How the Law Can Serve You

bankruptcy: voluntary and involuntary. The services of a lawyer are required in either case.

Estate Planning, Wills, Etc.

The Archbishop of Canterbury in the 1600s wrote, "There are two things in which men, in other wise enough, do usually miscarry: in putting off making their wills and their repentance until it is too late."

What was true in the 1600s, still holds true today. Repentance aside, few people make wills allowing, instead, the state to dispense of their property and leaving their heirs problems sometimes causing arguments and jealousies which split the family permanently. The time is now for all of us to consider the disposal of our property, and the simplification of our estates.

If you own real estate that has become a management problem, you may want to consider selling it and investing the money somewhere else. Many financial counselors feel that the older generation tries too hard to leave the heirs a sizable estate and in trying to bring this about, they refuse to touch the principal. As a result they eke out a sometimes spartan existence on the scanty income from dividends and interest on their modest holdings.

A lawyer is very helpful in planning final arrangements. Whether you have a small fortune or only a few personal belongings, you will want certain things to go to certain persons. There are several ways to provide for this, but the best way for you depends on several factors, including the inheritance laws of your state.

The Ideal Life

You can place some or all of your assets in joint ownership, but the legal implications depend on the exact wording of the agreement and the laws of the state. Once a joint ownership is established, the person may have complete control of your assets. Contact your lawyer before entering into any such agreement.

Establishing a trust allows you to transfer legal title to some or all of your assets to another person for a specified use for your benefit. This agreement should be prepared by your lawyer. It is best to set forth the manner in which you want your property used to your benefit, with disposition of remaining property to be made at the time of your death.

In drafting a will, the document must meet several formal requirements to be valid. A lawyer is aware of these requirements and will insure that your will is valid. He can help you plan your estate in the most efficient manner.

The purpose of estate planning is to employ tax reducing procedures that will permit the transfer of assets to heirs with a minimum shrinkage or reduction of the estate's value. Some ways to do this are recommended only for large estates (those over $500,000); but there are tax saving methods for smaller estates as well. The Federal Tax Reform Act of 1976 makes it important to review existing estate plans with the new tax code in mind, to assure that the most appropriate will is made to achieve the greatest tax benefit. Taxes are levied at

How the Law Can Serve You

death by the Federal and State governments. Some states have no inheritance tax and others are quite high. Recent law makes the transition of wealth by gifts or through wills effective at death. Administrative costs such as probate, executor's commissions, attorney's fees, funeral costs, and charitable bequests, along with the important marital deduction are all subtracted from the estate, which results in a substantial reduction in the amount to be taxed.

In 1981, the new, liberalized $250,000 marital deduction (or fifty percent of an individual's adjusted gross estate, whichever is larger) and the equally new $175,625 tax permits a person to leave more than $425,000 worth of business and other assets estate-tax free to his or her spouse. But don't be misled, for without careful planning with your lawyer, the use of the marital deduction may merely delay taxation until the death of your spouse. By using a two trust will, an individual can reduce death taxes and protect most of the estate from tax levy at the spouse's death. For example, with a proper trust plan, it's possible to save $54,000 on estate taxes on a $400,000 estate.

State taxes are another matter, and point again to the absolute necessity of having the advice and skill of your attorney, bankers, tax accountants and, also, your heirs. Some states tax the recipient of an inheritance, and heirs should be aware of it. You can take steps now to make drafting your will an easier experience. The habit of frugality and lifetime penny-pinching is a hard one to change, but your estate will be much

The Ideal Life

easier to administer if you start eliminating the clutter of a couple of Series E bonds, a few shares of six dollar stock that may have become virtually worthless or an old savings account in which you have about fifty dollars. Cash them all in, and simplify the number of securities you have. If you own real estate that has become a management problem, you may want to consider selling it and investing the money somewhere else.

What can happen to your estate if you die without a will? States vary from one to another on how property and money is distributed when no valid will exists. The laws of each state provide rules of inheritance for persons that have not made a will or made some other arrangement for disposing of property. You can let the state handle your estate, but there is no assurance that your property will be distributed among your heirs the way you planned.

When you let the laws of your state handle the distribution of your property, the court will appoint a trustee or executor to supervise the settlement of your estate. Most of your property will be frozen for several months, which can make things hard for surviving dependents. In some instances the widow receives the deceased spouse's property unconditionally. In most states the widow receives one-third of the spouse's property with the other two-thirds going to the children. The widow cannot spend any of the children's inheritance. The widow may be appointed legal guardian of

How the Law Can Serve You

the children, but in such cases the widow must file an annual account in Probate Court of why and how the money was spent to care for the children. If the widow remarries, the new spouse can receive one-third of the widow's inheritance without being required to spend a cent on the family.

Whether it is your will, income tax returns, savings bonds and certificates or any other important document, it is essential to safeguard such records. Good record keeping can keep you out of financial trouble and up-to-date on all the dates that are so important to successful retirement planning.

A safety-deposit box at your financial institution should contain your mortgage, titles to your house and cars, contracts, stock and bond certificates, important letters, leases, gold and silver coins, jewelry, loan agreements, personal records and papers, and a copy of your will.

A filing cabinet in your home should accommodate other important documents such as life, health, auto, and home insurance policies, warranties, income tax returns and records, cancelled checks and paid bills, and the original copy of your will. The original copies should be kept at home because safety-deposit boxes are sealed at the time of an individual's death to insure that the government can receive estate taxes on all property. Both federal and state governments have their freedoms to attack this income regardless of the survivors' circumstances.

The Ideal Life

It is a good idea to talk with your bank about the regulations of the state regarding the sealing and inaccessibility of the safety-deposit box to the surviving spouse who may be facing an avalanche of problems. It is wise to have separate accounts so that the surviving spouse will have funds available to cover expenses until settlement of the estate.

Make Your Own Decisions

The old saying, "The person who acts as his own lawyer has a fool for a client" is true, especially in these days of changing laws and intricate personal affairs. Our attorney friend sees his life after fifty as "when the kids are no longer underfoot, and you sometimes wish they would still occasionally kick you in the shins." Unexpected legal problems often feel like a "kick" in the shins"; but if you have carefully selected a lawyer you can trust and put your legal affairs in order, the hurt will only be temporary. Then, you can face life after retirement with the attitude of our attorney friend: "I want to work, but not too hard, play and keep physically fit as long as possible, participate in community activities, maintain an interest in politics without involvement, and maintain a tolerant attitude toward the young. They are as impetuous, idealistic and challenging as we were in our youth. I would like to emulate those of my elders who still understand and want to be a part of the young at heart, who are still searching for the truth and who maintain a sense of humor toward life."

Second Careers

The fifty year mark can be a declaration of freedom for many career people. Following, is how Tom and Peggy Weber of Mississippi declared their independence from the frantic pace of New York and the confines of a nine-to-five business day.

"After many years of living and working in New York City," Tom says, "my fiftieth birthday hit me so hard it made me sit down and think about the future. My wife and I had many talks about the time remaining to us on this earth. We started to feel better about life after we made the decision to leave New York and return to our beloved Mississippi. At age fifty-three, we took the giant step and made the big move. We have never regretted it nor experienced any guilt feelings about 'dropping out.'

"The ideal life after fifty is to do what you want to do and be relaxed about it. I do know this, that once you make up your mind to think of yourself and your

The Ideal Life

desires, the location of your personal paradise is within yourself. The geographics helped in our case, but we did not try to 'go home again.'

"We promised ourselves that I would no longer work regular hours, but when and where I pleased. This means we are independent in the strictest sense. It surprised me to find out how easy it is to find work with large or small companies if one is willing to stay out of the corporate tent. My assignments are confined to the southeastern part of the country—snow is out! My wife and I think we are very fortunate to travel around, stay in different small towns (no cities) for awhile and then return home to Mississippi. If I have a long assignment away from home, we rent a small apartment and live there for a month or two. We meet many wonderful people and thoroughly enjoy seeing each new place and experiencing its ambiance. We hope to continue our part-time gypsy life for as long as we live."

There seem to be as many ways for people to plan or stumble their way into new occupations as there are people doing it. There are painful ways to make a new start and some that are enjoyable.

Dislocation because of corporate mergers, bankruptcies, or termination because a phase of the business is discontinued is not easy to cope with. It does, however, offer an opportunity to get out of a rut and pick up a challenge in a new field. Many people have interests or activities outside their regular job, and

Second Careers

these can be revenue-producing sidelines. In that case, switching from one job and to another in a different field can be relatively easy.

Others acquire some training in an area in which they've always been interested. Frequently, a person who has expertise in a particular operation can hire out to a number of organizations as consultant—stay outside the "corporate tent" as Tom Weber so aptly phrased it.

Over half the people who have been working for someone else over the years have a desire to be their own boss and start their own business. One way to do this is to work for someone who wants to be rid of his business. You will be able to test yourself and learn while working with the owner. If you decide that the business is not only a profitable one, but also one which you would enjoy, then you can take steps to purchase it.

A friend of ours took over a business in a similar manner. After some years working for the owner of a clothing store, he bought a very small interest in the shop. As time passed, he bought a little more and a little more of the shop until he was half owner. He continued buying interest in the business until he owned it all. It is not often that this "installment buying" is possible, but it is worth checking into if you are interested in a privately owned business.

Whether you are an accountant, a typist, consultant, salesman, whatever, there are countless oppor-

The Ideal Life

tunities to start a business in your own home until you can expand into a shop or an office building. It is a way to get a new career started without risking sizable amounts of money.

Natalie Everett wanted to be at home while her children were growing up, so she left her job in publishing to run a typing business at home. She advertises on almost every available bulletin board in her area, and she now has two additional typists working for her. She won't be looking for a second career when the kids leave for college.

You will need to check your residential zoning laws before posting signs on your property advertising your business. A number of people run appliance repair services out of their homes. This type of business is a natural one for husband and wife teams. For example, the crew who treated our property for termite control last year began as a man and wife team. She took orders at home and kept the accounts, and he went out and did the work. Today, they are millionaires because of good service combined with good management.

These small businesses run from a home result in low overhead and good profits. With the mounting costs for small jobs necessary around the home, some enterprising people have joined their skills and other professional work at a savings, again working out of a home. These are retirees or sideline workers who have pooled their abilities. Some are masons, plumbers,

Second Careers

carpenters, painters, and electricians who, together, offer complete home repair work from one location. Local advertising usually provides about all the work a group needs; but of course, if a job is well done, the best kind of advertising, word of mouth, doesn't cost anything.

If you are thinking of a second career, don't overlook a sales opportunity. Taking on a product line with which you are familiar, or a combination of related products from different manufacturers, can be rewarding if you enjoy traveling. With many companies, you may be able to work out a small territory, which will allow you to spend only a few days a week on the job. A friend does very well with a small line of gift items. She checks in every two weeks or so with gift shops within a territory of 200 miles or so and keeps the racks and counters stocked. She makes as much money as she requires and finds that she can adjust her sales schedule somewhat, which leaves time for her personal schedule.

It is important that a salesperson sell a product with which he is familiar and one which he can believe in. Some years ago, Fred Digott began his own school supply business. He had sold school supplies for some of the leading manufacturers and knew a lot of school district business managers. He rented office space, hired two salesmen, and became a distributor for several manufacturers. He soon became the number one supplier in the state with everything from chalk

The Ideal Life

and blackboards to bleachers, seating, gym and athletic equipment. With his son now running the business, he and his wife have this to say about the ideal life after fifty: "To us, the most essential condition is to have the good health to do the things one always wanted to do if, in mature wisdom, one still wants to do them. The fifties, ideally, would provide a pause, a breather, a time to keep up without racing, a time to examine the options, the obligations that are still valid, and the dreams that still have time for fulfillment. A change of lifestyle may not be the end of the world, but a beginning."

There are some people who lack some of the qualities necessary for running their own business, yet still desire to be their own boss. These persons seek a partner who possesses the skills they are lacking. Partnerships can be fragile, however, so it's good to consider the arrangement and the skills and personality of your prospective partner. By all means, draw up a legal agreement, spelling out the complete arrangement. Husband and wife teams make the most successful partnerships, since marriage seems to be the supreme cooperative effort.

Some years ago, an acquaintance who was a linotype operator for a publishing company decided with his wife, who worked as a secretary for an interior decorator, to go into the contracting business. The first year they built one house. They checked the work crew in the morning before going to their own jobs,

Second Careers

checked them at noon, and then checked the progress again at night. The next year, with the bank's help, they built three houses, and the following year, six or eight. The husband managed the financial end and the workmanship, and the wife supervised the building designs and interior decoration. As partners, they moved on into sizable home development plots.

The opportunities for second careers and new businesses are as varied as the people beginning them. Here are a few of those businesses begun by people across the country. Most grew out of a previous interest, some from a new idea.

We had a neighbor who, when waiting for a train, saw postal workers dragging bags of mail across the concrete floor to load onto the train. Acting on a hunch, he began researching the cost of all those worn-out mail sacks and learned there was a place in New Jersey that had a work force sewing patches on the bags. Our friend had a better idea: iron-on patches. From this idea, grew a successful second career for our friend.

It is surprising just how many retired people come up with better ideas or even new inventions. If you seek this route to fortune, beware of those "Invention Ideas Wanted" ads. They may promise to make you an instant millionaire, but what they are often after is a few hundred or thousand dollars from you to search the idea through the patent office.

According to the Federal Trade Commission, a

The Ideal Life

good many of the complaints about these outfits come from people near retirement or retired, who have time to think of new ideas and need the money. Protection for an invention can be had by getting a "disclosure document" from the Patent Office. After filling out the form and including the drawing, file it with the Patent Office to show when you first began work on the idea. It is then protected for two years. If there is no conflicting patent on record, you will have a first and the patent will be protected for seventeen years.

You can get full information on how to protect a new idea and how to conduct a Patent Office search, etc., by writing Commissioner of Patents, Washington, D.C. 20231.

A popular second business is selling antiques. Many people operate this business out of their homes until their growth demands larger quarters. A friend told me about his retired brother who has bored with nothing much to do. So he suggested he begin collecting antiques at auctions, on farms and in small towns. The brother followed this advice and became fascinated with antiques. He even rented an old barn in which to store his collection. There was a problem, however. He took such a liking to each item he bought that he didn't sell anything — he just kept filling up the barn.

Hanging onto things is fine if you don't require a cash flow. And the lack of a cash flow is what puts

Second Careers

many people out of business. The costs of rent, help, utilities, taxes, and countless small expenses keep piling up. It is essential that merchandise carry enough markup over the original cost to pay for a new stock of replacement merchandise as well as pay the fixed cost (the burden), and hopefully, net something for the entrepreneur.

To make a go of the antique business requires that a person keep learning. You never know when treasures will turn up at flea markets, garage and yard sales, in someone's attic or basement, at auctions or even in another antique shop. It can be a lot of work and requires physical stamina; but once you begin, you'll love every tiring minute of it.

If you like animals, there are a number of enjoyable businesses that range from showing animals and breeding stock to beauty parlors for cats and dogs. There are pet stores, of course, and kennels for looking after pets when the owners are away.

Another unusual business is fish farming. Cousin Arnie Fladoos, who manages the Dubuque Golf and Country Club along the Mississippi River, told us, "We have a fish dinner at the club once a week and we used to serve catfish from the river. The fish came in uneven sizes and some had too much fat. We always got some complaints, but no more. Now we get our fish from the fish farms. They're fed a prepared food which accounts for lean meat, and they come to us in even lengths. They make a beautiful, tasty platter."

The Ideal Life

For a person interested in this type of work, fish farming may be worth looking into. Check with your County Agent for details on how to begin.

A Wisconsin man I visited with on a plane had another type of animal business. He had a dairy herd replacement business. He bought extra heifer calves from dairy farmers and sold them to other dairy farms in this country and as far away as Italy. The sellers found themselves with an excess of heifer calves and the buyers were either building a herd or had the opposite problem, too many bull calves and not enough heifers.

What this Wisconsin man does with cattle can be done with just about any product. Many people are "finders" and they collect a finder's fee for their services. At one time, a neighbor had a business of installing printing presses. He became acquainted with most all of the printing operations in the country, and knew who wanted what kind of equipment and who had it for sale. He brought the two parties together and got the job of disassembling, moving and installing the equipment. You don't need to be that big of an operator. This can be done on a community level by just investigating as to who has what and who wants it. This type of business spreads best by word of mouth.

Some second careers involve going back to school and learning a trade or brushing up on certain skills. George Maas lost his job when a local branch of a large

Second Careers

national corporation closed down. Having a lingering interest in electronics, George went back to school five hours a day for a year and a half. He is now as busy as one person can be with his own television repair shop. He keeps his rates down because he is able to hold down his overhead. This type of business doesn't have a "men only" sign posted. Women are finding this an interesting and challenging occupation, too, even though it involves heavy lifting when it is necessary to take a set from a home back to the shop.

Many people enjoy the challenge of small mechanical parts. Every once in a while one runs across a clock repairman working out of his home in some quiet residential area. The ones we know keep busy and don't seem to have any "time" on their hands. Another business associated with small mechanical parts is the locksmith. His business is helping those who lock themselves out of their house or lose their keys with the identification attached. In this day and age, this calls for a quick change of locks. In each case, to become proficient, a person needs to go to a trade school to receive proper training.

A number of small booklets are available for those seriously considering launching their own businesses. *Small Business Management Series* and *Starting and Managing Series* are available from the Superintendent of Documents in Washington, D.C.. The Bank of America's *Small Business Reporter* publication includes some particularly helpful issues at $1 each:

The Ideal Life

"Financing Small Businesses," "Avoiding Management Pitfalls," and "Steps to Starting a Business." Address requests to Small Business Reporter, Bank of America, Dept. 31201, Box 37000, San Francisco, California 94137.

There are so many types of businesses for a person to consider when thinking of launching into a business of her or his own, it is a good idea to go to the local Small Business Administration or write the main office at Washington, D.C. 20416. You can be supplied booklets on just about any type of business you want to know more about.

Another way to begin your own business is to buy a franchise. This offers the advantage of a well-known name and national advertising; but the initial outlay is often considerable. If there is a specific franchise you are interested in, you can check up on the franchise at your local Better Business Bureau and the National Better Business Bureau at 230 Park Avenue, New York, NY 10017. Your local and state Consumer Protection Agency, along with the Federal Trade Commission in Washington can furnish additional information.

For more information on buying into a franchise, write the Office of Management Assistance, Small Business Administration, Washington, D.C. 20416 for *Franchise Index Profile* (85¢). Two books are offered by the U.S. Department of Commerce and are availa-

Second Careers

ble from the Superintendent of Documents, Washington, D.C. 20402. These are *Franchising Opportunities Handbook* ($3.60) which gives names, addresses and details of hundreds of franchise companies in the U.S. and *Franchising in the Economy* ($1.50) packs more helpful information. Free from the International Franchise Association is the *Classified Directory of Members*. Address requests to 7315 Wisconsin Avenue, Washington, D.C. 20014.

For anyone thinking of getting into a business in his own community or another community, it is absolutely essential to research the area to find out what the needs are. The local Chamber of Commerce can be helpful. If competition exists you may want to check out the competitor's operation—the quality of service, merchandise, and prices. There may be an opportunity to offer the public something similar at lower prices or higher quality at higher prices.

You should spend enough time with your computer to be absolutely certain that you are sufficiently capitalized to maintain a comfortable cash flow when there is a tightening economy. Small-business loans are available and usually necessary. Most people borrow too little. Keep in mind that your business will probably take eighteen months before it can operate in the black.

The Ideal Life

Whether you choose to launch an independent enterprise or a franchised business, having a head for business just isn't enough to guarantee success. Following, are seven characteristics a successful entrepreneur must have. If you lack one or several, consider a partner who possesses the qualities you lack.

1) *Initiative.* You must be a self-starter and able to motivate yourself to success.

2) *Leadership.* You must be able to command authority. A leader is a good judge of character in hiring and a diplomat when dealing with disgruntled employees and customers.

3) *Organization.* The many details of running a business translate into dollars. This is no place for sloppiness in accounts or planning.

4) *Industry.* A drive to succeed must be translated into hard work and requires a high level of physical energy.

5) *Responsibility.* When the business is yours, "the buck stops here"—at your door.

6) *Knowledge of your product.* Running your own business is not the place for learning on the job. Become an expert in the field *before* you jump out on your own.

7) *Competitive spirit.* Successful entrepreneurs find competition challenging and fun. They have the inborn drive to want to succeed.

Second Careers

In the years ahead we can look for career spans lengthening, work weeks shortening and more uncertainty in the world. We will probably discover we need to be more resourceful with good faith, good will, and good sense. Owning your own business or just being your own boss requires both inner resources and sufficient finances. With the experience gained by the time a person reaches fifty, the challenge can be fun.

Getting a Job

Retirement. Freedom from hectic days and occasional long nights at the office. Freedom from irritating rush hour traffic. Freedom from busy lunches and daily schedules filled with meetings, appointments and deadlines. Freedom from jetting around the country to and from business conventions, shows and conferences. Time for happiness, relaxation and recreation. Not a care, not a worry.

Bob Karolevitz is one of the few very fortunate individuals who have successfully adjusted their lifestyles to fully conform with this idealistic definition of retirement. He expresses his feelings on this subject this way:

> I don't believe in the ill-conceived philosophy that when you get your gold watch

The Ideal Life

or hold your final auction, the next thing you have to do is rush right out and buy some mushroom spores or angleworm breeding stock and start a whole new career.

Retirement, for my money, is synonymous with a well-earned vacation, and I don't propose to work most of a lifetime just to qualify for pitching the stuff that mushrooms grow in or for being midwife to a cellar full of night crawlers. I'll take my mushrooms in a fluffy omelet and my angleworms on a No. 8 snelled hook.

As far as I'm concerned, one good career is enough for anybody. For every success story you hear about some retired farmer making a fortune raising polka dot chinchillas, you can be sure there are many, many more failures with nest eggs down the drain and some tear-jerking stories which are almost pathetic enough for daytime television.

I figure that if a person has been hardy enough to survive three-score-plus-five in this wild world of ours, he's got a few ideas of his own. Maybe he'd just like to play a little checkers or sit in the sun. What's wrong with that?

Mr. Karolevitz has a refreshingly positive attitude toward the life of leisure after retirement. In all

Getting a Job

likelihood that attitude will allow him to completely forget about work and live the type of life he has planned. But many of us cannot adopt a new life filled with recreation and relaxation while completely forgetting the working world ever existed. Surely leisure will become more prominent in retirement; but after being subjected to the work ethic for so many years, the transition from the nine to five world to Bob Karolevitz's can be a very hard one to make.

As a person approaches retirement it is extremely important to retain an attitude of purposefulness and self-satisfaction. This isn't easy if one's mind becomes cluttered with the intellectual and emotional "downs," or "blues," sometimes associated with retirement. The two primary sources that foster feelings of pride, purpose and satisfaction are family and work. With the children graduating from college, getting married, and starting their own families, the parents' importance to them is diminished somewhat... and so are the feelings they once derived as heads of the family. That leaves work as the primary source.

Work has probably been a part of your life longer than your family has. For most people, work is the major time-consuming interest during a lifetime. Work has been and still is a primary source of purpose, satisfaction, status, identity and even companionship. Losing all this at once can be traumatic if not viewed in the proper frame of mind.

When work is totally eliminated from one's en-

The Ideal Life

vironment, it is easy to feel deprived of useful purpose. The American Medical Association has documented that compulsory retirement and the cessation of productive work and earning power often lead to serious depression which can cause a decline in overall physical and mental health. For many, an end to employment means an end to usefulness. Work has been such a driving force in their lives that many persons really haven't had the time or opportunity to learn how to relax and enjoy leisure time. Working part time can afford the time needed to adjust to the more relaxed pace of retirement.

Many persons continue working after reaching retirement age because of economic hardship. In these inflationary times it is extremely difficult for the retired person to live on the income provided by Social Security, private pensions and personal investment. For these persons the need to work is not emotional or intellectual but simply a matter of survival.

Other people continue working just to continue a feeling of usefulness or who feel that a job, even part-time, provides the schedule necessary to their lives. After being disciplined to a work schedule for most of their adult lives, they find it impossible to function without one. Those fortunate ones are those who are self-employed and thus are able to simply cut their

Getting a Job

hours, working just enough to satisfy their own inner need while enjoying the freedom of semi-retirement.

The reasons for continued employment are many. A 1977 Roper poll showed that approximately sixty percent of the persons approaching retirement preferred working to some degree after retirement, although only about fifteen percent actually remain employed. Today, those who choose to work cannot be forced to retire at a specific age. The Mandatory Retirement Act assures us that right. Prior to the act, a person could expect to live at least one-third of a lifetime in retirement. It was virtually impossible for a person to make a job or career change after age forty-five.

The Mandatory Retirement Act

This act was passed in 1978, and became law on January 1, 1979. The Mandatory Retirement Act created many new options for the older worker and his employer. No longer would an employee be forced to retire because of his age alone; no longer could he be passed over for promotion because of age. Presently there are two exceptions to the act: tenured teachers whose coverage will not start until July 1, 1982, and executives who have an immediate, irrevocable pension of at least $27,000 (excluding Social Security). The act does not require that a worker stay on the job. It simply states that it is the right of the employee to choose at what time to retire. It also assures the employer that he need not retain an employee over

The Ideal Life

sixty-five who is nonproductive and cannot function efficiently. Federal employees cannot be forced to retire at any age, and there are an increasing number of employers in the private sector who are already eliminating all mandatory retirement age limits. If this trend continues, it is possible that the older worker may be retrained for a career changeover.

The Mandatory Retirement Act will create an additional work force of 250,000 older persons according to Labor Department estimates. Already three million persons over sixty-five are in paid occupations, and a group of four million say they would like to work if they could find jobs. At present there are very few jobs available for retirement-age individuals.

When one considers the financial condition of the Social Security system, it is not surprising that Congress has made an effort to extend the working life of the older person to the age of seventy. It is conceivable that there will be as many elders as youths by 2030. Further projections suggest that by the year 2011, when the postwar babies reach sixty-five years of age and become eligible for retirement, a crunch will develop, because of the increasing longevity and population of older Americans. Eleven percent of the population is over sixty-five at the present time, and by the year 2000, it will be at least thirteen percent. The point of these statistics is to emphasize that people are living longer and our present birth rate of 1.8 percent is falling.

Getting a Job

Consequently, there will be fewer workers to support the Social Security system, as more people become eligible to draw from it.

This act gives new leverage to the potential retiree in securing the best possible arrangement with his employer. The latter may decide to increase the worker's pension, provide medical insurance that will fill in the gaps of the Medicare Program and continue a portion of his life insurance—all to be available to the employee when he leaves. Some employers may also provide severance pay. The other alternative might be part-time work that would fit in with the Social Security earnings limitation laws. Working full-time will result in the loss of Social Security benefits, but creates a deferred one percent per year increase in such benefits after retirement at age seventy. Pension benefits may or may not be increased after sixty-five and should be discussed with your employer. There are many possible options that will allow each of us to earn more money and care for ourselves independently in retirement.

The same injustices and prejudices that women experience in employment in general are every bit as evident in the retirement job market. Discrimination in hiring, promotions, and pay scales continues to be a major obstacle to equality of women in the labor market. Starting salaries vary considerably for women and men, with the same educational background and in the same occupational field.

The Ideal Life

It was estimated that in 1978 forty-two percent of women were working in the civilian work force. In a Labor Department study entitled "The Earnings Gap Between Women and Men," it was reported that men's median weekly earnings exceeded women's by $116. Women have to work almost nine days to gross the same earnings men gross in five days. "Although women workers are as well educated as men in terms of median years of schooling completed, there are differences in the kinds of education, training and counseling they receive, which directs them into traditional and low-paying jobs," the study revealed. Women working in nontraditional roles may expect larger salaries than other female workers across the country. Those in government received wages and salaries sixty-eight percent of men's, whereas in the private sector, they could earn only fifty-nine percent. The earnings gap is narrowed a bit among professional and technical workers, with men earning only fifty-two percent more than women, eleven percent more if physicians or dentists, twenty-five percent more among the computer specialists, and twenty-eight percent more as elementary and secondary school teachers.

Finding part-time employment appropriate to your desires and experience requires persistence. You have a lifetime of expertise and knowledge to offer a prospective employer, so the challenge is not finding a suitable job but finding an employer who needs your experience, skills and talents and is not prejudiced against age.

Getting a Job

Although age discrimination was prohibited in 1979 by The Mandatory Retirement Act, many employers are not willing to hire qualified retirement-age persons. Enforcement of the law is new and discrimination is still quite prevalent. Be prepared for it and seek help in your area. Several employment organizations specialize in placement services for retirement-age persons. The law did open several eyes, and many employers are recognizing that this segment of the population can still make many valuable, ageless contributions.

Statistics support some employers' rationale for hiring retirees. Older employees tend to be more reliable, to work harder, to be more productive, and to accept responsibility willingly. Some employers have adopted the practice of hiring two part-time retired persons for one full-time position. Several progressive companies are developing programs to educate and prepare employees for part-time careers after retirement.

A problem area is overqualification. After acquiring experience and knowledge over the course of an entire career, white collar workers occasionally have problems finding part-time work in their respective fields after retirement. They are overqualified for most part-time positions. These persons probably have enough expertise in their fields to be hired by related organizations as consultants. The hours are relatively short, schedules are somewhat flexible and the income is substantially higher than most part-time work.

The Ideal Life

Finding meaningful employment after retirement requires organization and work. There are bound to be disappointments. Assess your ability to work. Each individual has physical and mental limitations. Know yours and select work suitable to them. Explore all the possibilities well in advance of retirement to assure yourself of enough time to accumulate the necessary training and experience.

Finding Suitable Employment

What kind of a job will be ideal for you? Certainly you want something that is interesting, challenging and offers recognition for making a contribution. Of course, you will be interested in a paycheck, but if the work is boring, chances are you won't deliver your best performance and the paychecks may come to an abrupt halt.

Assessing Yourself: Taking an honest, critical look at yourself is most important. Perhaps write down points to make a self-inventory of your likes and dislikes, your attitudes toward others, your personal appearance and, most of all, what you expect a job to do for you. It isn't likely that you will drastically change your personality or develop dramatic new abilities to impress a prospective employer. Be honest with yourself and your employer.

Adalaide Lalor assessed her abilities and found the ideal job for herself. She didn't wait for all five of her boys to leave home before entering the job market.

Getting a Job

A few years ago an uncle offered her a commission to sell a used car for him. "I just love to sell," she says. And sell she did, before moving into the greater promises of insurance. "I'm having the time of my life," Adalaide reports, "studying, taking exams, selling, learning all about this mysteriously complicated world of insurance."

What are your strong points? Are you articulate? Are you energetic or easy-going? Are you meticulous? What do you like to do most and least? Looking back over your experiences, what were your most satisfying accomplishments? Chances are, those were the things you put your heart into because you liked what you were doing. Try to find them in part-time employment.

What an employer wants is someone who is reliable and can perform a specific job, someone who is experienced, knows what he or she is doing and is not a management problem.

Impressing a prospective employer is more convincing if someone else "sells you," tells how good you are and about all of your fine accomplishments. If you sell yourself too hard, you risk appearing to be a braggart, leaving the impression that you may not be able to deliver once on the job.

Most all of us are persuaders to some degree, regardless of where our talents and abilities lie. A person is persuading when he gets someone to do something he hadn't considered doing. The best salespeople are creative, inventors of reasons why someone

The Ideal Life

should accept a concept, a service or a product. Just as it is difficult for a salesperson to sell something he doesn't believe in, it is difficult for an individual to persuade someone to hire him if he doesn't believe in himself, his abilities and what he has to offer.

The person doing the hiring in an organization is not likely to be in the personnel department. Arrange an interview directly with the manager of the position or department you are interested in. Learn as much as possible about the function and history of the organization, its financial status and management philosophy, its products or services and its rank among competitors, to improve the chances of making a positive impression and getting the job. The more you know about the company the better equipped you are to point out areas where your abilities can develop more efficient production, lower production costs, open new markets, outdo the competition, etc.

The Resume: A resume should precede you in making a personal application if you don't have an advance man to recommend you. A resume will serve as the other person telling the prospective employer all about you. It is an inventory of your skills, talents, work history and the like. If you are fortunate enough to have an acquaintance or former employer who is willing to give you a "to whom it may concern" letter vouching for your abilities and integrity as a responsible person, attach a copy to your resume for more impact. What you are doing, while selling yourself, is

Getting a Job

helping an employer in a decision-making process when it comes to comparing the characteristics of various applicants for a particular job.

The public library can supply an abundance of information on how to put together a resume that will get attention and spark action for an interview. There are several approaches. A good resume is designed to focus on a specific job and spotlights accomplishments with experience directly related to the job opportunity. Keep it short, crisp and to-the-point—no more than two pages. Sentences should be short and direct. And there are some things to leave out: no first person pronouns, no laudatory adjectives, no references that might indicate age, such as dates and years on a job, no reasons for leaving a job, no race, no religion, no political leanings, no geographical preference, and no mention of salary.

Here's a suggested resume format:
    Heading - includes your name, address, and phone number.
    Objective - should describe specifically and concisely the type of position wanted.
    Related experience - the heart of your resume, should describe for the employer how your experience qualifies you for the job you want. The employer's primary interest may be in this statement.
    Employment chronology - presents a record of your employment in reverse chronologi-

The Ideal Life

cal order, giving job titles, organizations and location. Group earlier employment experiences (over fifteen years ago) except for those of special significance. Give descriptive, functional titles rather than little-known formal titles.

Education - should be featured in relation to its importance for the job you want. Include colleges, universities and special schools and degrees. List your highest degree first and where you received it. Give any foreign language competence.

Activities - lists activities you have engaged in other than your job: club and associations, memberships, speeches, published articles, volunteer work and other activities related to the job you are seeking.

Personal status - gives the family status, condition of health, health maintenance, outside interests.

Resume distribution is up to you. If you have recommendation letters to attach, you may have success with a broad distribution. On the other hand, you may find it valuable to concentrate on a select group of possible employers.

Leave No Stone Unturned

When you are job hunting ask friends, relatives and associates if they know of any positions available

Getting a Job

in the area for which you might be qualified. You never know who might say, "I know a company looking for exactly what you have to offer." Check clubs and associations to which you belong and keep an eye on newspaper help-wanted ads. You may want to run a position-wanted classified ad to test the market. Talk to someone who represents your age bracket at the State Employment Service and to private employment agencies, but be sure to read and understand any contracts you sign. File your resume at all the placement services in your area. Listed below are several employment services that may be of some help to retirement-age persons.

Free placement services are offered by U.S. Employment Service (USES) offices throughout the country, and the special services provided to older workers are being expanded. USES has an operating budget of around $700 million and is particularly helpful in finding administrative support jobs. In some areas, however, it maintains services for those seeking professional and managerial positions. These offices also have job banks which provide job offerings in the area; however, not all local vacancies will be listed in the job bank.

Skipping around on temporary jobs is an excellent way to get acquainted with what's going on in the outside work world, if this is your first adventure in several years. It really won't matter what the jobs are, because you will just be shopping. Most communities

The Ideal Life

have some form of temporary job service. Check the yellow pages.

Senior employment services of one name or another are mostly nonprofit, community organizations. They develop employment opportunities for older persons in the community, counsel persons on finding marketable skills within their vocations or avocations, and sponsor community programs that meld available skills with neighborhood needs.

Cooperative Employment Services such as Forty-Plus are in several cities around the country. These are cooperative, nonprofit organizations of executive and professional men and women who band together to help qualified persons over forty years of age get jobs. To qualify for the services of Forty Plus you must have earned over $15,000 when employed, have a record of employment in responsible managerial or professional positions, and have good business and personal references. Some of these offices offer a counseling service, hotline telephone answering service, office space, typewriters, and benefits in a group whose members help one another.

The Educational Career Service in Princeton, New Jersey, pioneered the concept of a nonprofit, confidential clearinghouse, and remains one of the major placement and recruitment organizations for positions in teaching and school administration.

Civil Service offers an opportunity for the job

Getting a Job

seeker. The law provides that there shall be no upper age limit for entry into the competitive Civil Service. A mid-seventies study showed that nineteen percent of the people hired by the Civil Service Commission were forty and over. Write your congressman for more detailed information.

State and local governments offer a variety of job opportunities in city management, budget-planning, public information, personnel management and administration of Federal grant programs.

Whenever and however you go about finding a job, it's important to remember that you have much more to offer an employer than the "youngsters." You have experience—life experience and work experience. This is often the ranking qualification in the mind of an employer who needs reliability, sound judgment and good, productive work habits. It doesn't matter if the employer is the president or a department manager, he is performing against a budget: he has only so much money with which to accomplish an assigned job. He must rely upon his help, working as a team, to come out ahead at the end of the budget year.

Hastings College in San Francisco is one of the country's outstanding examples of putting experience and wisdom to work. The college decided to hire only retired professors for its faculty. As a result, it has not only achieved worldwide recognition but has developed one of the outstanding law schools in the country.

The Ideal Life

Private employment agencies profit from filling orders quickly and rarely have time to counsel on career changes. They are oriented toward employers instead of job candidates. Before registering, check the agency's reputation and make sure you understand the fee-paying arrangement.

Sharon Smallwood, a successful executive in her early forties, was a victim of a corporation changing ownership. She is a personable and outgoing woman and has a positive attitude toward life and work. Before seeking a new job, Sharon sought the advice of another person in the matters of hairstyle and the latest fashions for the businesswoman. Her coach accompanied her to one of New York's fashionable shops and helped her choose the proper attire for a woman executive.

Instead of answering newspaper ads or visiting employment agencies, Sharon took another route. She made appointments with executives in corporations and visited them, saying she was seeking a position, but not with them. She just wanted to learn more about this type of industry as it compared with other types she was investigating to see where her interest might best be served and, at the same time, make the greatest contribution to the employer. She did not make cold calls. Instead, she developed a chain, talking with one person who knew someone who might give her advice and who would recommend that he visit

Getting a Job

with her. Sharon then followed up with a phone call to set a definite date and time. Before she had completed the circuit of "visiting around" a job was offered that was completely foreign to all those she had considered. She took the job, however, and finds that she enjoys it and the pay is good.

Sharon's experience may suggest a new approach for men and women fifty and over who sense attitudes of prejudice toward them as they move along the traditional paths looking for a job.

The Interview

To this point you have analyzed your strongest assets and have determined what type of work you might enjoy after retirement. Based on newspaper ads and suggestions from various employment agencies and services, you have compiled a list of prospective employers. It may now be time to limit your concentration to a few promising targets. It will take some research to develop a general awareness of the organization to see where your abilities best fit. Your purpose is to locate the person who will actually do the hiring, the decision-maker for the department in which you are interested.

A short, to-the-point letter, directed to the department supervisor is one way of getting your foot in the door. Write letters to each company on your list and enclose your resume in each letter. Saturate the market with your name and availability. State in the letter that

The Ideal Life

you will phone on a specific date to see when (not if) you can fit a brief meeting into his busy schedule. When you phone keep the call short and acceptable. After all, your primary interest is in setting up an interview with the person. Remember that he has seen your resume, knows what your background and capabilities are, and may already have some idea how you might fit into the company operation.

Preparing for an interview can be a trying experience, especially because it probably has been several years since you were last interviewed. There are countless methods and theories to interviewing, but the best for you is what has worked best for you in the past.

Facial expression, while it must not be contrived or excessive, can tell an interviewer what you want him to know. Smiles are great indicators of character and self-confidence. Eyes that are bright and alert and comfortably focused on the interviewer further enhance the impression you make. Combining facial animation with erect posture and a firm, assertive handshake will immediately suggest vitality and self-confidence.

Hairstyles and clothing, reasonably in keeping with the time, promote the impression that you are both flexible and alert to the world around you. Balding men may wish to create a more youthful appearance with a carefully fitted, fine-quality hairpiece. It is best, however, to become completely comfortable with a hairpiece long before any interview.

Getting a Job

Fashion may be of particular concern in certain areas of employment, and dressing moderately in contemporary styles demonstrates awareness of major trends.

Try to pack more personal sell into a short interview by preparing ahead of time. Come up with ways to boost the company's production, cut expenses, enhance the company's image or the image of the products to increase sales. Think through ideas very thoroughly to avoid inviting a short lecture on how all of the suggestions have been tried and were miserable failures. Don't suggest anything merely to appear knowledgeable. Research; discuss the company's products or report on seeing them in retail outlets and watching customer reactions, etc. Knowledge of the market, the primary objective of company effort, can usually find an attentive ear anywhere along the departmental chain of operation.

Some years ago Joe Carr was seeking an editorial job with one of the country's top magazines. Because Carr had a degree in horticulture, he focused on one of the magazines related to that business. Instead of telling the editor what a good job he could do for him by writing editorial copy, he told him how much more plant food and related advertising he could attract to the magazine. Advertising income is what keeps most magazines in business. Carr got the job because he had gone well beyond step one.

It is possible that you may not be able to control the interview. The person behind the desk may have a

The Ideal Life

series of questions for you, many of which may seem unfair, suggesting a hint of prejudice. Be prepared for them and answer candidly.

"Don't you think you're a little old for this job?" Even though it is illegal to turn down job applicants because of age, employers can often say, "You are overqualified for the position." How can you respond? It has been said that a good salesman sells his prospective customer on the prospect's objections. The obvious response to such a statement regarding your qualifications is that the employer would be getting more for his money. Beyond that, convince the prospective employer that an overqualified person will be a better leader by setting new standards of work performance for his associates. Again, the company will benefit. Improved performance means increased production and greater efficiency, which will reflect well on the supervisor in the eyes of management.

"Why were you terminated on your last job?" Honesty is the best policy in response to this kind of a question, because the answer can be had with a phone call to your former employer. *It* might not be a fair answer. Take the opportunity to set the record straight, but remember that complaining about a former company, former boss or other employees is not advisable.

"How come you've jumped around so much from one job to another?" As a rule, no one wants an unstable employee who finds it difficult to follow company procedures. Again, be honest. Seeking better

Getting a Job

salary, more experience, or more responsibility are all plausible reasons.

"How much money are you asking for?" This question can best be answered by turning the question back in an effort to find out how much is budgeted for the job. The figure you stipulate may be too high or too low. If forced to come up with a figure, start high. You can always come down.

There are countless other questions that may be asked. Try to anticipate possible questions and prepare truthful, thoughtful answers.

Should a decision be made at this short interview that you are not the suitable person for the job, don't be disappointed. Most people don't receive a job offer after the first interview. It takes a few practice runs to improve your technique. It is essential that you maintain a positive outlook.

Thank the interviewer for his or her time in considering your application and ask if you may stop back in a few weeks to check on any other positions that might open up. Ask him to suggest other companies where you might fit in. Be sure to leave with a hearty handshake and a smile on your face.

The job search at any age can be frustrating or exciting, depending on the reasons for seeking employment. When financial considerations provide the impetus, stress can develop if the search proves fruitless at first. Generally, however, the search for a job at age

The Ideal Life

fifty can be looked on as exciting; for the years of experience and added knowledge offer greater qualifications, while decreased family responsibilities offer fewer financial pressures. For most people who seek jobs after fifty, the experience can be the one time when the job seeker can feel free enough to explore unusual possibilities, think about different places, and examine possibilities that twenty years before would have been hastily rejected, if presented at all. So to those looking for employment, relax and enjoy the search.

Families

"Our creator had to know what he was doing when he put us, in our fifties, in the middle of our families," said Jean and Harry Kenny. "We've had enough experience in complex problem solving, making tough decisions and stretching shrinking dollars to face up to the difficult hurdles ahead. This is the time when the grown children are just about ready to push off on their own, if they haven't already. They'll be back, of course, if in our upbringing we have convinced them that we may just have some problem solutions they haven't yet thought of.

"On the other side of the fifty marker are our parents, who have even more answers than we do, more experience, too. Fortunately for us, at this point, we still have more vigor than our folks, so we can be helping look after them in exchange for some of their accumulated wisdom."

The Ideal Life

Because all families have different structures, there is no ideal solution to all the problems confronting the family in the middle. How do you balance off responsibilities to your parents with obligations to your children? The easy advice is: do the best you can. The one thing to keep in mind is that you have passed through all or most all of the experiences facing your children but you haven't lived your parents' present experiences yet. So it may be worthwhile for you to learn more about the other side of the fifties from such an excellent source.

The ideal credo for the older person to live by was summed up succinctly by Dr. Ethel Andrus in her credo for the American Association of Retired Persons: Independence, Dignity, Purpose. Most every person wants desperately to maintain his or her independence and then some. Respect from others helps a person maintain his or her self-respect and dignity. And always there is the inner urge to be useful, have a reason for being, and a purpose in life. This permits people to hold their heads high with dignity and self-fulfillment. So, the thrust for independence, dignity and purpose seems to guide all of us in our life of activity, but never does it become more important to us than the time when we fear we may lose some or all of it.

To each of us, if we are lucky, friendships are a continuous life pattern—always changing because of death, moving away, losing track of one another, and sometimes just plain "falling out" and not wanting to

Families

continue the relationship. Some losses are replaced by new friends; but as the years go by it may take more effort and motivation. Samuel Johnson once remarked "If a man does not make new acquaintances as he advances through life, he will soon find himself alone. A friend, Sir, must keep his friendships in constant repair."

Dale Carnegie had something to say on the subject as well, "You can make more friends in two months by becoming interested in people than you can in two years by trying to get other people interested in you."

Older people may continue to belong to voluntary organizations, if such groups have had their membership for a number of years; but generally, older persons are not joiners or active members in new clubs and societies. The exception to this rule is the participation in church and religious groups throughout life. Community centers and their activities may appeal to this group and those retired may inspire interest and involvement by others. Retirement communities also plan programs of interest for the older group. In response to activities, friendships are formed.

As people age, they become more neighborhood-bound. Perhaps this will be a growing trend for all ages, with the shortage of gasoline and the decreased use of the automobile. This reduced mobility causes former interaction with friends outside the neighborhood to diminish. The loss of personal contact can

The Ideal Life

leave people very isolated and lonely (as well as depressed), if no effort is made toward forming and keeping happy relationships with those about them, especially in cases of emergency, shopping, trips to the doctor, and sometimes as advisors in crucial decision making. Simply visiting, sitting, talking, going for a walk, or sharing a sandwich can add something of interest to an older person's day.

For the age fifty couple, there is little difficulty in enjoying the fun and satisfaction of many friends and community activities. A move for this group is a challenge and a welcome change.

For the older person, moving from an old neighborhood to a new community is a strain, particularly if a person knows no one and is confused and baffled by the change. In these situations, the person is apt to withdraw and give up on previous activities and interests. Physicians say that too many changes compressed into a short period can adversely affect the health of an individual, regardless of whether the change is good or bad, and moving certainly could be one of those changes. The individual misses his old neighbors and friends and community support systems, so the move may bring on a period of loneliness and depression. Such community programs as the Crisis Intervention Program, The Town Watch, The Telephone Reassurance Service, Meals on Wheels and others may be quite valuable in making the individual feel more comfortable and at home in his new environment.

Families

The only way to have a friend is to be one, someone said, and we guess that's true. But how does a person go about being one? Well for starters, he might set off some ripples by simply smiling at others. Small children have no hang-ups, as a rule, in making friends; they approach the stranger with openness, without guile, and with complete confidence, that the stranger will, of course, respond just as joyously. So one should forget his self-consciousness, reach out and make some effort to get to know others. Get involved in activities, volunteering, and learn to to make friends on the basis of reciprocity and mutual help, sharing generously in the fun and companionship. An individual will make no headway, however, if he does not get out of the house each day and get interested in life about him. A neighbor discussed some friends that were permitting "life to pass them by." They sat in their apartments each day filled with gloom and grumbling, talking monotonously of the "good old days." Now, those are not fun people, and positively no one at all will ask them for an afternoon outing.

The happiest people are those who have friends of a variety of backgrounds and ages. One can consider himself lucky if a little neighbor child rings his doorbell to show a lost baby tooth, or Rosie who operates a roadside fruit and vegetable stand is bubbly and relaxed in her conversations, or the college student drops in seeking advice on how to roof a house, knowing that he will see a demonstration. In seeking some vitality and color in life, the retired person will not

The Ideal Life

limit himself to parading about in a goose step with only one friend, but will include others, as well, in recreational pursuits. And if his overtures toward friendship-making seem pretty unproductive, he will consider the words of George Sand: "Guard within yourself that treasure of kindness. Know how to give without hesitation, how to lose without regret, how to acquire without meanness."

This is the life George and Helen Kolbenschlag of Kent, Ohio, write of. "My first priority," says Helen, "would be to accomplish all the things I have wanted to do and should have done through all the years. To be inspired to do more painting, to do more traveling, spend more time with my friends, get caught up on my reading. I would welcome new experiences, new adventures, and meeting new people. We would hope to see our children and their families more often and to have more satisfactory communication with our teenage grandchildren.

"I would like to be selfish, without feeling guilty—to consider my own wishes rather than 'going along with what others want to do' (usually!). One thing I often long for is to have a cabin in the deep, deep woods—just to be available to me when I want to 'meditate.' After fifty, one should feel free to 'pull up stakes' and go where one wishes—but not a retirement area where there are no young people (a matter of choice)."

George responds, "To me, to arrive at the age of

fifty places me in a crossroad. I can look back at the successes and failures of the past and learn a lesson from them. I can hope to correct the mistakes I have made and get pleasure from our successes. We must plan the remaining years of our lives and benefit from what we learned in the past. At this time, we can be happy and proud that our children have apparently chosen a way of life that will mean success and happiness to them in their later years."

The majority of older persons try to maintain independence, either by themselves or with a spouse or relative. For as long as they can, they cling to the spirit of rugged individualism, freedom and independence and strive to maintain their own home, regardless of how modest. This does not mean that they are estranged from their adult children; not at all, rather it seems to be a mutually agreed "best" plan for the two or even three generations. In fact, the incidences of three generations living together under one roof have shrunk over the past twenty-five years. One authority questions whether the numbers of families living together was ever that popular, pointing out that the longevity of persons thirty and forty years ago was far less than it is today and, therefore, there were fewer grandparents to come and "live with the children." In the Social Security booklet *Planning for Later Years* advice was given to the over-sixty-five person to be cautious about making plans to move in permanently with the children, because of inevitable friction and strain.

The Ideal Life

When we see three generations living together today, the cause is usually poverty, the frailty of the elder member who needs help and care, the inability to find suitable alternative housing. The adult child will postpone as long as possible the institutionalization of his parent; and if it develops that this becomes necessary, the "child" may suffer guilt and anxiety. As age and chronic illness increase in the parent's life, his children will assist him in maintenance activities about his home, trying to help him retain his independence and autonomy. The family is always the chief source of help when a problem arises.

Although we live in an industrialized society in which there is considerable mobility and geographic separation, along with fragmentation of the family structure itself by death and divorce, the family, as a group, tends to want to stay within easy distance of one another. It is said in "Working With Older People" that seventy-five percent of the senior group live within an hour of at least one child; and that, furthermore, eighty percent of the group report that they see their children every day or so. Some groups have especially close ties with one another. The working classes tend to remain together in the same general neighborhood as a closely knit group, regarding one another not only as blood relatives but best friends as well.

The role of the family in enriching the existence of each of its members is unchallenged. Family life—growing, changing, enduring, flowing with all of life's juices—the babies, children, young people, wives

Families

and husbands, grandparents, aunts and uncles all add to its vitality. Families are the suppliers of love and security, memories and kindness, loyalty and compassion; they are the confidants, the support and comfort system, assuring one another that someone cares and can be depended upon to help.

All through life, each member of the family has changing roles and responsibilities and this is accepted by the changing values of what one member expects of the other. For example, in the early years of the adult child's marriage, the parents may still assume an involved and financially supportive role. By the same token, the elder at seventy-five and over may require more assistance from his children. The adult children may respond with emotional supports, the "talking it over," the family council, the listening and encouraging, the visiting, the transportation to the doctor, the grocery store and church, the parties for birthdays and anniversaries and other events.

Older people are especially likely to experience painful changes in family situations as spouses die and children move to other parts of the country. The stress and grief are compounded by the loss of support that a family can give. Geographic separation from members of one's family may not be exactly to one's liking, but parents should accept the fact that they cannot live their lives through their children. The parents should develop their own lives and be happy about it. You, the parent, have raised the child to be self-

The Ideal Life

directing, independent, strong and self-supporting, and you have succeeded. If children live across the country from you and have developed different lifestyles, you have freed them to do so. Our psychiatrist friend says, "It takes a strong kid to leave home." Freeing him or her, so there is no guilt or conflict in the leaving, may be one of the more mature acts you can do. One lovely mother says of her grown children living in different parts of the country, "I hold them close with open arms."

It is true that grandparents have no assigned role in society requiring much of them except not be a "burden" to anyone, and the middle-aged group is battered from all sides with demands, goals, taxes and fantasies. One writer soothes our worries by saying that our lives are in a state of adjustment; and when the smoke clears, we will, as one eighty-six-year-old retiree says, "finally get the hang of it."

The significance and closeness of family bonds are all too apparent in the letter from Regis Mulherin of Chicago in which he does a capsule review of their continuity. He writes, "It has been written that 'life begins at forty.' No so. I really believe that the ideal life begins at fifty, and I will tell you why. This is the time of life when the children have left the household to make their own way, and the house is empty except for myself and my wife. We are free at last to think of our own futures. Retirement isn't too far away, maybe five, ten or at most fifteen years; and we know that we are

Families

going to enjoy planning for it. Where shall we live? In a warm, sunny climate? Or should we stay put and possibly buy a different, smaller house or a condominium.

"This is when the joy of after fifty comes to life. We are free to explore the United States and its beauty to find the answers to our questions. Since the children are settled, we do not have to worry about them, and we can take all the time we want in our travels. We enjoy the beautiful countryside, the cities with their lovely homes, golf courses, tennis courts, shopping centers, and the fishing spots.

"Yes, it is a beautiful life, we have fun every day and thank God we are able to enjoy it. We leave worry to someone else. We take greater part in community affairs, attend clubs, museums, theaters, all the things we missed when the children were growing up. Then one day, our whole life changed with the arrival of the grandchildren and we spend more time at home, just having a good time with the little ones. They come visiting for a few hours, overnight or even to spend a weekend with us. And as they grow, we are interested in their school and activities, and we share the ballgames, shows and picnics with the family. Holidays are the happiest times of all with the children and grandchildren coming home and Grandma fixing the turkey. It is a time of great pleasure; and we know, indeed, that the most ideal time of life is after fifty."

Enjoying such an ideal life presupposes an ideal

The Ideal Life

family in which members enjoy strong family ties of loyalty each to the other. Unhappily, this is not always the case. It isn't easy to get the kids grown up without sibling rivalries that sometimes run quite deep, jealousies over another's accomplishments, accusations of unfair attention by parents, etc. The real tragedy is that too often brothers and sisters allow their childhood differences to follow them into adulthood. Strained relations split the family and the members go through their entire lives as strangers.

Psychiatrist Dr. Joel Goldstein advises, "Constant communication within the family is essential to continuous family harmony. Sure, there will be differences of opinion. Whenever you put two people together, regardless of their relationship to one another, there are bound to be opposite opinions on many subjects. The value of discussion, communications, is to lay it all out on the table. Don't keep a tight lip and let some petty difference fester inside. Out with it!"

After the kids are grown and strung from one end of the country to the other, this same family spirit will usually live on and will most likely be passed on to the following generation. But what happens to the family members who let their differences grow and become imbedded? They have one of two choices. They can carry on and pass the differences on to their own children, becoming the family aliens; or they can summon their courage and say to themselves, "How stupid can you get?" It takes some courage to be selfless, to extend

Families

yourself and admit being wrong even though you may not be the offender. The essential thing is to start communicating, planting a seed to grow on.

Because we live in an interdependent society, every lasting relationship involves a measure of commitment and sacrifice. The mounting number of shattered families points out the increasing unwillingness, for one reason or another, to live up to prior commitments which has given rise to a thriving investigative research effort by all of the professions that work in the field of human relations. Amitai Etzioni, Sociology Professor Columbia University and Director of the Center for Policy Research, states, "At the present accelerating rate of depletion, the United States will run out of families not long after it runs out of oil. This is not to be taken as a prediction," he added. "It simply projects a past trend into the future at the same rate of acceleration. The projection suffices, however, to show that the family is an endangered species, which it may require a conscious collective effort to save as part of our social ecology. Clearly if this decline is not to continue, some powerful forces will have to intervene to reverse the trend.

"Despite all the experiments and all the talk, marriage remains the vital cell of our society," Dr. Etzioni states. "Preoccupied though we are with the material aspects of our societal existence, with prices and jobs, shortages and energy, we dare not neglect the

The Ideal Life

institution of marriage. The disintegration of the family may do more to harm a society than running out of its favorite source of energy."

Some students of human relations have singled out the trend of individualism as the principal reason for the plight of the family—an overriding interest in personal happiness with little or no concern for others. The urgent need seems to be one of curbing the cult of self and working toward altruism and concern for others.

We cannot shut ourselves off from our families, our youth, our fellow humans and their needs. We must end our immaturity—whether we are twenty, forty, sixty, or eighty. Consideration of the other person and his struggles goes on forever, and there is nothing old-fashioned or "queer" about one generation reaching generous and loving hands to the other saying, "We love you; we'll help you if you need us."

There are increasing numbers needing help today. America has over fifty percent of its mothers of school-age children involved in the work force, and four out of ten of these mothers have children under six years of age. Fourteen million of these women are employed full time, and a large proportion of them are the sole support of their families. This means, according to figures available in 1977, ten million children (one in six) were living in households with only one parent, usually a mother. Good day care centers or other alternative arrangements that are desirable and affordable

Families

are sometimes difficult for the hard-working young mother to find for her children. Because women have not been able to command salaries that are commensurate with the demand on their purses, the support of these young families is often accompanied with anxiety and concern. If the mother is not able to arrange for supervision for her child after school, the "nobody home" syndrome occupies the life of both the mother and her offspring.

If our population had remained less mobile, would the extended family have provided some support system in situations such as these? Is the traditional family our cherished goal? Is it worth the effort? Would each generation arrive at a common answer to all these questions? We know that our nation itself is changing with inflation, divorce, liberation of women, disillusionment with religion and the political system. We know that the family structure is in for some rough going.

Studies indicate that most persons surveyed state that they still believe family life is the most important source of satisfaction and encouragement in their lives.

As more and more people move away from their home communities and many relatives, they are finding that they have inherited all the responsibilities and services which their families and relatives had been doing for them more or less routinely. Now, they find that they alone must take care of their babies, be vigilant of their teenagers' behavior and development,

The Ideal Life

be concerned with progress on their jobs, pay their own bills, and write the hospital social worker about what kind of nursing home is available for taking care of Grandma.

From Margaret Speers of Cedar Rapids, Iowa, who maintains strong family ties, came this response to our survey: "What is the 'ideal life after fifty'? It depends a lot on what my life was before fifty. Expecting life to be different, to give me benevolences and favors, just because I've lived fifty years or sixty or seventy, is to set myself up for disappointment, disillusionment and a miserable old age. From my point of view, how I see life, what I put into it, what I get out of it, and the way I value it depends upon what I genuinely believe in my innermost being. The word on the bottom line is *faith*. As the years pass and maturity is more advanced, I am discovering how profoundly important it is to have right relationships—*beginning with God.*"

Margaret has developed a "joy" formula to keep her on the track of serving God, humanity and eventually herself. She says of her "formula": "It has worked before fifty, is working now in the fifties, and I expect it to work as long as God allows me to reside in this world. Sometimes I've lived the formula poorly, to be sure. I've stumbled and bumbled with the best of stumblers and bumblers. But failures are opportunities for growing and maturing; and along the way I've experienced an array of wonderful intangibles that put a smile on the face and a spring in the step."

Families

She concludes by saying, "I haven't reached the ideal life yet, but in keeping with my 'Joy' formula, I may be getting closer." When she talks about her interrelationships with others, she is guided by the biblical, "Do unto others as you would have them do unto you." She tries to focus precisely on the person she is with at the moment. "In practical ways," she continues, "I am trying to understand where a person hurts, giving encouragement, lending a hand, appreciating his uniqueness, sharing his joy and sorrow, allowing him to be himself, and listening (a great thing to do after fifty)."

Being a good listener is commendable at any age, before or after fifty; but at almost no time does listening yield bigger dividends then when trying to maintain secure family relationships with teenagers. There are times when parents would rather blow their combined stacks than bite their tongues. We know. Keeping one's "cool" and listening accomplishes two things: (1) it offers the child an opportunity to be "grown up" in a one-on-one discussion of some pretty disturbing (to parents) beliefs and experiences; and (2) it allows parents time to sort things out and come up with some ideas on how to deal with them once they have settled into a calm after what can often be a shocking experience.

Blasting children at the mere mention of an offending subject can often cause them to clam up, keep on doing what they're doing and, as they drift away, develop such a chasm that it may take years of heartaches to bring relations back to a somewhat normal

The Ideal Life

level. It isn't as easy today as when we were teenagers. (Although our own parents may not agree.) We didn't have nearly as many temptations, nor as much money, nor easy access to transportation. The world wasn't moving as fast as it is today. So, parents, take heart from this wisdom of Ralph Waldo Emerson:

> Finish every day and be done with it.
> You have done what you could.
> Some blunders and absurdities no doubt crept in;
> forget them as soon as you can.

> Tomorrow is a new day;
> begin it well and serenely
> and with too high a spirit to be cumbered
> with your old nonsense.

> This day is all that is good and fair.
> It is too dear,
> with its hopes and invitations,
> to waste a moment on the yesterdays.

Retirement: The Best Time

What Is "Retirement?"

A distinguished Senior Judge of the United States District Court, William C. Hanson, gives this view: "Continue to utilize all your physical being, bearing in mind, of course, that you probably aren't as strong as you once were.

"Free yourself from dwelling exclusively on your life's vocation. Develop some stimulating avocations and explore new interests. Keep abreast of the times; keep your mind active and alert. Read! Don't retire from the world at fifty (or any other time), even if you could. Foster and encourage the *good* you see about you; challenge 'evils' of society which you recognize from your years of experience. And lastly, exhaust your talents. Build on your past knowledge and experience. If you have a particular strength in a certain area, pursue it."

The Ideal Life

Ruth, his wife, responds, "Keep on being busy doing useful, constructive things *together* (if you are still lucky enough to be together). Take time out to do things you've thought you couldn't afford to do before, like taking a Caribbean cruise, which *she'd* like or a canoe-fishing trip in the Canadian lake country, which *he'd* love to do again. Or get started on some new hobbies, even though you already have more projects than you know what to do with.

"Allot a little time and energy for community or volunteer work which is so needed, and which you now have time to enjoy. There's a lot of satisfaction in helping others, whether it be through a religious or charitable organization, or some remedial reading help in the public schools.

"After you have done all this, *slow down a bit*, and not only 'take time to smell the roses' but just let a little grass grow under your feet." Both conclude by saying that one should take time to "live, doing the things which seem most satisfying, most important and meaningful to all of us."

Retirement Syndrome Attitudes

Attitudes toward retirement are interesting. Some persons, who have no other identity than their job, declare in a tight-lipped way that they are going to "work until they drop." This group is likely to talk socially of only one topic: work. A second group may be those who have had boring, tedious, backbreaking

Retirement: The Best Time

jobs and who can't retire soon enough. A third group of retirees are those who have not been productive, those who have always been afraid they were going to get sacked and who welcome retirement as a way out and a respectable way to turn in the washroom key. And there are some who are happy and content to be free from the pressures, demands, stress and responsibilities of a job.

There is a special group, who are unlikely to leave the work force. These are the specialists, whom the company wishes to stay. In this group are the achievers, the creative thinkers, the specialists, writers, musicians, artists and inventors. They are found on corporate boards, in trade unions, among legislative and judicial bodies and in political offices. Lawyers and physicians of this group can work to the end of their days. But sad to say, most of those who are in the employ of others cannot.

At retirement age, many persons firmly believe they can work at full capacity and prefer to continue working a full schedule. There are also some who feel, because of economic hardship, there are no other alternatives than to stay on the job; and frequently, a sympathetic employer will arrange either full- or part-time work for them. A self-employed person may opt to continue his work, arranging his own schedule, hours and intensity of pace.

Counsellors in the field of retirement recommend that the process of disengagement from the work force

The Ideal Life

be a gradual one. But too many people retire at sixty-five with no plans, no goals, no dreams—only to putter, and use up their days aimlessly, fretting that no one pays any attention to them and time is passing them by. Others who have problems and cause problems for others belong to the "foot-tapper, let's-get-some-action-going group" who are obsessed with "staying young" even though the perpetual motion leaves them and everyone else exhausted. Authorities point out that constant activity is not synonymous with satisfying or fulfilling activity. The opposite type of retiree is the passive, dependent, "take care of me" group. Effort should be made to build up the confidence and self-worth of these people.

All people require a continuing sense of identity, relatedness, and security and this is no less needed in the retired person in order to maintain a productive life. Families and friends can give praise to the retirees' effort and work to support their families and develop the retirement nest egg. It takes skill to switch from one phase of life to another, and we all need as much help as we can get.

Retirement

When retirement occurs, good communication and good agreement on roles are important in a marriage. One wife, who was active in many clubs and groups, had a thorough understanding with her husband before he retired. "Tom," she said, "don't expect me to stay home and keep you company, for I won't."

Retirement: The Best Time

And she didn't. They all survived. Another friend tells of the noon lunch syndrome. Her husband loved noon lunch and visiting with his wife. After a month of lunches both of them were developing round little stomachs and could see that ahead of them was a big future. So out the window went the noon lunch. A better solution might have been a salad lunch and continued communication.

Beginning in the middle of your career, you should realistically start facing your retirement years, and utilize every resource available to determine where you are and where you want to go. This is the time to start developing hobbies, taking college courses to train for second careers, and securing retirement counseling, frequently available through the company for whom you are employed. It is this pre-retirement planning that helps people become better prepared and informed as to retirement options. Tomorrow will not take care of itself, but perhaps you can.

Because there are so many of the over fifties in our society, it is fitting and right that we should provide some input of skills, knowledge and wisdom into our communities by teaching, volunteering, and advising younger persons so we might attain an "ideal" life for all of us. We can keep in mind the words of Seneca: "There is nothing more dishonorable than an old man heavy with years, who has no other evidence of his having lived long except his age."

What does it mean to you to retire? Is it a welcome

The Ideal Life

chance to quit work, its drudgery, and rest and live quietly for a while? Or does it offer an opportunity to take a fling at something different, something that you have long wanted to do? Or is it fun time, a chance to travel and work on hobbies? We have heard of a near eighty-year-old General Motors retiree who travels extensively but sets aside some time each year to live and work with the Indians. There is an over sixty-five-year-old woman who translates books into braille and two seventy-year-old women, now retired from the school system, who teach (without pay) vocational education, remedial reading, and language skills to immigrants.

We've also met a retired executive who organized a band and is having the best time of his life. And a very proper professor retired and began guitar lessons, singing in the church choir, and painting with water colors (if he ever can find a minute). There are many who are going to school, teaching poetry, making wine, painting and gardening. There are men puttering in their garages working on secret inventions and women making patchwork quilts for sale.

Don't be afraid to experiment and put some zest in your life. Inevitably your lifestyle will be changing, and you will be engrossed in making the next years more fulfilling than those past. If large, earthshaking changes are not possible, take off for an auction, or have one. Or how about inviting your neighbors, kids and all, to strawberry shortcake with ice cream served on your patio some Sunday afternoon?

Retirement: The Best Time

Retirement is a time to begin searching for yourself, a luxury you have not had before. It is a good, unhurried, happy time; and authorities concur that if you were happy and resourceful in your middle years, the same disposition will follow you into retirement. Being flexible, adaptable, and optimistic are qualities that will keep you vital and in tune with the changes in the everyday world. If you have been a political activist, you may decide to give more time to politics and study, figuring out what issues and problems are most important to the well-being of our country. Around the clock leisure without any meaningful activity can not only be a bore but will contribute to listlessness and despair.

In *Working With Older People—The Knowledge Base*, published by the Department of Health, Education and Welfare, it was emphasized that there are many myths and stereotypes of the older person, so that sometimes the public sees him not as an individual but a depersonalized caricature. Chronological age does not determine when old age begins, but health and other criteria probably do. Certainly people in the over-sixty-five age group are not a monolithic population but a very heterogeneous group. They are not all sick, lonely and neglected, but are occasionally some of these. We would argue that most of them are resourceful, independent and conscientious, and a group dedicated to "carrying their own weight" in society. These twenty-four million persons make retirement big business, spending billions of dollars annually. Their

The Ideal Life

sheer numbers make for clout in the political arena and they vote.

Is work all that important for the retiree? It depends on the individual and the lifestyle he wishes to follow for himself. In our mini-survey, we found that there were many persons who were happy and content with the increased leisure time that they had earned for themselves. Sociologists who study the effects of retirement on individuals have discovered that neither retirement nor "the empty nest" is a major crisis for many persons; in fact, both events may be anticipated with pleasure. There are those who have said that work is an essential ingredient to a happy and normal life, but there has been a long term decline in the numbers of older people in the work force. It is estimated that in 1977, thirteen percent of older individuals were working —or approximately 2.9 million. This only makes up about three percent of the U.S. labor force. About one-sixth of the men were in agriculture or in self-employment jobs, and that force has been declining over the past decade. Some of the decline may have been brought about due to obsolescence of certain skills and the decreasing need for work on farms. With the availability of Social Security benefits and private pensions, the retiree may have some doubts whether the work ethic is all that great. (Statistics from Office of Human Development).

Employment and Volunteer Work

There are some so-called "volunteer" jobs that

Retirement: The Best Time

pay minimum wages and are open to people with low incomes who are sixty years and older. These are the Foster Grandparent Program, a twenty-hour-a-week program offering older men and women an opportunity to give love and attention to institutionalized and handicapped children, receiving in return the minimum wage in the community; and the Senior Companion Program which offers the over-sixty-group an opportunity to work with adults who have special needs. The assistance may be given in the adult's own home, nursing home or in institutions. Other employment for the retiree includes: staffing of local committees on aging and other service programs for the elderly; the project Green Thumb which pays for part-time work in beautification, conservation and community improvement projects in rural areas; and the Department of Labor's work training and job opportunities program for low-income people. Federally aided programs, reimbursing volunteers for transportation and other out-of-pocket expense, for which the older person is eligible are the Retired Senior Volunteer Program (RSVP) which sponsors a variety of volunteer services; and the Service Corps of Retired Executives (SCORE) which uses the skills and experience of the retired businessman who wants to help the small struggling business to succeed. Since 1965, SCORE volunteers have helped more than 175,000 enterprises succeed. Other programs that might be of interest to the over-fifty-group are the Peace Corps,

The Ideal Life

Volunteers in Service to America (VISTA), a national corps of volunteers working in urban ghettos, small towns, rural areas, Indian reservations or wherever there is poverty. VISTA volunteers serve one year and may re-enroll if requested. For their service, they are paid a monthly living allowance and a cumulative monthly stipend when they leave.

In 1979 the U.S. Department of Labor received an appropriation of $10 million for a new Older American Community Service Employment Program. Final decisions on the operation of the program are not available. The pilot projects that it sponsors include Green Thumb (National Farmers Union operating in twenty-four states) which provides part-time work in conservation, beautification, and community improvement in rural areas. Applicants should have a rural background and must take a physical examination. Senior Community Service Aides, sponsored by the National Council on Aging in eighteen urban and rural areas, provides part-time work in Social Security and state employment service offices, libraries, hospitals, and in many other areas.

Senior Community Aides, sponsored by the National Retired Teachers Association and the American Association of Retired Persons in thirty-one cities, recruits, trains and finds part-time work for aides in public or private service programs and assists in child care centers, vocational education classes and in clerical positions.

Retirement: The Best Time

After you retire, if you are an expert in some field, there may be opportunities to fill a part-time faculty position, and there will certainly be choices of many courses available in community colleges, adult education, junior colleges and technical institutes.

The possibilities for a useful life are endless in today's world. There is so much to be done and so many less fortunate people in the world, that retirement certainly should not mean a retirement from a life of service to our fellowmen.

So just what is an "ideal life" after retirement? A beautiful, retired school administrator, answers thoughtfully. "Retirement is an inauguration, an opportunity to eliminate all things insignificant, a chance to bring meaning and substance to one's life, to develop serenity of spirit.

"It gives one time to sort out one's thoughts, desires, ambitions. It means long walks, kicking the leaves and smelling the autumn bonfires. It means raising one's eyes upward and seeing the flight of geese winging their way to a familiar watering hole. It means taking one's delightful grandchild for a walk and reading aloud a favorite story before bedtime. It means becoming acquainted with this wonderful world—sometimes by traveling or by reading or by merely encouraging one's senses to absorb the beauty of the day. It means renewing old friendships, sharing ideas with new acquaintances, giving of one's talents and time in helping others. It means giving zest to

The Ideal Life

one's life by getting a part-time job, learning new skills in a vocational school, or taking a political science class to become better informed about the issues of the day. Retirement is the recess, and the best is yet to come."

ABOUT THE AUTHORS

Authors Gordon and Mary Elliott are well qualified to write a book on planning for retirement. Gordon, before his retirement, was Editorial Consultant for the American Association of Retired Persons (AARP) and for the National Retired Teachers Association (NRTA). This position followed a career on the editorial staffs of *Look Magazine,* Meredith Publishing, Curtis Publishing, and *National Wildlife Magazine.*

Mary's career began with a B.A. in journalism from the University of Iowa; but her graduate training was in social work, gaining her membership in the American Association of Social Workers. After the birth of their two children, Mary devoted her career to volunteer work; she has served on the boards of Legal Aid and Day Care and as Chairperson of the Council of Social Agencies.

Today, the Elliotts live in Bryn Mawr, Pennsylvania, where Mary continues as a volunteer for the local hospital in the departments of Social Service, Discharge Planning, and Professional Standards Review Organization. Gordon is still active as a free-lance editorial consultant. Both find retirement life to be *The Ideal Life.*

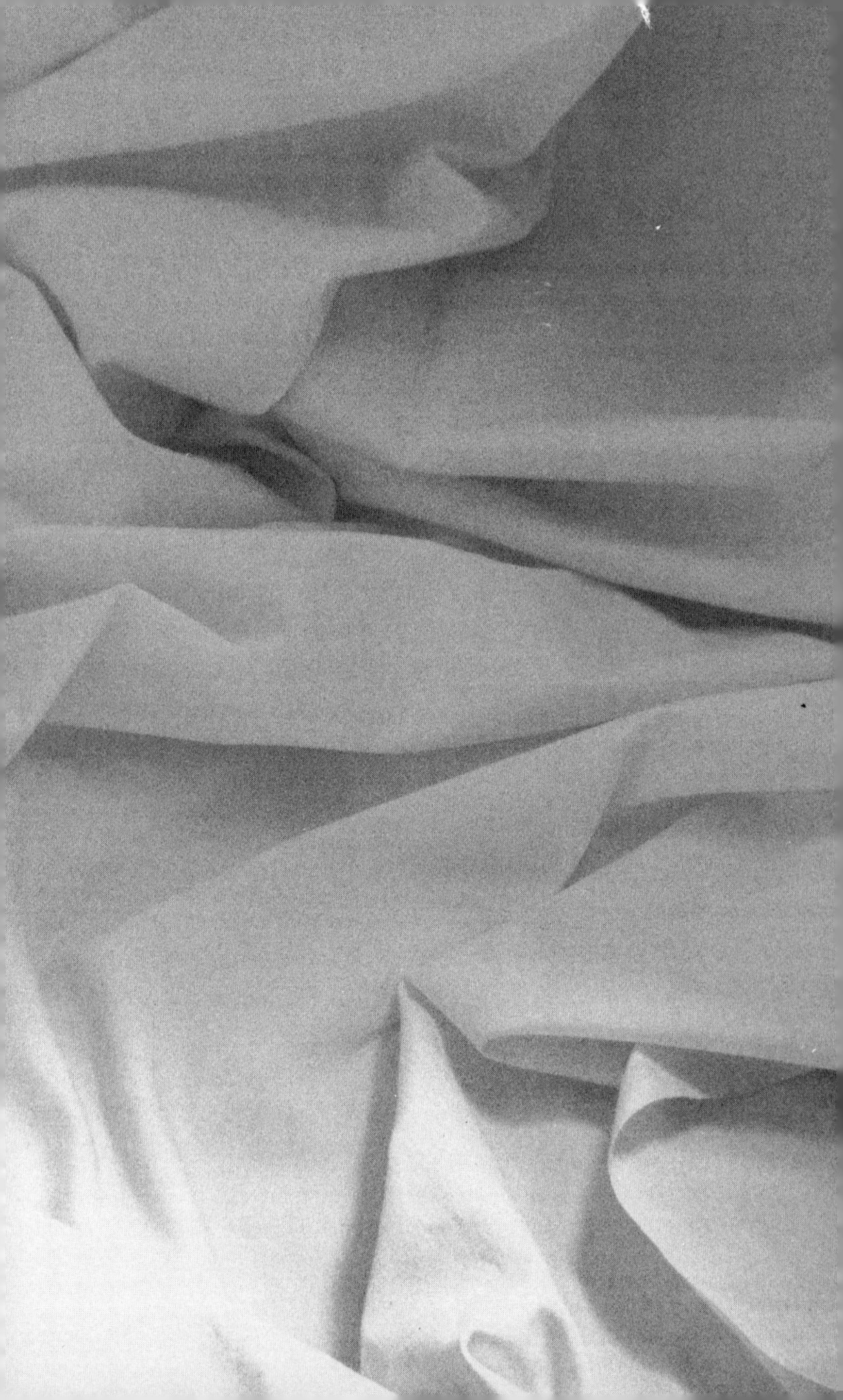

Growing
Through
the

Ugly

A Novel

Diego Vázquez, Jr.

An Owl Book
Henry Holt and Company
New York

Henry Holt and Company, Inc.
Publishers since 1866
115 West 18th Street
New York, New York 10011

Henry Holt® is a registered trademark
of Henry Holt and Company, Inc.

Copyright © 1997 by Diego Vázquez, Jr.
All rights reserved.
Published in Canada by Fitzhenry & Whiteside Ltd.,
195 Allstate Parkway, Markham, Onterio L3R 4T8.

Library of Congress Cataloging-in-Publication Data
Vázquez, Diego.
Growing through the ugly: a novel / Diego Vázquez, Jr.
—1st Owl books ed.
p. cm.
"An owl book."
ISBN 0-8050-5744-7
1. Mexican Americans—Texas—El Paso—Fiction. I. Title.
PS3572.A987G7   1998   97–43689
813'.54—dc21   CIP

Henry Holt books are available for special promotions and
premiums. For details contact: Director, Special Markets.

First published in hardcover in 1997 by
W. W. Norton & Company

First Owl Books Edition 1998

Designed by by BTD / Beth Tondreau
Photo on pages 2 and 16 © B. Tondreau

Printed in the United States of America
All first editions are printed on acid-free paper.∞

3 5 7 9 10 8 6 4 2

To Marjorie Lin Kyriopoulos

Grateful acknowledgment is made to the Jerome Foundation, Minnesota State Arts Board, and The Loft.

Parts of *Growing Through the Ugly* appeared in different form in *A View from the Loft*, The Loft, 1992; *Do You Know Me Now?*, Normandale Community College anthology, 1993; COLORS magazine, Four Colors Productions, 1993, under the title "Some Whispers Never Leave"; and *Speaking in Tongues*, The Loft, anthology 1994, under the title "Nam Paso."

Special acknowledgment is made to the Estate of Pablo Neruda for permission to reprint lines from "Cuerpo de Mujer" from *Selected Poems: A Bilingual Edition* (Houghton Mifflin, 1990). Originally published in England by Jonathan Cape, Ltd. First American edition by Delacorte Press, 1972.

M.L.K., your time, heart, soul, and support in helping to shape the "raw ugly" into something publishable will never be forgotten.

Thanks to Jill Bialosky for taking that leap of faith.

Growing Through the Ugly

Prologue	13
I. Buzzy Digit Gets a Name	15
II. Mercado	25
III. Little League	39
IV. The Bird Cage Was Not Perfect	51
V. A Carpenter and a Writer	59
VI. Lottery Winners	67
VII. Some of Us Are Missing	77
VIII. Bienvenidos to the South	85
IX. Travelling with Men	105
X. A Visit to the Hotel Cortez	115
XI. The Flight Home	131
XII. Poets and Listeners	139
XIII. Travelling with a Woman	155
XIV. They Came Home Before I Did	175
XV. Everywhere I Turned, One of Us Was Dying	183
XVI. Sky Come Get Me	187
XVII. Return to Sender	199

Growing
Through
the
Ugly

Prologue

August 31, 1969. This is my first day of being dead but I want to return to my abuelita's house. Granny's little red brick casita. Memory is stuck inside this box with me. Soon there will be memorials, but I am the memory. Cold feet jumping on a hot fire. Memory shows me things in small fragmentary bursts. Funny thoughts tingle through my fingers. Me at six. Still chewing my toes. Then suddenly, the week before I turn fourteen, leaving El Paso for the last time. Today. A brief glimpse at the white colored brightness the day before yesterday. It is the third week after my eighteenth birthday.

This box is getting stuffed into the huge cargo bay of an old warhorse air carrier where memory stacks up like a bunch of old Sunday morning newspapers. Yellowed articles record that the best for me was during those too few years in El Paso. Yellowed articles with bold headlines detail the first day I am with abuelita, mi Nana Kika, at the Mercado Bustamante on Calle Paisano. Nothing has been written to tell why I leave home so soon, just before I turn fourteen. The desire to know more increases with each new murmur. I am just pieces now, but I am getting stronger.

1

Buzzy Digit Gets a Name

especialmente, *monarcas*

The importance

of butterflies

has to

do

with

their

offspring

growing

through

the

ugly

and

always

flying

away

beautiful.

Doña Kika Soldano

(translated by Buzzy Digit)

When I was six, I knew things. I knew the sound of strangers when they approached from behind. I knew you could eat potatoes with the skin if they got washed real good. Not so with jicama. If you eat jícama skin, it jangles the feel of the earth onto your tongue for days and days. I learned this from my grandmother, mi abuelita, Nana Kika.

Nana Kika sold tortillas de maíz and two choices of tamales all day, every day of the week, at the Mercado Bustamante on Calle Paisano in El Paso de Tejas. Six was an important age for all of her grandchildren because it marked our first trip to the mercado to help her work. Our abuelita was famous. Nana Kika would amplify a lecture on the importance of keeping our lengua in working order, insisting, "The best hope for keeping your mother tongue intact is in this marketplace." In my early Mexican Spanish, I always defined lengua as "beef tongue for dinner." La Doña Kika Soldano did not want our tongue boiled and lost in the puffy steam of this caldron de los Estados Norteños.

From the day I turned six until three months before I reached the small age of fourteen, my El Paso home was with her. Her three-story yellow house was a little rumbley sometimes because the Southern Pacific ran right off the backyard. It wasn't really a backyard. Maybe fifty feet, and one tree separated the back door from the railroad tracks. When cousins or friends came over to play they usually stayed in front of abuelita's "big yellow bird cage." Except for me. I was always drawn to the backyard. The adults would warn me not to lead any of their offspring toward the tracks. "Don't be playing on those tracks when you hear the trains coming." Then, of course, they would offer any one of numerous stories about a small child becoming a bundle of blood on the rails.

Nana Kika was gentle and great. My old skinny grandmother, with the eyes of a rain-charged mudslide and the hair of a snowstorm, had the tall sense of an old Ponderosa with broken limbs all about her. La Señora Kika Soldano was the Ponderosa loggers would leave stand after a clearing.

For years, abuelita appeared to me as the tallest woman on earth. My head reached her waist. She was just under five feet, seven inches tall but she towered over all her grandchildren. I was frail, with cream skin and round eyes like my mother. The dry mood of my darkness came from a lost father. Nana Kika was my father's mother. Whenever I walked with granny, I would hold her hand, believing she could see beyond the horizon. Beyond the dirt crusted Rocky Mountains.

I must rely on legend to transcribe my name. My real name is Bernadino Soldano Dysyadachek, Jr. But I've been Buzzy Digit since I was a child. The exact moment it began is lost for me. Abuelita Kika used to ask how many Juniors could one family stand. It is said my favorite books as a child were books about cats. Children's books called cats "pussies." When I said "pussies" it came out "boosie." My older cousins, who were farther along in their command of this New World englich, played on it. Boosie became pussey, busy, boogsie, booze, boozy, Buzzy. My mother's Chicago-Polish last name was a burden to all. They took Dysyadachek and turned it to Dissachikie, Disastick, Digitstick, digs shit, dig it, Digit . . . my cousins were kind. They decided against calling me a pussy that digs shit. They invented Buzzy Digit. Because my mother was from the Windy City, I decided my real birthplace was Chicago. A Chicago Chicano, Buzzy Digit.

Abuelita Kika was also a diplomat. When I claimed to be her favorite grandchild, she would smile and lift the gentle, dusty importance of my desire into a look in her eyes that would send me into storms of joy. In private, she assured me of my most favored status, though I was never able to get her to confirm this in public. All my cousins, who were direct descendants of Satan and not worthy of Nana Kika's affection, also considered themselves her favorite.

My abuelo, my grandfather the baker, died of a heart attack when I was three. Nana Kika often spoke of the gentle heart of her Don Pablo, her huge baker macho de hombre who had seeded her with nine children. He was struck at the panadería, his bakery, a few minutes after midnight as he prepared to bake bread for a November Wednesday morning in an old West Tejas smelting town. I don't remember abuelo, but his bakery and his land became a legacy that survived all the debts his sons piled up against their inheritance.

The wars of inheritance raged as soon as abuelo was put into the ground. Nana Kika had four sons who served this country during la Segunda Guerra. Only two saw combat. One died three days after coming home from Nazi Europe. The other, my father, came home with malaria and the horror of the siege on Guadalcanal. He saved himself from those horrors by abandoning his familia—all the familia, his two little girls, his tiny boy, and a disbelieving wife.

Two versions of my father's disappearance evolved. The first, and most prevalent, blamed his duty as a Marine medic on that island as having permanently stolen his soul. At family gatherings, an uncle or auntie would pat me on the head and whisper sorrow for my terrible fate. It was good for tips, too, because they would stuff money into my little palm, telling me his return from la Guerra had affected him in ways no one could know. They insisted it was not his lack of love for me that caused him to run, but rather the toll of too many bodies he could not fix. The terror this caused his inner world could not be mended.

The second and least talked about version of my

daddy's fugitive status involved our almost-teenaged cousin, Gloria. She was the first grandchild, the oldest cousin, and epileptic. Exactly one year after my grandfather died, my father took Gloria to her swimming lesson at the downtown Y. The sun rose, promising to cover the desert with more heat. In the early morning, my dad gave Gloria the ride to her final swimming lesson. He drove away with the top down on his latest "demo," a red Chevy Bel Air. Sixty-seven minutes after Gloria waved goodbye to my dad, Auntie Margie received the call that would affect all our lives for the rest of time. The young swimming instructor cried to my dearest tía, "Everyone thought Gloria was holding her breath under water. She was in the shallow end of the pool and all the other girls were doing the same thing. The others kept coming up for air, thinking Gloria was just ahead of them in going back under. They thought she was winning." When the instructor witnessed a color of purple contrition on our Gloria's face, it was already too late. The small puddle of chlorinated water had poured a flood into the territory of a young girl's life. The water forced itself into her lungs without waiting for her seizure to stop. The water took Gloria as a gift. Our oldest cousin, almost a teenage girl, had been taken back. Gloria became an angel.

Only one time did I hear Nana Kika mention my dad in the same breath with talk of Gloria's death. Only one time did I hear her say she thought it was the one ride that destroyed him. All the other excuses for his abandonment centered on the war. The second big war. I became a believer of the drowned version.

They say my mother is beautiful. But she abandoned me after my daddy ran, her brave heart broken and saddened. I only recall her screams. Once, some crazy ghost screaming from an abandoned graveyard made her slice the skin on my head with a jab from a broom handle. I locked myself in the bathroom and cried while my head dripped blood onto my hands. When she finally opened the door, the blood had dried. She told me it was nothing and not to say anything to Nana Kika. In most pictures, she has eyes that look like the desert green of small lizards. Abuelita said they were the deepest green she had ever seen. They were eyes that made people feel as if they were looking into the center of the ocean.

My grandmother spoke softly of my mom and dad. "Mi'jo, they were so pretty, O, pretty together. But the war ruined him. Tu padre signed up with those Marines without telling anyone. At seventeen, he was already filling prescriptions for Hidalgo's pharmacy. He told the Marines he was going to be a doctor so they made him a medic. Y tu mamá, mi hijito, tan hermosa, and so strong."

"But, abuelita, if she was so strong, why did she hit me and where is she now?"

"When your daddy ran away, she left with a Mexican painter from Chihuahua. After that, she met some writer, or poet, from Chile and they went back to his home in a place

called Temuco. The last we heard was her letter telling us of a place called Antofagasta. It is the place on this earth where the sun is always the toughest. She said you will be sent for when they get settled."

"They" included my two older sisters. My mother pleaded with Nana Kika that girls needed to be with their mother much more than a boy did. Granny never turned away a child and this is how I came to live with her. I was one of many cousins who would ask Nana to be my mother.

I had a favorite dream during my first year of school. It gave me a second chance at choosing a mother. In waking, I told myself that since the first one was lousy, the next one would not have to be so pretty that her eyes need to be green. *I just want her eyes to see me when she looks at me. That will be fine. She can wear short dresses. I want her to walk with me. If she wants to hold my hand, I will let her. She can touch me in public. She can be old, like thirty-three. She can have dark hair, short ears, crooked nose, and wide soft lips. Her breath will be from the heart of a strawberry. And when I sleep, she will kiss me. If I wake from broken dreams, she will let me sleep with her. I can lay my head on the inside of her thighs, or her belly, or on her breast like I used to when I could put my lips on her nipples. She will let me sleep on her buttocks if I want. She will take me like the ocean returning to gather all its stranded creatures. Her skin can have sand in the pores, but her eyes will remain clear. She won't hit me with crazy broom handles when I cry. I promise to choose a mommy who will tell me it is not necessary* *for tears because she knows how to be funny. We will laugh at men's jokes. And, because she wants me to grow protective of her, she will tell me about men. Then, she will let me warn her about things she already knows. As the night gets darker, she will let me be her child.*

When I was six, I knew things.

11

Mercado

Nana Kika is from the angels who brought us to the border. She was firmemente, consistently determined to make us find our special guardians. When the last of the seven bakeries and the last of her equity from a big yellow house on the south side of the Franklin Mountains dissolved, abuelita went back to work. I was a poor student in a poor school in a poor frontier town. The teachers were bored with our Mejicano Spanish and could not reach me like my tough, skinny granny with the neon white hair and the most sparkling laugh.

When Doña Kika's sons depleted her tiny savings, greed covered these boys and their wives. Except for my dad, who jumped onto his isolated island home and never tried to blame anyone. His isolation cost me my heart. He left us all behind crowded with attorneys who never stopped sending raging divorce demands. I lost some cousins during the turbulent declarations of contempt. I lost a few aunties. Women whose smooth tender legs were blotted from the rights of la familia. Uncles cried nightly from rooftops. Their sons-of-a-baker's lips soaked with rum as their arms held onto hourly women. They gave up on their wives . . . soft birds singing about sons. Los hijos de Don Pablo rushed ruby red extemporaneous furies at the dull, bleached women who married them for a slice of Don Pablo's estate!

They got lost in a jungle of puterías, of whores. Nana Kika said those boys spent too much time and money con putas. It made them lose passion for their brides, who had, at one time, promised to let them stick it anywhere. While her boys grew uglier and stole Nana Kika's last centavos, mi abuelita de oro, my granny made of gold, got innovative.

Señora Bustamante, Nana Kika's comadre from twenty thousand lifetimes, arranged for abuelita to rent one of the most visible stalls in the Mercado Bustamante. Granny had only two fine slender hands, so her real strength was in selling tortillas y tamales that looked and smelled hecho en casa. Home made. But a business agreement with the real baker of the goods, Don Martín de Montana Street, kept it a secret. His hidden factory revealed important discoveries for the grandchildren who witnessed an early exposure to the conspiracy of adults. In the pieces of silence that bounce from secrets, Nana Kika and Don Martín reached their business agreements. Secretos of profit.

Don Martin was a giant with the roundest belly and the roundest face and the roundest smile and the roundest bald head a man could have. The first most-beautiful man I ever saw. Looking at him was like watching the night with a full moon and a million stars. He was full of everywhere. For the children in my family, meeting Don Martín was an event that rivaled that of waiting for presents on a December morning from el Santo.

Strange stories surround the grim assistant baker of Don Martín's hidden Montana Street factory. Chonte, a drunken gila monster, looked like a lizard but his moves were much more dangerous. My older cousins told stories about being at the young age where some kids can look like either a boy or a girl. And the ritual of being left alone with el Chonte. It only took a few minutes for him to coat the nipples of preteen girls with baker's yeast. It is a legend that girls who got it early from him would have sweet milk flowing from their breasts when they gave babies their nipples. If the lizard Chonte made a mistake, sticking the yeast on a boy, then the pobrecito would be certain to grow up to be a sissy.

History was big for us. All of my older relatives listened romantically when Nana Kika would demand, "We own more rights to this desert then estos Americanos want to admit. They even stole White Sands up in New Mexico so they could play with all their UFOs and kill all those innocent Japonéses. Buzzy, I know your dad hated fighting all those guys in Guadalcanal but you know what? He was still fighting a real war. He didn't hate those Japs. He hated their leaders. Now that these gavacho leaders have built that bomb right in our backyard what's to keep them from using it on us? Nothing! With the bombs that they own they are going to keep this land away from us for a thousand years. And watch, someday, just to make sure that no more of 'us' can cross la frontera, they will build a wall all across the desert like they did in China. But we were here first and those mad gavachos stole it from us... somos parte indio... all of my family has indio in them. We are not 'Spanish' just because we speak it. Those Cabroncitos robbed us, too, even worse than these gavachos at Fort Bliss, but at least we can say we are Mejicano."

But bigger history was made for us when we ate the biege leche quemada candy Nana Kika gave us. Her favorite candy. The fate of Nana Kika's El Paso grandchildren, when they turned six, was to help her work at the tortillería en el mercado. At the mercado, she took your hand and placed it on an ancient wagon with big, ugly wheels and a long, black handle. At one time, the old wagon might have been red, but by the time I saw it, it looked invisible. On my sixth birthday she pushed me through the most direct, yet discreet route to Don Martin's hidden factory. The path was familiar and boring until we passed the alley behind the house of the gavacho. The dirty gringo from Georgia, Leroy Harvay, who had shot and killed un negrito burglar on the front porch of his house one Thursday at ten-thirty in the morning. The Nazi Harvay was known for training killer dogs. Nana Kika stayed sharp and precise in warning me as we rolled quickly past his house. "Mi'jo, never go close to that man!"

Don Martín always conducted the indoctrination

of a new grandchild into the business world. The round Don Martín. Even his factory was round. Don Martín supervised the initial loading of the invisible wagon. Fresh tortillas and warm, soft tamales with secret ingredients. He stuffed a large round bottle in a wooden box and placed two blocks of dry ice wrapped in old rags into the box. His instructions were to not unwrap or touch the burning ice. "Because it can melt the fingers off your hand." Everything warm got covered in waxed paper, assorted pieces of old clothing, and pieces of cardboard. Each day included more than a dozen return trips to the factory. Nana Kika accompanied us only on our first trip. After that, she expected us to remember what to do. We were part of the routine.

On returning to her stall at the mercado, the warm goods were dropped into a large, insulated metal box, which kept them fresh and hot until they were sold. Nana Kika unloaded the specially wrapped bottle and placed it under the table where she sat most of the day. A false facade behind the counter gave new anglo shoppers the impression that her food was made on the premises. Anyone who has shopped more than once at Mercado Bustamante in the heart of the barrio segundo on the southwest side of El Paso, and each new grandchild after the first day of work, knew that Granny only sold the little corn miracles. Don Martín and his lizard assistant, the drunkard Chonte, took care of the rest.

Until I turned thirteen, my most important job was to get my grandmother's goods to market. I always had a desire to help her. I considered myself her most loyal and available grandchild. Abuelita's requests for help were necessary to me. All my older cousins from the "Red" Rosemary to the boy hating "Pulgas" seldom continued to make pick ups and deliveries with the invisible wagon. They would usually just stay in the stall with abuelita and help her cure the world of its blues. Along with spiritual assistance from the round bottle.

I was destined to travel every inch of the mercado. Once I saw it, I could no longer exist without the taste and feel of the daily, huge chunchunchun of life crowding and pushing its way into the lives of those who try to replenish a hunger for something beautiful and severe. The hunger of men whose stomachs were lined with the caked-blood memory of war. The hunger of motherhood shattered by boys returning from battles with broken eyes staring into a future of agony. The hunger of young, foreign, girls as their breasts fall between the hands of grim strangers who have paid for this affliction. The hunger of an old man as he watches teen girls running in their Catholic-school skirts. The hunger of a young boy being kissed under the light of small candles while the Salvation Army choir sings in the park. The daily hunger of a small world exploding with desire.

The effortless joke of my young life became an ugly laugh when I was caught alone with the lizard drunkard Chonte. It was almost the end of my second summer with abuelita at the mercado. I was seven years old. I knew how to read round clocks and I knew my days of the week. *It is four P.M. on a Friday. Don Martín is not at the factory. Chonte says to be quiet and stay still. He quickly lifts my shirt and places his left hand on my titty. Then his other hand grabs my other titty. The hand is holding a glob of baker's yeast. While he smears my chest, his big thing starts to show under his apron. It looks like it is watching me. I feel it touch me on my shoulder and his hard lizard hands are rubbing my titties. Everything in his power rubs its way onto me. I feel a hot splash on my neck and smell his sweaty, exhaustion. His beard looks muddy. I remember the face of a circus horse as it sleeps after having performed. Dreaming for a choice.* Chonte drops my shirt and whispers, "Esto es what makes the yeast rise." He never touched me again. He had too many children to choose from.

Outside, on the street, I swayed. The world had become nothing but brown desert dust. The beginning of the end for me was all the dust. Fear had arrived. It hid behind the seconds and minutes on the faces of clocks. At 4:19 P.M. on a Friday afternoon, the world stopped. I was trapped under a big, smelly, ugly foot counting dust for hours and hours. Chonte was the first person who led me to believe the plaza park preachers with their warnings on hand-painted signs, "The END is Near!"

The preachers in alligator park never stopped talking about the end of the world. On Sundays at three A.M., they could be heard screaming at the drunk soldiers who had jumped the fence in order to wrestle an alligator. "These animals are going to bite off your whorehouse dicks." Every soldier wrestling with his animal bride would jump, UFO-like, from that pool. The preachers would howl, "These alligators were put in this park by God so they can test any soldier who is returning from a night of whorehousing in Juarez. Presidente Brandy and an ally gator means one lost body part."

As the years passed and too much of the zone known as the "Preacher's end" surrounded me, I would run to the mercado to find my abuelita Kika in rampant dialogue with her comadres. They were always in the middle of endless conversations concerning their poached pain from the untold suffering inflicted on them by their sons and daughters. Their oral studies on the condition of our souls were sanctioned by cups filled from the bottle wrapped in dry ice. I would come alive with them and they were good at ignoring me, so I heard everything they said. Except for the time Señora Bustamante was talking about how she had started to use her fingers instead of waiting for him. When she saw me, the vieja Bustamante stopped talking and renamed me "Droopy." She said I always had sad eyes, even when I laughed. I wanted to tell her to go finger herself, but I wasn't sure what it meant. My Nana Kika said there was no room for new names. My cousins had taken to calling me ese Buzzie Digito, and she was certain that name would stick.

Summers with Nana Kika were pretty. Everything, except the drunk lizard and the grief of the prophets, had the ooze of dreams. Dreams that carried me home after the howls of dark invaders had motioned for my throat. Nothing compares to those first years. The world spoke to me in a West Tejas español, which was the clearest, slowest, and most perfect dialect on the planet. I studied death, stars, and my abuelita's tongue. Nana Kika had a large army of translators available for any ventures into the Norteños lengua. Whenever I asked her why she would not speak la english, her answer never varied. "We were here first." She would scratch her left ear and talk of a time when the only spoken tongue was her Mexican Spanish. "No, hijo. There is nothing but an invisible line dividing us from our people."

When I was ten and the end of summer was near, that bottle in the box saved my life. My routine with the invisible wagon was broken when Yolanda Bustamente forced me against the fence and kissed my tongue. After that, I found myself with shaking knees, pulling a squeaky old wagon into the territory of Leroy Harvay's killer dogs. One of Leroy's Nazi mongrels found my leg and sunk his teeth into the back of my left thigh. I immediately abandoned the idea of whapping the dog with tortillas or tossing a tamale to stop this mutt's trained response. In those full-kill moments, my two tiny arms grabbed the bottle from the wrap of towels and slapped dry ice into the mutt's mouth. As the four-legged Nazi singed his tongue, I broke the bottle over its bad brain and ran. I had been told stories of dogs stealing children so that they could be raised as animals. But this was not a steal. This was a kill. My pants were bloody rags and my left leg felt loose.

Nana Kika's sacred bottle was broken, so I returned

to the factory for a replacement. It was not simple because I had to listen to Don Martín give me his thoughts on the particular family history concerning my dad and my older cousins. "Buzzy, don't you know how hard it is to keep this bottle fresh? I can't tell you how long it takes to mix and blend and brew this. Because it takes a long time and it is a very secret recipe . . . it has some of the same medicine that that Coca Cola used to have before the government wouldn't let them keep making it. My abuelito gave me this old formula, which he swore that Coca Cola company stole parts of . . . difference with his was that he also blended in ron de una isla del Caribe, he would say, 'and that island rum is the strongest magic in the whole world if you mix it right,' and then he also used some special yerba. So once a week I have to go into Juarez into colonia Anapra and visit a curandera that makes a special yerba that I add to my mix. It is a lot of extra work, niño. But I do it so that me and your Nana Kika can stay healthy." He looks at me the way a priest does before offering Communion. "Niño, you are too young to be trying to do what your cousins used to do. Oye, at least they were teenagers when they first fooled me with that old pendejada of a perro story. This dog story is too old now. I know your daddy. I know how early he got started on that botella. Don't be starting so young, niño. Because this botella is just for when you are older. If you start tasting it right now it won't work . . . just bad things will happen."

"But, Don Martín, look at the back of my pants! I tell you for real, lo que pasó. I didn't drink that stuff. Besides, wow, I smelled it and I don't know how anybody can drink it . . . it smells like a gas station. I . . . I . . . had to use the bottle and the flaming ice to knock away that gavacho's killer dog."

Don Martín studied the drying blood behind my leg and whispered to God that someone should pay for this. He did not apologize to me for his disbelief. He replaced the contents of the protective box and sent me away. I thanked Don Martín and left him shaking his head.

At the mercado, when abuelita saw me torn and shattered, yet slowly pulling a full wagon, she screamed, "Sangre de Cristo, niño, que te pasó?"

"Blood of Christ!" I felt like a martyr. But my pants were sufficient protection against the jaws of the killer. There were no deep punctures. My deep hero wounds amounted to small scratches on my skin. I quickly decided to ride this wave of heroism as far as I could. First, I retold the Yolanda encounter in full detail and quickly discovered that was not the pathway to martyrdom. My granny's compassion dissolved as suddenly as the cheap Nazi mongrel took to my thigh. She said I was too young to worry about girls and warned Yolanda through me that she had better behave or her mother would be told.

The first piece of this puzzle came to life. Sometimes, adults say things to children that are meant for adults. Sometimes, they just say things that are meant for anyone nearby. I knew that Yolanda's mother would be told.

Nana Kika's scolding softened and my attention faded. She concluded that Leroy Harvay and I are both as goofy as each other, because, "los dos no saben . . . neither of us knows where we are going." I stood there, quietly thinking of the plaza park, plasma-donating prophets. And Señora Kika Soldano stated, loudly enough for all the mercado to hear my public flogging, how she wished that the madman Harvay with the trained killer Nazi mongrels had been stuffed into one of those ovens she was certain he had operated for the Germans. "Todos los judíos pobres got gassed so he could live and train dogs to kill in nuestros Estados Norteños." When she grew silent, I walked across the street in search of a preacher.

III

Little League

I played my first game of Little League baseball two months before I turned eleven. Because Chonte had coated my nipples with yeast and squirted on my shoulders, I knew I was destined to become a sissy. But I wanted to keep it secret. I was not a good hitter during the real games, only at practice. I told the coach I needed glasses for game days and that Nana Kika couldn't afford to buy them. Coach questioned why my glasses weren't necessary at practice. I explained, like a doctor, that it's only a sometime condition. That I had no way of knowing when my vision would turn fuzzy. This started a few years of being tagged as "Fuzzy Buzzy." I assured him that once la Doña Kika had the money to buy my glasses I would wear them all the time. Coach was too busy with other problems to worry about my eyesight. His team was in its first year of wearing new uniforms from a new sponsor. He let me play, in spite of my vision. In dark red, bold letters, the three lines across the back of my new shirt spelled,

COMPANIA don MARTIN
Tortillas y Tamales
(fresh daily)

I played second base until Bucky Renterría recovered from his butterfingers enough to catch a ball once in a while. He was bigger than me and able to hit the ball far on game days. I was slow, small, and stupid when it came to hitting the ball. I stood at the plate during a game, surrounded by an advancing army. The drubbing advance stopped to observe my desperation. I was a bone standing at the plate holding a feather against the cannon shot of an opposing pitcher.

It was not a fair war. Swinging aimlessly at the marauding shot, I discussed death with myself. I did not react in time to make contact. My next swing began as the ball returned to the pitcher. I was too anxious to wait for a bad pitch. To walk for me was a rare deed. I swung at each pitch. Not good timing for a lead-off hitter. In practice, I was consistent and ordinary. But, on game days, my coach would tell me to look up a word, "impotence." I thought it meant extraordinary. Coach eventually hid me in right field and placed my bat last in the line-up.

During practice, it was easy for me to face our team pitchers. Even when the coach yelled at Jan Halso—our best pitcher—not to let up on me, I could still hit his best stuff. But, I never took practice with me. On game days, standing in the batter's box, I recognized the monster on the mound as a member of the other team and suddenly that marauding army would appear. Surrounded in the field with every weapon pointed at me, I waited impatiently for the massacre to begin.

I played on the same Little League team with most of the best players in town. Mando "Sluggo" Enriquez. Anselmo "Flaco" Vázquez. And the "Vikings," Jan and Gabby Halso. Jan was our team's tall, blonde pitcher. Gabby, the "baby Viking" was huge. He played first base and batted clean-up. Sluggo batted third and hit more home runs than Gabby. In our Little League they were known as "Papa Sluggo and his baby Viking."

The Halsos were the first family I knew who spoke something other than Spanish or English. They talked Norwegian, which always sounded Puerto Rican to me. Or Cuban. I would ask them to repeat themselves and then they would repeat themselves in English. We laughed a lot then because their language always surprised me. I would begin listening to them, thinking they were talking in Spanish.

Everyone who went to Jan and Gabby's house would eventually call Mrs. Halso "Mom." No one knew why. They just did. I wanted to, but always stopped short before the word left my mouth. Mr. and Mrs. Halso owned the flower shop where my Nana Kika Soldano shopped whenever an occasion arrived. There were five Halso boys, the products of a wise florist and a tin-voiced, fat, drunkard husband. The husband was as mean as the Nazi dogs. But he had no bite. The boys were my first friends outside the border of our barrio. Jan and Gabby were twelve and ten. Erik was nine and couldn't play on our team yet, although Coach dreamed of the day when Erik would be old enough. The old-timer viejo scouts said that this nine-year-old was going to be even better than his two older brothers. I didn't spend time with Yule and Siegi because they were only five and four. The five Halso boys became my brothers.

Mr. Flower Shop Halso hated everything. The army had recently retired him. Of all the brothers, Gabby looked like his dad the most. Two Santa Clauses in one family. Not much else was known about old man Halso because no one could get a question in when he talked. When he started preaching, his lips pouted scary stories of apostles falling for evil women. The best story he ever told was of a bigshot company president falling for the brown eyes of an adulterous young teen girl. The old-time executive falls in love with a mexicana who lives in the whore house. The aged man divorces his wife of a million years to marry the young backroom beauty. Eventually, the old exec becomes too sick to satisfy his young bride and she begins sneaking out at night for encounters with strangers. Old man Halso, who emphasized the terrible life of sin in which the girl lived prior to meeting her savior, instructed us, "Once a whore, always a whore."

Mrs. Halso would interrupt, shaking her head, "You just can't be too sure. I don't believe that's true."

The man dies and leaves the young girl nothing. She returns to the old courts of enriched houses built for the satisfaction of men. She never again finds a man just as important to the rest of the team as the big guns. A team accepts everyone's weaknesses and plays together with their strengths." I listened when Ernie Banks had said to keep the pocket of my mitt trained.

I continued training my mitt. The names of the other Cubs escaped me. I couldn't remember Luis Aparicio at short stop. *No. Luis is a White Sox player. No.* When I was afraid, I tried to remember the baseball players and their teams. *Where does Ernie play? What team is he on? The mad house on the corner, bulging into light, becomes a ship in the night sailing off the coast of Chile. All things I know escape me. I am small and alone. Hidden in the darkness. Across the street, lights bathe me in a mystery of luxury. The top floors of the house glow in yellows and dim pinks and brightened windows explode on my skin. There is no punishment. I see creamy skin pausing against reflections of gentle smiles. A party for shadows.*

I heard the purchased breathing of women whose smiles and legs and arms and breasts I had seen in magazines that my older cousins keep hidden in their bedrooms.

He tells me to wait here. He is going inside to get her. I ask if he has a ball and, sure enough, he gives me one to help me train my mitt. I say I will wait quietly. He insists that I will be safe here and not to worry about the dark. Train my glove and wait while he goes to get mommy. I believe him and tell him so. He has never lied before. So, I believe. "Oh, and we have never talked together this much. I like the ball you gave me. Is it new?" *He promises to play catch when he returns.*

"O.K." I sit still and train my mitt. A big dog appears. It is huge with red, green, and brown fur. Through grey eyes, I know he is a boy dog. He stands across from me as if here to protect me. He is not a Nazi dog. I continue training my mitt. Punching leather in panic. A quiet breath. A silent watch. A beast in wild lights lighted by storm candles. The quieter I get, the madder the dog becomes. Magic flames get too hot and scary. The man who left me here comes back and holds me. "Daddy, you're back. Did you get mommy? Daddy?"

He holds me and I grab him tightly. "Hijo, wake up. Wake up, son."

His whiskers scratch against my Little League face. I do not want to let go of him. He feels brave. "Daddy, did you get mommy?"

His voice amplified. He dropped me onto the front seat of a car, "Hijo, what are you doing here? Where do you live, son?"

My fuzzy eyes tried to focus. Patent leather blue on a shiny hat glitter. Splotches of my muddy fingers on his thick, dark neck. I realized that these fine, large, shoulders were not my daddy's and that we had met during unknown moments of my sleep. He stopped when he saw my slumped frame on the bus stop bench. He wondered if I was wounded or dead. I laughed and said, "My coach thinks I am dead at the plate." Our time together was less than an hour. We laughed together like old sluggers, remembering all the bad pitches we'd swung at.

I have forgotten his name, but I remember that he was a gift. I remember, too, all the presents my father promised and never sent. That stranger in shiny shoes with a rough face and a fat, round belly above skinny legs anchored in me the belief that crossing the river was my right. I remember more of him than I do of my father.

IV

The Bird Cage Was Not Perfect

My abuela said, "This house is so big and yellow that all the canaries in the world think they were born here." Abuela would laugh and toss the niños outside when she had had enough of our chirping. "I spend the majority of my life at the mercado." When the first floor of the grand old canary cage got too boisterous with puny little kids, she would send us out. "I only get to be home for such a short time. You niños need to stay out of here so I can get some rest. Maybe I should just take my bed and sofa to the mercado and live there. How would you like that?"

My prima Red, my best cousin, would always respond, "Bueno, Nana, but leave us the tele."

Granny would laugh with Red and then tell us, "Now, go get some fresh air. You know how far to go. And I don't want any trouble from anybody. Buzzy, you too, go outside. Why do you never want to be outside? At the mercado when I have something for you to do you are always outside. What is that you tell me after I find you? When I tell you to go back to work. 'Nana. I was just outside thinking.' Well, hijo go outside now and do some more of that thinking."

The house was a very simple pale yellow with white trim. It was tremendous. There were five levels. Even though it was really a three-story house, cousin Red and I counted the attic and Tío Martín's basement "bachelor pad" as two separate levels. Red snuck into his basement more than I did. I was still playing Little League baseball when she first moved into abuelita's house. Red and I were in the attic when she first told me about a fake lock on one of the back windows of the basement. Red said she had learned all about writing from tío. And that he let her sneak into his basement. He told Red that if she saw him come home alone and if she felt like visiting him late at night, that she could sneak in through the rear window to visit him. For a long time in her young life, she felt like going there a lot. "I got tired of him always being busy with some new vieja de Juarez. Tío needs to stay on this side for a while. But Buzzy, he has so many books in there. Everything you would ever want to read. It's better than the library because if you sneak in when tío is at work, nobody will ever bother you. There is no phone down there and he keeps the front door locked like it is Fort Knox."

La Red and I were the only ones in the family who ever went up to the attic. It was the most enchanting room for me. Red said it was the most peaceful room for her. The other cousins didn't like to climb up the ladder that led to the entryway. More often than not there would be pigeons on the roof in front of the window. Whenever I climbed up there, either alone or with Red, the birds just seemed to be waiting for people to tell them to leave. They would hustle off the roof with a pissed-off coo, but they respected us enough to stay away until we had climbed back downstairs. The dirty birds, la Red, and I shared a rare space in that attic. It was one of those doors that so many on this planet search for. It was an unlocked entryway toward heaven.

The attic was warm and the screens on the windows were torn. There were only two large pillows in the attic. Cushions for the lethargy . . . a silent cloud on top of the roof. Above the street, above the spectacular laughter of Don Martín, abuelita, Tío Martín. Above the flame that left me alone, above the desire that drove Red into madness, raging at all men, all women, all things on earth that destroyed love, above the schoolchild first being sent away from school for not knowing how to read in English, above the joy of first kissing Yolanda, first sleeping between the earth of a sleeping woman, above the empty day when my mother left me, above the empty day when my father left me, above the empty day when my sisters were taken from me, queerly staying in the attic, too sick and stupid to come downstairs and say goodbye, too mad that they were going with her and I was being left behind, too little and too belligerent to know that we would never again see each other.

Tío Martín's room was the entire basement. When he decided to come back and live there, he blocked off the inside entrance to the basement. This left only one entrance, which was down the outside stairway. It led to his front door. Cousin Red, our wildest cousin, the writer, the carpenter who smoked mota, took me to the back of the house. The 3:33 Southern Pacific rumbled behind us. She said we would have to wait until it passed by. "You can't break in when the passenger trains pass by. Tío said he knows all the SP conductors and they watch his place. If they see someone trying to get in through this window, they'll pull the emergency brakes and stop the train." She showed me the fake lock on the tiny window. I had always noticed the locks on all three of the back windows and just kept away.

"Red, the only times I've been in his room, there are always two or three other cousins yelling at uncle to tell us more stories. I have wanted to sneak back into his room and be alone there for a long time. I feel like there is something in that room I need to find."

"Buzzy, when you grow out of your sissy-looking cuerpo de mujer, your new body probably won't be able to squeeze through this window. So watch how I turn this lock and remember exactly how to put it back on." My regular visits to uncle's basement began as I crawled through the window with the phony lock.

Red continued to explain, "One time, I was down here late in the day when I should've been in school and tío was out somewhere. I read his books and drunk some of his vino. Then I stole a bunch of his mota. I smoked too much and got really high and when I went back out the window, I forgot which direction he told me to have that little arrow pointing."

"What arrow?"

"Look at this lock. See that tiny little arrow? He scratched it in with something so that it always points down when it's locked. Sometimes he comes home and looks at his back windows before going downstairs. If the arrow isn't pointing down, he knows somebody is up to something. That is how he knew I stole his mota."

I still didn't understand how uncle knew it was La Red who stole his mota. "Well yeah, Red, big deal, how could he prove you from a burglar?"

Red told me that Uncle Martín made her promise him she would never steal any of his things or he would create a new secret lock and he would not tell her about it. She promised. He said if she didn't keep her promise, he would spank her, too. Red laughed the most curious laugh I had ever heard from her. It was full of something different. Somewhere, there was a secret within her that she was just finding. Many years later, the recollection of that single laugh would touch me in soft places when I had bad dreams. Red had laughed a laugh I would always want to know more about. We stared at each other as if we knew why. Then we climbed downstairs and ran into the shouts of other cousins who were looking for us to come outside and play with them.

Whenever Rosemary wore her carpenter's overalls she insisted on being called "Red." I stuck to calling her La Red all the time. We were walking across the street to buy some ice cream and I continued to ask her about sneaking down into the basement. She got nervous and told me, "Buzzy, quieto. Let's not talk about me and uncle anymore. Tío installed the phony lock because he needs a safety latch in case he loses his keys or something. He told me not to tell anybody. Nobody. After he caught me, I knew that I always had to pay attention to the arrow. I knew that if uncle came home with some vieja, I still had enough time to jump out of the basement and attach the fake lock because their voices would be so loud and full of wanting to get inside, it would take him forever to unlock that ugly front door. Sometimes, when he comes home alone, I wait for him to unlock his door. Then I surprise him. It is okay with him as long as Nana Kika doesn't know I'm staying up so late."

The yellow canary cage in a desert city so full of hungry birds. Cousin Red was the hungriest bird I knew.

V

A Carpenter and a Writer

Bertha Espinoza, Red's mother, had one daughter and one son. The oldest, her son Jimmy, moved to San Francisco at age nineteen. Everybody knew he liked to be with other guys. Her daughter, Rosemary, "La Red," said she was going to be two things in life: a carpenter and a writer. She wanted to sell best-selling stories to the magazines and she wanted to be a woman who could build things. She was also the brightest and prettiest red-haired, green-eyed girl to ever live in West Tejas. When Jimmy lived at home, he was La Red's fashion coordinator.

The marriage of Bertha and Arturo had been good for many years. Then, as suddenly as a bicycle thief on a kid's birthday, Arturo Espinoza, my dad's cousin from abuelito's brother, decided to leave El Paso. He left the desert with a twenty-one-year-old blondie from the west side of town. Arturo and Bertha had lived in a matrimony that the Catholic Church would have sanctified. Arturo was an engineer for the Southern Pacific. La Red's mother had worked at Texas Western College for ten years. Bertha was head secretary for the president of the college. If you wanted to know anything about the president, much less talk to him, you had to go through Bertha first.

They lived in a small brick house with a small lawn and two large trees. Because Arturo was on the rails so much, he never did anything around the house. Many functions at the college needed Bertha's time and effort. Little Red and little Jimmy saw more of the maids at home than they did their parents. It was fine. La Red was trapped in a cloud that did not allow her to see anything except the small footsteps to school, the jumping and skipping, the screaming on the playground, running and chasing other kids, silently sleeping through boring classes with boring teachers, walking home on the shade side of the street when the sun was too fuerte, and watching little Jimmy put on Bertha's clothes as they pretend to be sisters. La Red insisting she can build things and Jimmy claiming he can see things, and both of them laughing, laughing, and not once thinking that it could end.

When Red realized her life would never be the same, I was spending Saturday night with Rosemary and Jimmy. The phone rang right after midnight. Bertha held the phone to her breast for a long time after she finished her conversation. We had not gone to sleep and we watched her hang up. It looked like she was going to vomit and then she started to take deep, hard breaths. After a million deep sighs, Bertha softly reported that their dad was not coming home.

"Did the train break again, mommy?" Jimmy always worried that the trains would break.

Bertha wanted to say yes, but she didn't.

Rosemary paid attention to something that seemed to be wrapping sheets of wire around her mom. "¿Qué, mom? What is wrong?"

Bertha stood up and walked into the kitchen. She ran to the kitchen door and opened it. "¡Cabrón! ¡Hijo de puta! And he always promised me that he would put up a screen door so we could have a breeze through this house. Ten years we've lived in this house and the only door without a screen is this one. Maybe he'll bring her over and she can help him hang it. I'd like to hang the both of them." Bertha slammed the door so hard that we came running into the room.

Red put her arms around her mother and promised to learn carpentry so that someday she could make her mommy a screen door. Bertha wailed in a tone that none of us had heard since the death of our dear cousin Gloria.

Jimmy asked if he could see where his daddy is on the map and Bertha fell to the floor. He asked, "Mom, is dad dead?"

It took a few moments for Bertha to answer. She told her son that his father should be dead. "No one deserves to be treated the way he treated me."

Two weeks after the divorce was granted, Arturo moved to Tucson with the blondie. Jimmy left for San Francisco. Bertha put the house up for rent and dropped La Red off at Nana Kika's. Bertha told abuelita that she needed some time to find herself. It took her four years to return to El Paso.

By the time Bertha moved back into her old house, Red and I were constantly together. We would go visit Bertha frequently so that we could spend the night away from the endless traffic of family at Nana Kika's. Red was uncertain about moving back in with her mom full time.

Red framed the screen door. She was planning to hang it before morning to surprise her mommy, but the hinges were too big for the door. "Mom. Remember that day when you were so scared and you screamed in the kitchen that your Arturo had never put up a screen door in this room? Remember how I told you that I would learn how to do it and that someday, I would hang it? Mommy, today is your day."

"Sí, Rosie, pero mi'ja can you try not to be so mean?"

"Don't blame me. Blame it on that stupid husband of yours who drives trains." La Red picked up the too-large hinges and left the house. She drove an old Chevy flatbed with a broken fence that Tío Martín gave her because she was such a good apprentice. As she turned the truck onto the highway, Red fired up a joint. She knew there's nothing finer than wearing her carpenter's overalls and working on a project. The road was slow, so she thought about the hinges. There was no time to gather desire in her heart because she was working. And working, for her, always kept the boys away. She was fine with that, too, because being a carpenter, she knew how to use her hands.

Red looked at her just hammered thumb and yelled to God about his mother. She also called her a whore. "Puta, madre de dios." La Red is lefthanded, so her brown right thumb was bleeding and swelling.

"¡Rosie, no diga eso!" Rosemary's mom is the only one who was ever allowed to call this seventeen-year-old carpenter anything other than Rosemary.

"Fuck!"

"¡Rosie!"

"Fuck!"

"Mi'ja, go buy a dress or something and give up on that stupid door. Mauro said he would put it up next week. He has the right tools, too."

Red always called me her "primo Buzzy-ayúdame con esto-Fixit." Never Digit. When she was really high on mota, she peacefully revealed to me that she would marry me if I wasn't such a sissy... and then she laughed, remembering the time I struck out with the bases loaded and two outs in the bottom of the seventh inning when the panadero's team was trying to get past that fucking Lubbock team. "Of course I struck out, I didn't have my glasses on."

"O, Buzzy, everybody knows you're a sissy at the plate on game days. Yo quíero saber why you are. And just when it's time to win."

Red scratched herself in front of me and I felt like her sister. We settled into each other's eyes and streaked into the open desert with our blood hot and our lips soft and our legs heavy with the weight we carry. Our feet were toughened by splinters from thousands of thorns, thorns that gave themselves to protect the rose. For the soft belligerence of beauty, la little Red and I embraced in envelopes that would one day be mailed across an island . . . the island of dreams, dreams of peace, dreams of little girls first touching their softness, dreams of little fine dreamers surviving the first leathery mad howl of a mother cornered by a man. The first violent howl of a little girl being grabbed by a man with diesel, oil, beer, smoke everywhere on his body, with the small girl and her small fingers having to touch his horrible thing, with the smile from the satisfied, not knowing that the lost one is not the child. Then, with the smile of survivors, La Red and I danced in the blue sad light of her bedroom . . . a room filled with soft flowers and soft eyes of the toughest girl in the barrio.

VI

Lottery Winners

By the time I was about to get drafted into the Army, Red and Wanna became lovers. I looked at my watch before opening the door to a tornado of two women in love. I had just estimated there were four days, four hours, and four minutes left to my life as a civilian. I told Rosemary and Wanna. "Four, four, four."

I think they both answered at the same time. "Qué chingaos es eso¿ Four, four, four. What the fuck¿"

Red and Aunt Wanna stopped moving furniture. Both of them fell down onto the couch. Red started right away about her blond Aunt Wanna. Her aunt was wearing a dark green mini-skirt and a white top that revealed the destination of her nipples. Her wavy hair was pointing all across Tejas. Silently, as Red rambled, Wanna spread her legs apart.

"Buzzy, I don't know what your numbers mean right now, but do you know what my twatty tía just told me¿ She told me to stop using her. Buzzy, help me. Jee, fuck." Rosemary's spaghetti-strap, black dress was torn. Her top lip was swollen. Her left hand was scratched and the blood had dried across her knuckles. Aunt Wanna had harsh, bloodied fingers. Red and her first woman lover had just finished a lover's quarrel.

"I was counting the time I have left before I go into the army. I know you don't like to hear that I am really going. You think you guys will still be together when I get out? All you do these days is fight." The day was filled with numbers. I counted how many men I had been with. How many women. I had been with more men than girls. Girls always wanted to be my friend. Men wanted me cause I didn't care.

Red was in the process of moving in with Wanna but most of her furniture had been sitting on the outside porch for two days. Red wanted to move it inside but Aunt Wanna wanted her to wait until the Salvation Army came to haul away some of the old furniture from inside the house. When the slugging stopped, La Red had reached for the phone and pleaded with me to come over.

I didn't run to their house because that day I walked with a lonely shadow. When I was lonely I started to count numbers. All my other cousins had mothers and fathers somewhere within reach. I started counting how many girl cousins I had. It was too confusing. How should I count Red? Some of my cousins had brothers and sisters from a new mom or dad who lived in the same house. Or at least the same city, if they had to spend time at Nana Kika's in order to get away from family problems. How many postcards would they get if a parent went out of town? My father sent me many postcards, but none with a return address. In all the years since my mother left, I could count three letters from her. The last one being the most cruel.

I was twelve and playing my last year of Little League. My mother, Isabella, wrote that she and her husband and my sisters would all be there that summer. She did not know exactly when, but she promised. It was the first time I believed one of her promises. That summer, every night, I would stay in the front yard, refusing to go anywhere because I wanted to be outside when they arrived. I wanted her and my sisters to see me first. The summer ended without them. They never came.

Wanna's husband, Arturo's brother, had been dead all of our lives. Red was nine years old when she began to spend most of her time at beautiful Auntie Waawaa's house. Tía would encourage la baby Red to show off, "because it is the fastest way to make a man feel like loving you." She told her.

Wanna wore evening dresses that made the wetness inside her a widely available gift. She had a need to get tied into herself. A desire to attack dignity with a loud howling in the accent of a girl from another country. Young and old soldiers. She called them all "boys." They attacked her language with songs from their hometowns. With their religions. They said their homes were better places than this desert. As they invaded her, she listened to their stories. Still, their special courtyards walled out the pressure of loving. They were just passing through, on their prescribed passage with her for a fun fuck which made them men upon their return home.

Wanna's men behaved like they had been tossed from the arms of mothers whose milk had dried too quickly after they were born. Too many of them told the same story and were so alike that Wanna could no longer distinguish men from boys or tiny from big. Wanna got to know them all as she piously wandered across the military base called Fort Bliss. She had been there long before I was drafted.

One time Red got mad at me and tossed her dirty panties in my face. Wanna and Red had just begun their affair and I was mad because I was feeling left out of La Red's life. I let the panties sit on my face. Then, I chewed and sucked on the crotch. I tasted her blood. We laughed and she helped me finish my make-up. We were like that together. We came with each other many times. It was something to do while we searched for our mates. We promised each other that no one would ever know about us. I was a boy stepping into his sister's dress and we kept our secret in wisdom like the silence of gods. She liked me inside of her and she giggled when I told her to squeeze as many fingers as she could push into me. She said that if I had a cunt, I would be a big whore. And that she would make me into a big, rich, sophisticated one. We did everything together. We licked each other. I took her from behind. She took me from behind. I watched her do things on the toilet. She held me when I peed. I changed her pads when she bled. And we once watched ourselves together in the mirror. She got tired of pleasing me and I got tired of pleasing her, but we stayed together because we were in love.

"Buzzy, when does the mailman come?"

"Whenever he wants to put something in your slot, slut."

We were that way together.

"Buzzy Digit, you stroke my hair like you love me." Red and I were sitting in the attic on New Year's Eve. She was eighteen. A foamy flame thower. A girl that wanted me. A genuis of a girl because I wanted her and she knew that. Always knew that. It would be our last New Year's Eve together. I was going to war. A great gathering was already underway downstairs in Nana Kika's big yellow bird cage. The greatest parade of our time would wind its way in front of our home on Montana Street. Our canary cage was the last house on the right before the procession crossed the railroad tracks. I continued stroking La Red's hair and she started to laugh. "Remember how funny it was last year when the train stopped the parade? You know, the Southern Pacific has never crossed those tracks during the parade."

I stopped touching her and opened the attic window so that we could climb onto the roof. I whispered, "I remember how crazy the crowd got. Those vatos across the street started throwing all their stolen beers at the engine when it stopped in the middle of the street. The band from Bowie High was stuck there and they kept playing their fight song and ducking the splashing beer from the tossed broken bottles. Remember all our uncles going crazy and singing along with their old high school band while they were fighting with the train?"

La Red wrapped her soft hands on her breast and asked me how I knew that the beer had been stolen. "Red, half those guys across the street I knew. Do you remember that guy with the long hair and black hat? Last year, you couldn't miss him . . . he was the only one of the guys who dressed that way."

"Buzzy, you mean that guy that the cops took first? He was wearing Tony Lama's and those tight blue Levi's and his hair was almost down to his neck and his white shirt was unbuttoned and his belly was really pretty and his nipples were gorgeous and brown?"

Red Rosemary and I sat on the roof watching the night prepare itself for the next day. I asked her with a tortured voice, "How did you know his nipples were brown?"

"Well, Buzzy baby, I wanted to suck them."

"So did I Red."

"Buzzy, you're such a queer. If only I could get you to start acting like your cousin Jimmy, then we can keep you out of that fucking army."

Rosemary was with me when I reported for my physical after the papers arrived ordering me into the army at the whim of our Tío Sam. She did not stop talking. She yelled at the room full of sergeants that I was "as joto as the night is dark." Embarrassed by my guardian angel cousin, I sat on an iron bench with my legs crossed and my mind in a race to the everywhere of desire.

"Red, shut up."

"Fuck you, Buzzy. They are not taking you."

"Yeah, but don't be telling everybody about me."

"You *are* a sissy. They can't take you. I won't let them. What are you going to do when it comes to fighting? You don't even know how to use your knuckles. The other day when that stupid punk was trying to rape me, what did you do? Nothing. I hit the fucker on his huevos and kicked his ass out of the house. You, in the meantime, just pranced about like you needed to get fucked in the butt. You are a sissy. You fucking queer. I love you and nobody is taking you away from me."

The examining room was full of men. No one heard our conversation. The military clerks no longer listened to excuses from the draftees.

"Dysiaaiadidcheck . . . whatever the hell your name is, come to the counter."

Rosemary screamed at the men, "You cocksuckers! You can't have this fucking queer."

Sergeants exchanged cigarettes and notes on the "evaders." Not once did they respond to my sweet angel Rosemary. They ignored everything she said. They had heard worse. Yesterday, a mother had walked in with her son and broke a bottle of pulque across his head.

The stitches only delayed his draft by a few hours. The Tejas border was especially kind to volunteers who were needed to fight in southeast Asia. Rosemary was protesting to a room full of machines.

VII

Some of Us Are Missing

My two sisters were either a memory or a dream. Olivia was a tangerine. She looked like Elizabeth Taylor in *National Velvet.* She was a sweet mix of good things. Olivia is the oldest child. She always held my hand as we entered the school, which was run like a prison by the nuns of Asilomar. Old, rough women dressed in the blackness of Halloween. Asilomar is not by the sea. It is an abandoned monastery on the east side of El Paso near a chicken farm and two factories. A man-made lake nearby gives the workers from the factories priority boating privileges. My uncles used to laugh at this because the lake was so full of weeds that even if you owned a motor boat, it would get stuck and tangled in wet catfish weeds. And if you caught a fish, no one would eat it because of the smell. Not the fish smell. The smell of a sweating gavacho.

Leticia was the tough one. She was my defender once we entered the gates of this children's hell. She was like a sturdy plough horse. Leticia chewed bubble gum and spit all day long. Nana Kika always said that I remembered Olivia and Leticia more through my dreams than she could through her memory. I asked abuelita if she remembered Tío Martín coming to pick up all the kids in his truck during an emergency when the stupid Asilomar got closed down by some court order. Abuelita scratched her head. She remembered Uncle Martín taking us there every morning, but she said Asilomar was never shut down. I tell her my dreams wish it had been.

The water in the center fountain was brown and smelled like a raw sewer. The older kids threatened to throw me in unless I gave them my lunch. This happened daily. And daily, Leticia came running from her circle of toughs, chasing the thieves away and threatening to slice off their hanging huevos.

My sisters never hit me. They liked me and I liked them. Leticia said I was too skinny to be a boy and that I would probably be a sissy. Olivia told her to shut up. Olivia was a very proper lady. She already wore lipstick, stood straight, and wore ironed dresses.

The dreams stopped at Asilomar. The road to Asilomar was always gray. Even when the sun was shining on El Paso and on top of Nana Kika's house and all over the West Tejas tierra of old rocks and old drinkers and old runaway dreamers, the road to our nursery was always gray. Grandchildren between the ages of five and ten were convinced they had been sentenced to this chamber pot of nuns. We were certain the sisters who controlled this place were secret fugitives from a hardass back country controlled by Hitler. The nuns had given in to the other side. They did not know my god.

Uncle Martín blew the horn from delivery truck No. 1 of the Panadería Don Martín while he yelled to me and all my cousins that "the last one in would not get to lick frosting from the early leftovers." I didn't know about him. No one was ever the last one in. Usually, eight or ten of us were in the back of the bread van bouncing, giggling, spitting, farting, screaming, pulling something of someone else's, and generally making the morning as loud as possible. This, after having just barely opened our eyes, crying that we were too dead to move. Most mornings, once we stopped bouncing and wiggling, Tío Martín would tell us a story of his adventures of the previous night.

"A baker's day begins at midnight." A baker, like our Tío Martín, began his day during the hours before midnight. Depending on how far apart his current women lived, he could be out on the street as early as six in the evening. Abuelo left behind a legacy for his sons that said, "Bread must always be fresh and work must begin at exactly noon with an upside down moon." Tío Martín, despite his wild ways and beyond his rum, was always on time at the bakery. He was the jefe now that his dad was gone. But he had not learned as much about the ways of women as he had about what happens to the seeds that are planted in women. Muchos sobrinos y sobrinas. Lots of lost children.

In the early sparkle of the supernatural morning on our way to an eerie border town hell, our hungover uncle filled the van with the loudest, stinkiest fart and then told us his story. It was always about a woman for whom he had done everything. Even gave her a job at the panadería.

"You try to be her friend but she doesn't want a friend. She says she already has too many friends. She wants more than just a friendly night out. She wants to see baby tears on her breasts . . . I tell her I can cry but she says I be already too old and feo . . . but I tell her I'm old, and not too ugly—to pretend baby stuff." By then, the van became a rolling steel laugh box.

Leticia grasped her breasts and asks, "How big are her chi chi's?"

Uncle Martín suddenly got proper, responding priest-like. "Ay, mi'ja, what kinda question is that?"

I asked him about the color of her eyes and he told me that there is much more to a woman than the color of her eyes. I said I don't think so and he told me that my mother's eyes were the prettiest eyes he has ever seen. So many times he wished that my dad had . . . then tío trailed off into an adult silence.

Isabella, my mother, held me against her breast. She was saying goodbye. "Adios, mi'jo." I changed my smile to match hers. We were mirrors. I was on top of her. She kept her left hand in my hair. Isabella's right hand was on my buttocks. My face breathing on her breast. "My baby, I have to become his sister."

"Isabella, I will be your brother if you take me with."

"He only wants girls, mi'jo. I can pass as his oldest daughter and Olivia and Leticia can pass as my baby sisters."

"Mommy." I cried and she let me suckle her breast again. I was six years old on my way to being left behind at Nana Kika'a house. It was my birthday. Isabella gave me a blue Timex watch. She put her fingers around her nipple and continued to stroke my hair. I did not want to stop crying.

"Baby. Mi'jo. Honey. Listen to me baby, I will come back to get you. Just let me be his girl for a little while and then I know he will let you come with us. He is a good man."

I don't remember when I stopped crying.

"So much memory will destroy us . . . join me in my prayers. Join me in my prayers. I am the last woman who will ever love you. I am drowning but you cannot do anything about it. Remember Gloria? I drown like her. Take my hand mi'jo, and hold me against your heart. I am the last woman who will ever love you this way. It is cold right now. It is so cold. Sit on my lap. I know you think you're too big, but, angel mi'jo, you will never be too big to sit between my legs. I changed your diapers. I was so young. I am still so young. He wants me to be his sister. The girls will be my sisters, but I can't make you my brother. I can't make you anything . . . you are my baby boy. I will dream of you.

Sand on your fingers. The opposite eyes of mine. The tender small laughter. Boy of mine. I don't know how to ask you to forgive me. I can only say goodbye. I can only say . . . ."

I don't remember when I stopped crying.

VIII

Bienvenidos to the South

The preparations for the party started when Ricky Roy and Tío Martín got into a huge tearful discussion about Gina, pobrecita, and her need to feel accepted by todos en la familia. Poor Gina. She did not feel welcome. Our big Biloxi blonde wanted Nana Kika to make her feel like she belonged. It was a Wednesday morning. My oldest boy cousin and my oldest uncle were drinking beer, sitting in abuelita's kitchen. On the days when I knew the divorced Mrs. Triana was home, I would peek into her bathroom window from six-thirty to seven.

My oldest boy cousin, the twenty-five-year-old Ricky Roy Inclava, offered his house as a place "to fly away from the canary cage whenever you want to." It was at the end of my young baseball career. We were driving back from Odessa after having lost in the regional. "Look, you need to come over to our house more often. And when you want to, if there is work to do, Gina will tell you what to do. You can make some extra money."

The water in Nana Kika's bottle contained truth. Ricky Roy despised my attitude. My laughter bothered him. I was twelve years old and drunk for the first time. He was not laughing as he picked me up from the garage floor and promised me that I am going straight toward el diablo. Then I puked on his shiny, police-trainee shoes.

My big-shot cousin was a high school cheerleader's dream. But to me, he was a mutt. After my first encounter with the gavacho dog, I yelled at Ricky Roy, "Doggie boy Roy is the same as Leroy." The only Leroy we knew was the Nazi, Leroy Harvay. Ricky chased me, threatening to remove the most important of my young organs. Nana Kika saved me by yelling at him to leave me alone as I continued running and laughing that refrain, "Doggie boy Roy is the same as Leroy."

Ricky Roy returned from the Air Force after having survived the Nam by being stationed for four years at Keesler Air Force Base in Biloxi, Mississippi. But he did not survive the demands of a trio from the South. He married a big, loud, pink woman from Biloxi who already had two daughters. Gina Halinger said she was twenty-nine and continued to say this for several years after I first met her. I figured she must have been saying it for a few years before she arrived in El Paso.

Gina was a big opposition of a girl. She had pretty blue-green eyes like a mountain lake before winter. Yet she looked like a bully. The erotic pain of giving had absorbed her. Gina was the leather sting of a strap against the inside of a thigh. She wore brassy earrings and giant bright rings on her fingers. Her southern breasts were a tremendous escape from the oppression of segregation. She wore lips in colors sworn to secret, futile kisses. She had the look of forever as if she had just been saved from a bottomless pit of gloom. Her painted toes had curled over the fresh cut roses of many a dreamy lover. Gina's shoes never had less than four inches of heel.

I am inside their house for another of my frequent intrusions. No one is home. The two girls, Charmaine and Heather, are in school and Gina is at a baking class. I walk into her closet and begin an aroma test of her soiled undies. I start with a skin test of her married materials on my crotch when the bedroom door explodes open and my stupid cousin and his big, horny wife enter. I hide, in fear of my life, in the darkest corner of the closet surrounded by four-inch heels for more than forty-seven minutes. I tell myself that if I survive this burglary, I will keep it secret and take it with me to my grave.

The sweat of their exhausted bodies finally gave way to a joint shower. Once they were both under the gushing water, I bolted, clutching an imprinted pair of my favorite panties. Those that have been worn being filled with a man's orgasms.

My dead cousin Gloria's brother, Ricky Roy, married this woman with the Southern white English accent from Biloxi. Their wedding was held in the rain on the Gulf a week before they came back to Texas. In all his letters he had promised to bring back sweets. I figured it was going to be something better than leche quemada. I did not like her for anything except the leaked-on smell of her panties and the feel of her high heels. She was an interference in my lifetime of mourning for our familia's loss of the seizure-prone Gloria. No one could possibly expect to triumph in a deeper tragedy than mine.

The first story Gina told me was one of how she found her brother dead in a side creek of the Mississippi. His body had oozed in the water for several days. She said it looked like bread that had soaked in milk too long. "If you aren't careful when lifting the body out, it will fall apart." His rescuers wrapped canvas and sheets of plastic around her brother's body before removing it from the muddy stream. He was only twelve years old when someone did things inside his butt, then shot him and tossed his thin body into the river.

Gina's oldest daughter, Charmaine, was turning fifteen and was very much on my right-handed thoughts. Charmaine wanted to be proper. She considered us relatives, so she would not kiss me. She would kiss my buddies, but she would not kiss me because I was her "family." I tried to explain that we were family on paper only, but this did not convince her to kiss me. Even after I rescued her from countless cheap wine highs on the hillsides of our brown, desolate, suicidal desert town, she refused to kiss me and begged me to stay the way I was. I thought stealing panties from her mama's closet was a terrible way to stay, but since she insisted so kindly, I decided hers would be next.

Their house was the landing site of imported women. The other import, young ten-year-old Heather, immediately labeled me a pagan. When she arrived in El

Paso, she believed in stuff like the Resurrection and a responsibility to the meek through guidance toward salvation. She also feared that savages like me and my friends might someday rule the world. This poor, pink, prepubescent Biloxi brat with no straight teeth and wild grass for hair and big ears and wrinkled, freckled hands and big areolas on tiny tits, became a major pusher of brown Mexican heroin in West Tejas. If she had anything, she had drive.

A few years later, when I was stationed at Fort Bliss, before being shipped overseas, Heather was my best source for dope.

At seven-thirty in the morning, I finished my paper route and ran to la tolstoyería to watch the girls. A little house run by red skinny people dressed in the clothes worn by slaves in those bible movies. Nana Kika insisted it was a whorehouse but I kept telling her that those people were believers in loving for free. "Niño, qué es love free?" I never had an answer for her. But I told her that if she wanted to come with me to their house they would explain everything to her, too.

"Nana, they call themselves beatniks and they talk about how children do not belong to their parents, wives do not belong to their husbands, congregations do not belong to their preachers, workers do not belong to the owners." The guys who did all the talking looked like gladiators and had beautiful, big, thick-lipped women hanging around them. All these fine girls looked like they wanted to be somebody's mother. I always dreamed that two or three of them were mine and that I was their shared son.

Nana Kika called it "la tolstoyería" because she never knew who owned the house and who owned the souls. "That ruso, Tolstoy, tried to do the same thing in Mejico . . . cabrón, hijo de puta. . . ." She cautioned me that hanging around this place could give me the most confusing dreams of my young life. "They talk about war as if they know about it, mi'jo. Mi'jo, yo te quiero. I cannot begin to tell you about the razor's edge on us. We survive a thousand wars every day of our life." Señora Kika Soldano ignored my vague response and continued, "No one in there has lost a son to war. I lost *two!* I have more sons. I have more daughters. I have more life. But I *do not have* my two sons! I *do not have* my two sons. I *do not have* my two sons." The only time abuelita ever cried was when she talked of the war and of her lost boys.

I would finish my paper route at the beatnik house. The "wild Tolstoys" were never asleep at five in morning. I could always count on somebody to be laughing. And the girls in that house were so naked. Not that they had their clothes off—it was a part of belonging to the tolstoyería that made the women look naked. I would hand deliver the morning newspaper to that house because someone would be waiting on the porch for my arrival and they would invite me inside. The house had the same smell of Uncle Martín's parked car at a party . . . weeds burning. I would get a daily lecture from a guy or from one of those tremendous women, and I would walk away laughing at how they delivered their speeches to me. It was as if they were trying to save me from something. "Little brother, love should always be free. And the best mota coming into this country right now is from your raza's old country."

Then I went to Mrs. Triana's house to make my appearance outside her bathroom window. She had two morning routines. If her boyfriend's car was in the driveway, she ran through her bathroom functions as if all of time was coming to an end. Then the boyfriend would stumble in, spoiling my fantasy. Ugly man. When there was no car in the driveway and she was alone, I could count on her being lazy, slow, and lovely while sitting on her toilet. She would wipe her crotch, then move her flushed naked buttocks into the middle of my dreams. Watching her study the image of herself in the mirror I thought it was what an angel would do, if it could see its own face. Each morning after I watched her, I floated home with her inside of me.

Uncle Martín watched me walk in the door. He laughed, "Buzzy, you weren't peeking inside anybody's windows were you?"

"No, tío. Not just anyone. Only the redhead."

"Oye, hijo, is she really red down there?"

"I don't know, uncle. You'll have to look for yourself."

Ricky interrupted our fun with his long sad face and ordered me to go to bed. Then he continued talking with Uncle Martín. Ricky Roy and tío had been out all night because Ricky had had a big fight with his wife, left his house, and went to the bakery just as the bread was being baked. The two of them then went to Juarez in Uncle Martín's MG.

Ricky thought that I had gone to bed, but I stood in the hallway. His voice was slow with the dust from a hard night. "Listen, uncle, I feel so sad for her. Gina says Nana Kika won't talk to her whenever they are alone together. Gina knows abuelita understands English, so why won't Nana Kika talk to her en inglés?" Ricky swallowed his beer.

"Mi'jo, your abuelita loves everyone in her familia. Even new additions. Remember that vieja? Christina. You know, the widow you kids used to call, 'wicked witch of the southwest.' Bueno, pues, Cristina and I were going to get married. I was crazy for this woman, who no one else liked. My jefita, your granny, never interfered. She guided me out of that pendejada, out of being such a fool, with one of her crooked threats. And you know how she did it?"

Ricky was crying. "Did what?"

"Do you know how she got me to leave that woman? No? Bueno. Well, Nana Kika caught me with Don Martín's favorite niece, Angelita. She was the first one in his family to go to college. In fact, that old panadero was paying for her school. Don Martín swore her to secrecy because he was afraid someone else in his familia might make it into college and he would have to pay for them, too. But Angelita told me everything. It is a funny thing with virgins. The most crazy thing about them is that they will never tell you about their past. No matter how much they fall in love with you. All you hear about is their secret future. A man can never know how virginal a virgin is. But he knows how good she will be with other men. A virgin was never meant to stay with the first man. Little Angelita was the first one to tell me about her bald round uncle and mi madre getting together. Angelita even knew where they did it. Still, the fat fucker gets my respect. So when your Nana Kika walked in on me and the baker's no-longer-virgin niece, she stood still and straight and said, 'When the day comes that you decide to settle with just one woman, that will be the day I start talking in English.'"

Ricky Roy sounded like he was entering a seminary. "But, uncle, you have been married so many times, I lost count. What? Is it two or three?"

"Hijo, it doesn't matter how many times I've been married. I have never stopped believing in love. I just don't know who to stay in love with."

Nana Kika saw me in the hallway and quietly glided delicate, cold, skinny fingers across the back of my neck. I jumped and screamed like I was trying to leap across the copper canyon. Uncle Martín and Ricky Roy laughed so hard that Nana Kika told them to stop or they would wake every dead dog within a hundred miles. She ordered me to bed. Her laughter came from the belly of a giant.

Uncle talked to his mother like she was a business

partner. "So mama, diga me, qué mujer en esta familia tiene ansia por la felicidad¿ What makes a woman happy¿"

"Hijo, with the things my girls have to look forward to in their lives with men, how can any of our women be too anxious for married happiness¿"

Tío Martín was not too smart this morning.

Nana Kika walked up to him, pulled his ear, and told him to go to bed before she herself showed him exactly what it was that made women happy.

My uncle would not stop arguing with someone he would never win an argument with. "Mama, the women I know just want to get it."

"Quieto, niñoso, they only want to pull your huevos. Hard and mean. And you, being the son of my first old panadero, every floja around here wants to be your girl so she can see some of Don Pablo's money. And pues, tu, digame, how can I be happy when I am widowed from the biggest baker in town and now soltera, but very friendly with the biggest tortillero in town¿ Nothing but the kitchen for me.

Her son, the first Martín in her life, asked, "Y, qué pues con eso¿ I don't care if somebody wants me for my money if all I want them for is their body."

"Hijo, ya basta. Duérmate." Nana Kika ordered her oldest son to bed.

Watching Nana Kika in the kitchen in the morning was like watching the sun spill heat onto cold, small flowers. Suddenly the room was warm and coffee was being poured. Huevos con chorizo, carne asada from last night, tortillas, and frijoles refritos were served by a woman listening to two men crying about the impossibilities of women.

Tío Martín got up from the table the same way I did when the house was crowded con familia and granny ordered all the pinguinos, us little piggies, to get out of the way of the adults. Uncle moved like a man accused of murder, head to the ground, shoulders rounded and in trouble, feet so heavy—a man so wrong as to help himself immediately with praise for something religious. "Mama, que Dios te bendiga." He asked God to bless his mother.

Ricky Roy bolted upright and smiled at my favorite uncle. "Tío, nana never needs any of us to bless her."

"Rickie, ya vete a tu casa." La Sra. Soldano was firm and in charge. "Go home."

Ricky bolted and was gone in the flash of sunshine on broken glass.

More often than not, after finishing my paper route, I fell asleep before getting ready for school. My granny didn't get mean, sometimes she woke me with her favorite imitations of birds. Other times she sang old songs. Whenever she awakened me, I noticed a certain happiness, one that is restricted and found only in the soul of lost angels. But that day, with newsprint and the satisfaction of having watched Mrs. Triana's bathroom habits all over my fingers, I was startled when granny woke me. She was talking to me in English.

Abuelita was practicing speaking her new language for the party. She was spooky with her, Tejana dialect, "Wake up, niño. Escuela, school, it almost ready, mi'jo."

I screamed.

"Quieto, niño, qué te pasa¿" Skinny, white-haired granny flew a gypsy smile across my face. "Quiet, boy. What's wrong with you¿"

"Abuelita, I didn't know who you were. What did you just say¿"

"Nada, hijo. Nothing." She was both a bug and a ghost, hysterically biting me with her grin.

"O.K."

When I came home from school, big Gina and her southern girls were in the house. Whenever Gina wanted to bake, she would come over to use the big oven installed many years ago by my great and dead grandfather. The baker left behind almost a complete bakery inside the yellow bird cage. Gina was baking some kind of bread I'd never heard of and the girls were both scrambling around the house. Tío Martín told Gina that the family was planning a huge celebration in her honor. Upon hearing that a party was to be given for her, Gina's smile crossed the desert like rain. I began to feel miserable and didn't know why. I didn't want to believe it. After that day in her closet, whenever I saw Mississippi Gina, her smell became the gray beginning of life for me. It was a period of joy so absolute as to remain forever. The breath of yesterday spilled onto her thighs with the excrement of the moon. I wanted her to push my face into her crotch. I wanted her to show me how to kiss. I wanted her to teach me how to love a woman. I wanted her to be close to me. Something beyond a dream. I wanted her to lift my body up and bring me to the river of life. I wanted her to surrender her mothering to a little boy. To forget her own girls. I wanted her to kiss me and let me kiss her back with soft boyhood moans. I never wanted to be around her.

Gina survived my fantasies because she was not interested in me. I knew from the time she walked in on me when I was in the bathtub. I was soaking in the suds, watching my erection surface above the water line, pumping lather and soap on my twelve-year-old penis. When she walked in she only stared at me. Then she said to hurry up because the toilet was waiting for her. The door closed and my little pito collapsed. *Farm girl, Come back and secretly gather my wish between your long fingers and gently stroke me.*

Instead, Gina pounded on the door and told me to close the shower curtain because she couldn't wait any longer. "Damn, Buzzy, I gotta pee so bad my back teeth are floating." I obeyed her command. She stepped into the bathroom and covered the toilet with her Biloxi buttocks and peed. She was too fast for me. I couldn't figure out how to peek at her. I smelled and heard everything. I wanted to watch her so badly, the same way I could watch Mrs. Triana.

Tío Martín talked to his compadres at the Legion Hall and they decided to book the hall for us two weeks from Saturday. The American Legion building was a structure that has seen mayhem, agony, desperation, and many parties. From las bodas de sangre to the high school proms to the official celebration palace for the war veterans, it was the only hall our family ever used for big events. Now it had been scheduled for a welcoming celebration of our new Biloxi girl and her daughters. Ricky Roy was happy. I was nervous. Old man Acosta took control. He said the hall would be fixed up like it was a wedding. Nana Kika and Don Martín negotiated the cost.

When the big day came, it was hot. Nasty desert hot in the middle of summer. For me, that was always the best time of the year. Not only because of baseball, but because all woman smelled of desire in the summer. They stuck themselves full of douches that worked miracles against the air wandering onto the small crevice of their center. I bathed with them and held the nozzle. Deliriously. A small long climb into my lost mother.

A Saturday mass was held before the great ceremony. Cousins I hadn't seen in two years were there. Everyone who had ever worked at the mercado with Nana Kika was there. It felt like everything I had ever read about New York City. Millions of people and endless images. A confusion from the ordinary day. La Red and her new friend quickly hugged me and promised me thousands of smiles if I would steal some mota from Tío Martín's MG. Sure, fine. Girls. My legs are yours to move any direction. Uncle caught me with my hands in his trunk and smiled. "Buzzy, I know this mota is not for you. Who set you up?"

"Tío, I ain't telling."

"Bueno. Don't tell. But the girls don't get any if they can't ask for it themselves."

"How'd you know it was the girls?"

"Hijo, they both got you wrapped around their tiny curls. You don't do nothing for nobody unless it's for them. So just tell them they gotta ask me. Y no digas nada, don't say anything, to you-know-who. If Nana Kika finds out, she can still kick my ass. Tell them to come outside. I'll stay here in the parking lot for a while."

It was a tremendous party. Ricky Roy and all of his stupid police buddies couldn't stop slapping each other around. The women brought my favorite smell with them. It is carried by a woman wanting to be at a party. The uncles from nowhere were now important and talked loudly about their mighty positions in many different companies. Suddenly there were vice-presidents in our family... and corporate executives who single-handedly had saved their empire from collapse. One of my lost aunts was now a singer for a band... and they were travelling between Silver City and Alamogordo and even Tucson and Phoenix.... A vice-president of an oil drilling operation was talking about going to Alaska... nobody believed him. I did, and told him that a moose is called an alce. He ignored me.

They banded together with the blandness of lies.

Singers sealed my dreams. The band was eclectic. A tornado at sunrise was all I wanted. But Uncle Martín had told me long ago that El Paso never gets tornados because it is surrounded by mountains. I went outside to the parking lot and listened to him tell his mota-smoking nieces that they should never smoke that stuff with a guy, "unless you are willing to really go crazy . . ."

My great girl cousins asked, in unison, "And you, tío, you are the craziest vato in this entire familia . . . oye and why can't you stay with one slut, O. I mean why can't you stay con una puta no mas. . . ." They laughed big. Two girls who so wildly and quickly became women never stopped treating me like a little sissy boy.

Ricky Roy screamed through a megaphone ordering everyone inside for the special ceremony. Nana Kika welcomed Gina and her daughters in English. My MG uncle and half the vatos in the parking lot missed most of the welcoming ceremony because of their slow walk in to the hall. That night the hall was filled with dresses and dancing shoes, sharp suits, eyes pointing toward the reunion of a moonbeam, wet lips and dry mouths. There was just enough wiggle in my toes to carry a hand on my arm and just enough newness to make me believe I was headed on a trail that led in a straight line to heaven.

Gina, Ricky Roy, the girls, the drunken German priest, and the enormous goodwill and beauty of Nana Kika filled the stage. Ricky spent too much time talking about himself and the Air Force and the South. Gina cried. Gina's girls were oblivious. They must have been hanging around uncle's MG. It had never occurred to me that my grandmother needed to speak in English for anything beyond a simple yes, no, or no entiendo. The priest offered his blessing, but no one was listening because La Señora Kika Soldano was ready to address the crowd. She looked nervous and unprepared. At the mercado, she controlled the crowds. Tonight, she stumbled in words that were not hers. "Hallow, ebb re buddy." It hurt me to listen to her speaking in English.

She went on. "I want to welcome the South to our house." Then she publicly promised to speak more English to Gina and the girls. The high throng of bilingual partygoers gave her loud and lengthy applause. The cheering was so heavy it smashed my feet. Feet that moved me out the door and into the night sky, falling in an entirely new way for me. Never had I seen a sky look so gloomy while being so pretty. Stars were jumping off the hot desert floor of sunset. My favorite pinks were whipping the mountains. I felt lost and alone again for the first time in many years. My feet walked me to the freight yard. I was almost thirteen and ready to hop my first freight out of town.

It felt like I was six years old again and listening to Isabella say things that I did not want to hear. I did not want to hear my abuelita speak to anyone in English. I did not want her to change.

IX

Travelling with Men

I hopped the first of many freight trains from El Paso to Los Angeles. Southern Pacific ran a daily passenger train that left for L.A. every morning at 6:45. The one-way fare was $27.45, but I had no money. In the early 1960s, boxcars were free. The first freight I jumped onto contained five men headed for new destinies. No one volunteered a name, so by the time the boxcars were rolling past the smelter town, I had named four of them after my favorite baseball heroes. Ernie Banks was hunched in a corner smoking bright ashes. Luis Aparicio paced back and forth near the door. Jesús Alou stood still, waiting for the next pitch. Juan Marichal was kicking the side of the car. I could not name the last player because he avoided contact with everyone in the boxcar.

A dead body discovered on the side of the rails in Tucson prompted the railyard guards to chase everyone off the train. There was a long delay. The body had been found the day before we arrived. Big men in uniforms with well-fed bellies searched us and kicked us and insisted that we would soon be licking their boots. They said this was a lucky day for us because they decided they did not want their boots to smell like dogs.

Juan picked up a big stick and went after a cop. Ernie grabbed him from behind and scolded him. "The sons-a-bitches will kill us all if we fuck with them." Juan carried the weight of a madman in his eyes. He didn't respond. He was frozen. I listened, petrified, praying for Ernie to keep his hold on Juan. The Chicago Cub became a bear. Ernie held onto the wild beast long enough for us to live. The railyard monsters with badges howled at us to leave their land and their trains.

Ernie told me to follow him. Once we had strayed far enough away from the other travellers, I watched as Ernie rolled a thick cigarette. He handed it to me, saying that if I had never known a strawberry field, I would know one now. Marichal and Alou followed us. They laughed as soon as I took a hit. There was a brief pause in the history of my life and the next sound I heard was a loud scream from Juan telling me to hand him the puta mota. Jesús just stood there, waiting for his next pitch. Ernie finally grabbed my attention, laughing and telling me to hand the cigarette to Marichal, " ... before he goes and kicks something. A madman waits for nothing."

On the first day of my life away from El Paso, I saw my first strawberry field. A field of wild berries, most of which were not straw. Make-believe fresas. I stood there, in the Tucson desert, reminded of the tree I had moved for my grandmother. Abuelita Kika had insisted that transplanting trees in the El Paso desert was necessary for our survival. Cousins Leticia and Fernandino had been snapped away from us too soon after the death of my oldest cousin, Gloria, the angel. Once, I overheard abuelita tell a comadre that one of the big agonies of my young cousin's death was that it happened on the day of her first period.

A brick building with a tall chimney startled me. It stood against the edge of my horizon as I inhaled the smoke of my strawberry dream. A door opened and a thousand miles of smoke poured onto the flat, brown, sunny landscape reminding me of the Plaza theater during a Saturday matinee. I always loved to leave the noon grip of a West Tejas sun and enter an igloo air-conditioned theater with a sky full of stars on the ceiling. In the early years of cinema, I had a joyful and constant career of attending matinees.

The baseball player with no name walked past us as we shared the mota. He grunted something about hopheads being worthless and spoke to God in four languages before he disappeared into the dust. Louis walked up to us carrying a jug of clear, white liquid. Half of it had already been drained into him, but he shared the rest with us. Ernie smiled and whistled to Jesus. "This stuff is hotter than my last woman." Jesús Alou swallowed his share and continued to stand in the batter's box. Juan said that drinking it made him want to throw his best stuff at the Dodgers. When I took a drink, I felt the desert sand scrape my throat. I coughed and choked, and my heroes howled. Ernie's eyes were gentle. He said I'd get used to it quicker than I could know.

I left El Paso, carrying a small suitcase filled with two pairs of pants, four shirts, a bunch of unmatched socks, and an extra pair of shoes. I was able to squeeze in an extra pair of shorts and one huge wool sweater. The last stuff packed was a writing pad, four pens, and six pencils. The ball players watched me write and a silence enveloped us. I wanted to write a letter home. Their laughter still rides on my shoulders. I stopped scribbling and we headed toward the main gathering of travellers. A campfire had been started and had become a magnet. I heard new noises and began falling into a foreign world. A world more bizarre and musical than any circus or band of gypsies that had ever passed through my West Tejas. A crowd of men were walking into the Sonoran desert. Men with no spare change in their pockets. Each knew when to leave and each knew when to speak and each knew they had given up on nothing. Patience was their pay.

The player with no name sat against a Tucson lightless sky. He was not a member of the group, yet he remained within sight of everyone. Ernie said those kind of guys don't like to be noticed. He asked me where I came from. I was shocked to be asked something so personal because from the time I straggled into their boxcar as the train rattled past the smelter on the west side of El Paso until this moment, not one of these travellers had asked me a question. I had been offered cigarettes, directions, booze, mandates, timetables, dope, advice on love, more advice on losing love, and simple quick responses to living, such as, "just keep jumping on the next train outta town," but not one of them had asked me a personal question.

I told the great Ernie Banks that I come from the home of the Chicago Cubs Triple-A farm club, the El Paso Sun Kings. He asked whether I go to many games. "Man, I tell you, if it wasn't for my stupid friends who get caught sneaking in with me, I would be at every home game. My abuelita knows two concessionaires and when I go alone they let me walk in with them. Whenever I let a pal tag along, the vendors get anxious and swear that it is not good business for me to be spreading secrets. Then they walk faster and when the guard notices the distance between the adults and children, he asks for a pass or a ticket. The beer vendors are gone by then and me and my stupid buddy get thrown out of the park. So I miss out on a lot of games by trying to be nice to my buddies."

Jesús stepped out of the batter's box. He overheard the conversation. He swung at my first pitch. "Listen, just don't stop being nice to your compadres. It makes a difference in war and in peace."

"What do you mean?" My shock had aftershocks.

Louis and Jesús spoke at once and Jesus backed off, letting the great shortstop respond. "Hey kid, it matters if people are your friends. It don't matter who you play with if you're running a game. You can win a game with enemies on your team. But you can't win friends with enemies as your friends."

Ernie coughed, contending that Louis was trying to make sense, but so far nothing does. We all laughed together. The cool night brought chills. I reached into my small bag and grabbed my huge wool sweater. Lawyers and doctors and sons of bakers were adding branches from the desert to a transient fire. Those without warm clothes nudged ever closer to the heart of the heat.

A red cardinal informed me that it was time to sleep. The party of roadside men stampeded into the night and no one had acknowledged any kindness from the night before. I lay on the ground, hugging my large wool sweater. Ernie and Louis said they were going to ride a train back to Chicago. Jesús said he'd wait for the next pitch even if he has to wait forever. Juan raged that his destiny is L.A. and that he'll send for his family once he beats the Dodgers.

The next morning, Ernie was gone. Louis was still sleeping and Jesús pushed Juan's shoulder, telling him the train was leaving. I grabbed my bag, not knowing whether to continue on to California or turn around and go back home.

Trains moved in a thousand directions. My head was tired and my eyes were cut open by a large scorpion sunrise. I jumped into a railcar that quickly gained speed and felt like I was riding a rocket. A rocket taking a child back home.

The bodies are in the air. We are alone. At least I am not buried. If the plane falls into the ocean, that might be all right. I think my body still needs to get burned. I hear something in the cargo hold. An airman has walked into our area with a guitar. He tunes up for a long time. I cannot yet communicate with the other dead. I want to talk. I am talking, but there are no receivers for my new language. Nana Kika used to remind us about how my dad had declared that the language of the dead is not learned until the body is given its final resting place.

The airman sings amongst the war dead. He is polite. The guitar becomes another singer. We are offered a delicate entrance into this new place where we dead must go.

X

A Visit to the Hotel Cortez

President Kennedy was coming to town and the city went berserk. The Hotel Cortez is quiet and proud. The President of the United States of America will be staying in their penthouse. I have been a part-time dishwasher in their kitchen for three months. Bruce Cortez, my little league buddy, got me the job. Brucie's jefe owns the joint and his dad wants him to learn things from the bottom up. So Bruce helped me start at the bottom, too. Because we are only eleven, we are paid daily in cash and instructed to get the hell out of the sinks whenever the bell captain howls, "Just drop your aprons and go out into the plaza. Go play for a while and when the coast is clear, I'll let you know."

Bruce was the best third baseman in the entire Little League. He had the fourth best batting average. With the President coming to town, we're told to take a small vacation. But we still get to hang out at the hotel while JFK is in town. We just didn't have to do anything.

The President's plane landed in the afternoon. Bruce and I timed it so that we would disappear from baseball practice early and get to Five Points just in time to sneak through the crowds and shake his hand in the limo. We were determined that our pictures would be in the papers. Two Little Leaguers shaking hands with Mr. Kennedy. Too bad his wife didn't come with him on this trip. They say she was saving her energy for Dallas.

"Bruce, let's go before Coach sees us." I took my last drink of water before our great escape.

"Buzzy, stop being so fucking nervous. Coach will notice all your wiggles. I think he is already on the lookout." Bruce acts like he is tightening his baseball mitt.

I am pissed off. "Are you chickening out?"

"No."

"Let's go."

"Go!"

I never ran faster. We heard the vague screams of Coach, but we never looked back. We stopped at the railroad tracks to catch our breath. Bruce looked at me and grinned. I smiled back. We were happy. We were five minutes away from Five Points. We decided to run. Good thing we ran because the presidential entourage was moving fast. When we got there, the motorcade had already stopped for pictures of Kennedy with some babies.

We were wearing our scroungy practice uniforms. The President of the United States shook my hand and asked me what position I play. I didn't know why I answered, "I play left field." Left field and pitcher are the only two positions I have never played. Bruce responded that he played third base and the President's voice sounded like a baseball announcer, "Maybe someday the Orioles will need you as a replacement." I guess Kennedy could tell I didn't know what position I played. And that was that. The motorcade took off down Montana Street.

The finest things a grand hotel has to offer are all presented to the President. He stayed only one night. He was in El Paso for the signing of the Chamizal Treaty. The Rio Bravo changed course and clipped off a small piece of old Mejico. She wanted her land returned. So, Kennedy gave it back. Bruce and I ran wildly through the hotel. Because I was with the owner's son, we weren't held back from anything. When we got to Kennedy's floor, we stood guard with the Secret Service. There were three of them. One at the elevator and two at each stairwell. They joked with us that we looked like young assassins and if we didn't get the hell out of their way they'd send us to Leavenworth.

"For what?" I asked.

The agent at the elevator threatened that they will send me away for not being a good hitter at the plate.

"How did you guys know that?" I feel trapped. Now they do know everything about me.

Bruce chimed in, "How do you guys know that? Buzzy ain't worth a shit on game days, but man, at practice he tears them apart."

The south stairway agent joined in. "Because we have been monitoring you, kid. What do they call you? Buzzy? Well, for one thing, you are too damn skinny to hit anything with any power."

The elevator agent ordered us to go stand next to the south stairway. The elevator opened and a doctor and three nurses walked off. They were led into the presidential suite. The hallway was hot with silence. Bruce and I did not move. I don't think we breathed. A few minutes ago, the agents were clowns. Now, they were machines. Suddenly, even their skin changed. Earlier, their pores sweated in the heat. Now they looked like the soldier of fortune guys in Ricky Roy's girlie magazine pictures. These were tough guys.

I knew that Mando from La Bowie High and Jorge from Cathedral High could grow up to be like these agents. They had the same way about them. Mando once said he wanted to be a cop but then, in the next breath, he said that was too low of a dream. He wanted to go bigger. Jorge was the same kind of tough but he was short. Mando said the Feds would never take him, just the way the majors would never take him as a pitcher, because he was too small. "The scouts don't like chaparrito pitchers. They want them to at least look huge. Size intimidates. Plus, we are Mejicano bred. And that leaves us out of everything except washing dishes." Mando then slapped Jorge with a wet towel and they started chasing each other around the kitchen.

Mando's uncle, the chef, screamed at both of them to stop the shit. They both went back to the dishwasher. Bruce and I stood there, talking about what we have just seen. I asked Bruce a question, "Did you see three nurses walk in?"

Bruce gestured like he was smoking a pipe and

thinking hard thoughts. "Yes. Yes, sir, I did see three maids, I mean, three nurses and one doctor walk into the room of the President of the United States of America."

"How many walked out?"

"Two nurses and one doctor."

Jorge and Mando were wild with envy. Jorge was short but he was very loud. "What the shit! Are you guys halando our huevos? Don't be yanking us by the balls. Is this for real?"

"Sure." Bruce was the patron's son and they believed him.

Mando's uncle again yelled at all of us to cut the shit. "Brucie, cabroncito, you and your sissy compadre can just get the hell out of this kitchen. Stop fucking around or I'll tell your jefe. So just get out and let those guys do their work."

I got mad at the chef. "Why you calling me a sissy?"

"How many hits did you get last night against Odessa?"

"Nobody got a hit against them. They no-hit us."

"Yeah, but you still looked the worst. At least the other guys got some fouls balls. If you don't start hitting something, you're going to be lavando trastos, washing these same dishes for the rest of your life. And I will be watching over you on each plate. Not even your Nana Kika will be able to save you. How would you like that? Huh."

Bruce and I went outside into the plaza. We felt

like big shots because there was an enormous crowd lined on every street leading to el Hotel Cortez. San Jacinto Park (alligator park to us) was mobbed. There was no room for any new bodies. Bruce and I wore security passes around our necks. But, before we walked outside into the crowd, a ground floor agent advised us to stick our security passes into our shorts. "Keep them hidden. And stay invisible once you are outside."

No one noticed two Little Leaguers in the crowd of dreamers. The crowd wanted to sing to the President. Maybe give him a smile. Maybe share a dream. Maybe help him. It was a massive assembly of border town humanity.

"Brucie, look at that one, those are huge. Man she looks good." I stared at a woman who was probably thirty years old. She had enormous breasts and was blessed with legs that could walk across Texas.

"Buzzy, she's too old. She would probably eat your dick and keep it."

"Yeah, I'll let her."

"You probably don't have enough dick to keep her happy."

"Want to bet?"

Bruce spotted two girls our age and motioned for me to move quickly. One was dark-haired with short curls and bangs. The other one was blonde. She had breasts the size of the thirty year old. Her eyes were a new blue and she was exactly my height. Brucie started talking with the dark-haired girl and I began to stutter with my first ever conversation con una hueda. A blonde first girl and me.

Her name was Danni and she went to school at Loretto Academy. I told her that everybody called me Buzzy. "Danni, you mean you are in high school already?"

"No. Loretto goes from kindergarten through senior year. I will be in sixth grade next year. What about you?"

"I don't know. My uncle tells me that I should just give up on school now and go straight to college. But, yeah, I'll be in sixth, too. I have lived in this town forever and I was sure that Loretto was just a high school."

"Well, you're wrong." She smiled with a grin that said she knows how to be in many places at one time. Her eyes turned into opium. I was getting addicted to her.

Her friend, Yvette, was from Canada. She only spoke French and some Spanish. Danni spoke French, Spanish, some German, and of course, English. Danni was a military brat. Her dad had been stationed all over the world. Yvette was just visiting for a few weeks. They were trying to get a glimpse of the President. Bruce and I were afraid to let them know how important we were. After two glances at one another, we didn't miss a thing.

Bruce spoke to Yvette en español, stating proudly that his dad owns the joint where el presidente is staying. She laughed at him and mentioned that about an hour earlier, two soldiers had told them that they were here on special guard duty for their commander-in-chief. She said that they promised to sneak them in to see the prez. "So why should we believe you guys¿"

"Really, my jefito owns the joint. You guys want to come in with us. Buzzy, show them your badge."

"No. Man, it's in my shorts. Show them yours. I ain't taking it out here." The girls both laughed and said that we were even funnier than the soldiers.

Bruce pleaded with them to wait for us while he and I walked downstairs into the men's bathroom so that we could take those passes out of our chones. They laughed and ordered us not to be too long because then they would know we were doing something dirty in there. We got downstairs and the bathroom was empty. Bruce had to take a leak anyway.

"Buzzy, how much hair you got¿"

"I don't know. A little."

"You got any¿"

"Yeah."

"Let's see." Bruce turned around and I saw his penis. But I couldn't see if he had any hair.

"Let's see yours. I bet you don't have any."

Bruce unbuttoned his blue jeans and lowered his shorts. He didn't have that much hair, but he had more than I did and his penis was hard. I showed him mine. My hair was very fine and just starting to grow in. My penis was soft. He grabbed it and I watched it get hard. "Let's see whose is bigger when they get hard."

I grabbed his dick and we both tried to get ours bigger than the other. Then we put them next to each other. It looked like a draw. When we heard someone coming down the stairs, we quickly buttoned up.

The girls were talking to some big high school football players. We stood around and waited a while. Then, we got too impatient and started to walk away. Danni yelled for us not to leave. "Hey, I thought you guys were V.I.Ps. Aren't you going to take us inside?"

After almost jacking each other off, Bruce and I did manage to take the passes out of our shorts. I answered, "Yeah, we can get you in, but just you two."

The football players did not believe us, so they scowled at us. Bruce and I walked across the street back to the entrance of the Cortez and waited for the girls. They ran fast across the street and joined us. The guard signed them in as our guests, after he talked to Brucie's father on the phone. Mr. Cortez was in his finest hour. Granting wishes for those who have been denied. The guard commanded us to stay out of the way and said the big shot Mr. Cortez promised to kick the shit out of us if we got in any trouble.

We took the girls up to the Kennedy floor. The same guards were still on duty. The elevator one let us walk off the elevator and the two stairway guards started snickering at the girls. South Side said, "Watch out girls, because the little skinny one can't hit anything. And I'm not sure about the tall one. He looks like he could be weird."

North Side spoke his first words. "You young ladies look way too old for these little boys. You need to be looking for a real man."

Bruce shrieked, "You can go to jail if you try anything with these two. They are too damn young for any of you."

North Side mumbled a slow response. "You will never know how impossible it is to put us in jail. It would be easier to have us killed than to try and jail us."

Elevator gave North Side a look of contempt and then ordered him to shut the fuck up. North Side obeyed.

Yvette and Danni looked scared until South Side got decent with us. "What grade you girls in? Someday, if I have kids, I hope I have daughters that grow to be just as pretty as the two of you. Now, if I have boys, I sure hope they don't grow to be as ugly as these two. O. I would have to toss the poor things into a river or something. Hey, do you guys have any friends? And girls, how could you want to be seen with these two monsters?"

We laughed together and because the elevator guard was in charge, he promised us that he would ask the President for autographs for us. "But we must wait until after the nurse leaves. Do you guys have something he can write on?"

Danni said he could sign her bra. Yvette said he could sign her stockings. I said he could sign my shirt. And Bruce said he didn't need anybody's autograph.

Then he wished aloud that he had brought his mitt with him.

Danni walked over to North Side and started a conversation with him. It was hushed and I couldn't hear what they were saying. He wrote something on a card and gave it to her. They continued talking while Bruce, Yvette, and I traded jokes with Elevator and South Side. Elevator was as old as Mr. Cortez. He was divorced and had three children who lived with their mamma in Atlanta, Georgia. South Side was almost thirty. He had never been married. Too much travel. He said that he was only home about four or five days out of a month.

North Side looked like he was barely twenty-one. We didn't know because none of us, other than Danni, talked to him. They talked together for a long time. She laughed and he moved around her like a hungry bear who has found a river full of fish. Danni glittered in his shadow. They looked splendid. The river is green and fast. It is running with the waters from ancient glaciers. He finds the bend where the fish are pooling. He looks for her. He waits until she crosses his path. Large arms scatter the water. She was there. Her need was to become filled with his desire.

The nurse was leaving but she was no longer wearing her nurse uniform. What hair. Big, long, blonde and wavy in a strapless dress that looked like waxed paper wrapped around her. And what eyes. The precious eyes of a great one. She commanded more respect than the elevator agent. He obeyed her completely. She giggled at us. "Are you kids in line to see Mr. President? I just spoke with him and his back is hurting him very badly. You might not get to see him. But I hope you do."

The only operating elevator to the President's floor arrived and another agent escorted the nurse into it. She waved kisses to all of us and threw in a wish. "I hope he talks to you kids. He misses his own children very much. Bye. O, little girl with the blonde hair, you are gorgeous. Stay outta trouble, if you can."

Danni proudly rested her hand on North Side's arm. Elevator looked away from them and South Side talked with us as if he really liked kids. Once the door closed, the agent in charge suggested that it would be a good time for us to ask the President for autographs. He ordered us to knock on the door. Danni came running over. Leaving North Side with his mouth wide open. Four brats were knocking on the President's door. It felt like Halloween. That we would be greeted with treats.

Two giant agents answered the door. We expected the President. Both of them looked like the last time they smiled was at birth. Elevator gave them some secret kind of code, which must have meant we were all right. They allowed us to come in and sit down by the window. One guy looked like Sam the Sham of the Pharaohs. The other one looked and talked just like Wolfman Jack. We sat and listened. Wolfman grumbled, "Which one of you is the owner's kid?"

Bruce was silent for a long time before he answered. "Why do you want to know?"

"Because your old man said that I could lock you up if you and your pals get outta hand."

Bruce had grown tired of their stupid jokes. "You guys are so fulla shit. If I want to get outta hand in my place, I can. And so can my pals . . . in fact, if I want you guys to lick my shoes, you might have to because I got connections. And maybe one of you perverts will get assigned to dishwasher duty if you don't stop fucking with us . . ."

John F. Kennedy walked into the room. His Irish smile surrounded us. The smile that always connected him to us Mejicanos on the border. "How in the world did all you kids get into my room. I think I'm . . . I am going to have to trade all my Secret Service guys for Brinks agents or something. If they can't keep kids away from me, how can I ever feel safe." He gave us that smile that only the gods can give.

We were all standing at attention. Danni's blue eyes became an ocean. Yvette suddenly understood English. Bruce was rigid. I slouched with my grand question. "Mr. Kennedy, do you feel that the Rio Grande has the same significance to Mexicans as the Berlin Wall has to Germans?" I had practiced this question for a thousand days.

Kennedy placed his left arm on my right shoulder. "Son, the schools here are more advanced than I thought. Have you been studying European history already? What grade are you in? Ninth or tenth?"

"No sir. I am in sixth grade. I studied these things on my own."

"You are . . . I hope someday you become a politician. I like your style."

The President signed all kinds of things for us. My shirt. Brucie's. He even signed Danni's bra, but she had to take it off in the bathroom and bring it to him. Everybody laughed and laughed. Yvette spoke a few small pieces of French with him. Bruce talked to him about the stock market. Kennedy advised Bruce to respect his dad. "He runs a great hotel. Mr. Cortez is a fine Democrat. His employees are a sign of good ownership. They all have high praise for the way he runs his business. Pay attention to these things, son, they will be invaluable to you later on in life."

The president looked tired. He had smiled so much it almost became painful to look at him. We had acknowledged our president in our most studied and reverent way. The two bears walked us out of the suite. No other words were spoken inside that room. In the hallway, the shock kicked in. We all acted like car wreck victims. None of us talked. Elevator put us on the elevator. The only one to say, "See you later" was North Side. South Side and the old man both said, "Goodbye."

XI

The Flight Home

To: APO SF, CA
   Box 08444

August 30, 1968

My Dear Buzzy,
I miss you so much. We all need you right now. Did the Red Cross get hold of you yet? Nana Kika died tonight and I called them. I wanted to let you know right away ... Did they reach you? O, Buzzy, please come home. Please. They said they might have some trouble reaching you, but I know you get my letters, 'cause you have answered all of them.xxxx

   I didn't realize she was almost seventy-four. Did you know that?

   O, Buzzy, I miss you so much. Your Rosemary. Tu Red. I laugh and laugh when I talk about you coming home. I am going to play the piano (*like I know how to play). I bet Nana Kika would just listen to me play because she was so patient with everybody.

love always. Red

To: APO SF, CA
    Box 08444

Sept 4, 1968

My dear lost Buzzy,

The woman at the Red Cross told us your unit is on an "unreportable mission." She almost cried as she giggled, "It is kinda like you don't exist."

We so terribly wanted you here for Nana Kika's funeral. Granny's magic was never the same after you left... She kept trying to go back to the mercado, but after you left, she couldn't walk without that stupid cane. Well, one day I was talking with her while she watched, no, no, actually, we were both watching una de sus novelas. I can't remember which soap opera it was right now. O, it doesn't matter. Anyway, she reminded me of the time you and Alfredo replanted a tree for her in the backyard. She was so proud of you. She said, "To this day, it is the only tree that keeps growing." With that funny look of surprise she gets when no one else knows, she told me how Alfredo tried to discourage her from moving it. He thought the tree was at the point in its young life where it was too big to move.

Remember Alfredo, our patron saint of the garden? Nana told me all about him. Did you know that he is already sixty-two years old? He still looks forty. I love the way he looks—that dark, rough, desert skin of a man wearing boots. That fine gift of his smile is always there for me.

Abuelita said it was the first time you ever wanted to own anything. She said you insisted to Alfredo that with your help, the tree could still be moved. So the entire rest of the day the two of you dug and dug and dug ... first you had to dig out the tree. Then you had to dig a new hole for it ... she said you were on a mission to get it all done that day ... Nana Kika smiled that hilarious sonrisa of hers when she started to talk about how tired you looked that whole day. And Alfredo, with that miracle smile of his, moved along with you in everything you did, but faster because he was so used to moving through the daytime of a summer desert. Nana Kika said you were so used to moving through the nighttime of a winter snowfall ... your having been born in Chicago must have caused this. She cried when we walked outside to sit under your old shade tree. You know, there's a bench and a pond underneath now. She looked up at the branches and cried, "Red, this is Buzzy's tree." All of us other kids our entire lives never knew that the most beautiful tree in Nana Kika's backyard, actually, I remember you called it the Southern Pacific's backyard, was there because of you. Your work gave a tree to all of us.

Buzzy, my sweet heart, please come home as soon as you can. Even though you were not here for the funeral, I will let you know what happened. I played the piano, of course. It made everyone cry. Then I asked Jimmy to sing "Amazing Grace." And when the piano playing was over, you would not believe what happened. I heard Nana Kika laughing and telling me that her patience with having to listen to me play the piano was over. Everybody always knew that Jimmy was joto. We all knew. But you were hard to figure out. I remember how I wished that you could be my girlfriend. And I always wished that I could find a man like you. Something about our border makes me want to keep crossing all frontiers. I felt your breath on my neck when Jimmy and I played the final music for Nana Kika. I saw Gloria standing next to Jimmy as he sang. I wanted to see you sitting next to me.

The services were held at Nuestro Señora de Guadelupe. I thought of all those times you and I took the bus with Nana Kika on Sundays when she decided to go to church . . . Nana Kika and you would get into these big discussions. The music stops playing and all I remember is me, you, and Nana Kika on a Sunday morning bus ride to that church. You would squeak at abuelita that this church was too damn far to go just to hear the servicio en español. You couldn't understand why St. Joseph's didn't have any services in our lengua. It was in our own backyard. It was surrounded by raza. What did you used to say . . . "Nana, with our country so full of indigenous and oppressed, why can't these Catholics make every church talk to us in our language?" . . . something like that. Remember how we all used to laugh at you when you would start philosophizing?

The priest was going to continue with the funeral program, but "my" uncle Martín and "your" cousin Ricky Roy walked up to la Señora Kika Soldano's casket. Each of them placed one hand on her box and the other on his heart and began to sing to her. Without music, it is called a cappella or something like that. The walls of the church have never held in what we saw.

Nobody knew that they were going to sing. Our hearts became tabernacles of grief as we listened to these hard men offer their soft voices to a woman whom they loved. As our abuelita from about a thousand lifetimes slept inside her box, two of her men poured her favorite song to everyone. "Cariño Verdad" from Los Churumbeles. Everyone has heard uncle sing a thousand million times, but I had never heard Ricky sing. It was the first time I ever saw them as beautiful. We sent Nana Kika away full of the love she gave us.

Buzzy, please come home. I want to be the one to take you to see her, O.K.¿ We all miss you. We all want our hero to come home, Buzzy. We are waiting for our misdirected angel to come back to us.

love, Red

Nana Kika was getting ready to visit la Señora Bustamante at the mercado. She fell just as she was about to open her bedroom door. She was almost seventy-four but I always felt like she was my age. Tío Martín was walking into the kitchen when he heard the kind of scream that means trouble. He ran to her room and she couldn't move. Uncle had to push the door against her body in order to get in. Her hip gave out for the last time. Many years earlier, before I had helped Alfredo replant Nana Kika's tree, I was the only one home the first time she fell. She broke her wrist and I carried her all the way to the hospital. Good thing it wasn't that far, because I sure got tired. The family always laughed about that story. They would recall skinny little me running three blocks to Southwestern General carrying wild, screaming abuelita. "I can walk. Let me walk. Buzzy, put me down."

And there is no moon left for you nana . . . recuerdo que mi lengua es de usted, recuerdo que me corazón es de usted, recuerdo que mi tristeza es de usted. I will never forget my language is yours, my heart is yours, my agony is yours, nana, and there is no moon left for you . . . in these hills that you never saw . . . recuerdo que mis ojos son de usted, recuerdo lágrimas, sonrisas, el sol jugando con Gloria. My eyes are yours. I remember to cry. I remember smiles, and the sun when it played with your tears as you promised me that I just had to ask God anytime I wanted to play with Gloria . . . there is no moon left for you nana.

The messenger is objective but I color him pale. I know what to look for. It is the notice of my abuelita's funeral. She was my mother for seven great and gentle years. She carried me with her from the day I turned six until I hopped on my first freight train from El Paso at the small age of thirteen. I am in a jungle, tightening the growl. The heat is different here. You sweat and sweat and stay wet. In El Paso, you sweat and get wet but you can dry off once you change your shirt. Nothing here can change the wetness. It is full of blood. Everywhere I look, en route to the villages, I see the lonely ghosts of these people's ancestors. Our unit prepares to move on and the message drops to the ground. Hundreds of blood-stained boots trample it into the earth.

XII

Poets and Listeners

Girls from the new side of town thought Chuey Vargas was delirious. Chuey told white girls who asked him his real name that he was "Jesús." They didn't know that Chuey is a nickname for guys named Jesús. He was a monster for his age. At fifteen, he grew a full beard.

I first met Chuey at my cousin Sandra's quinceañera. It was Miss Baca's coming-of-age party. Everyone seemed to be fifteen. I had not yet begun to shave and I had never kissed a girl. Chuey was dressed in "borrowed" purple robes from the sacristy of the Iglesia San Martín. His bearded brown face was punctuated with dark green eyes handed down from a religious fugitive. The first impression he had on many people was that he could have been an escapee from a Federal prison. A maximum one. His voice was purple. The first thing he asked me was whether I thought Sandra could be saved. I asked from what. He said from him.

Chuey, the mad prophet, wondered why I was the only one who talked with him after he floated into the celebration of Sandra's fifteenth birthday, yelling to the crowd that he could walk on water. My Uncle Nestor screamed at him. Sandra's younger sister, Pulgas, tried to bite him. We called her Pulgas because she acted like a flea. She never stopped trying to bite boys. Pulgas was twelve and already considered boys dogs.

Chuey's entrance left people stranded in mid-sentence. Silence, then loud confusion. I laughed and waited for the fury to die. Then I welcomed Chuey by handing him a stolen, paper-wrapped quart of Pearl beer. I had taken it earlier from the backyard where all the older neighborhood vatos and my uncles were singing and sipping and praying. Chuey, the Jesús from the south side of Zaragoza in the armpit of West Tejas, blessed me for my offering and thanked me publicly. Loud enough and mad enough for all in the house to hear, he declared that we should go outside and bless the old men in the backyard who were suffering for their sins. We glided outside.

Pito Echeverría, the west side's mortician, swallowed a drink of extra suave pulque and asked Chuey, "Vato, why you always fucking with that priest shit?" The men laughed a laughter sprayed with fear.

Chuey chugged another hit of la Perla into his Jesús throat and hit the hardened men with a soft response. "Because I love."

The silence was drunk.

Uncle Nestor walked into the silence and woke everyone by asking the young madman, "So, why'd your parents name you Jesús anyway¿ You're too loco to be anything other than un zero a la izquierda."

Young Jesús ignored Nestor and asked the crowd, "Any you guys ever hear of the poet, Pablo Neruda¿"

As the group of small-town drunks shook their heads into the unknown, my Uncle Roman told me that if my dad were still around, he would know who this punk Chuey was talking about. Chuey tossed another one of his savior smiles at the negative nodding and pulled a small book from under his ecclesiastic robe. He began reciting, *"Cuerpo de mujer, blancas colinas, muslos blancos,"*

The men did not defend nor accept Chuey Vargas, but they did listen. Chuey decided to start over in English.

"Body of a woman, white hills, white thighs,"

No one made a sound as the gray eyes and the gray mood and the gray agony of the men surrendered to Don Pablo and his crazy disciple.

"But the hour of vengeance falls, and I love you," Chuey stopped to light a cigarette. The silent men waited.

"Body of my woman, I will persist in your grace.
My thirst, my boundless desire, my shifting road . . ."

Those hard men with bruised hands and swollen faces cried as the salt air from Neruda's poetry exploded in their lungs.

"Dark river-beds where the eternal thirst flows
and weariness follows, and the infinite ache."

Uncle Nestor re-sparkled the drunkenness with his

response. "Chuey is a great example of the infinite ache." Jesús/Chuey suggested that we not drink with the men because they would eventually get too mean. Some had already begun their cries about the horrors of their women. No. They had all begun to moan about the terror. The constant lament was opaque and brief. "She always wants something I don't have."

Uncle Nestor had too many quick answers. "You just give them what you got. If she don't like it, kick her ass out on the street. Then she can learn what it is to be white. Those gavachas just love pretending they can survive on the street. And all they want is dark cock and a green wallet."

Jesús interrupted. "Oye, Nestor, how do you know this?"

Then Nestor stumbled as he tried to punch Chuey. Too drunk to make contact, my bien borracho uncle fell against the rock fence. It cracked the skin on his scalp and suddenly the attention of the older men changed as they helped one of their wounded. Jesús stood there with his full beard and his crooked smile and his broken face and his fifteen-year-old soul, proclaiming "Nestor is not an idiot. He is just lost."

Chuey and I walked back inside the house to join the women and their young. Sandra smiled. Chuey and I were the only men in the house. We sat on the living room sofa, which was used only for special occasions. Weddings, funerals, and coming-out parties.

My Tía Yolanda and Uncle Nestor had three daughters: Irma "la Rubia," Sandra, and Pulgas. Three sisters from three different countries. Irma, at nineteen, was still the only natural blonde in our family. When we would tease her that she was from a wandering lechero, she would always answer. "No. Not the milkman. It was the priest." She was a soft and dark-eyed beauty with the funny colored hair. Our Blondie discovered early that her beauty could get her out of town. A film crew from the United States Information Agency was producing a local documentary on "Spanish" border towns. The producer promised a free ticket to freedom and she fell for him. Tía Yolanda declared that it was la Blondie's fault for getting in bed with a Federal agent. My aunt has always charged that the pain inflicted upon her by her eldest daughter was the most severe.

Blondie had no other name to us. But for the producer, she used her real name. "Irma" sounded funny when we heard that skinny tall gavacho with yellow teeth and a bald head call her by her real name. He looked to me like the pervert, Oscar, who owned the laundromat. Oscar was known for giving free loads of wash to any woman who was willing to watch him shake his thing in the bathroom. I remember watching him a few times. The legend of Oscar was that his thing was so tiny, he was embarrassed to put it inside a woman. But he liked sitting in a dark corner, shaking it and watching a woman touch herself. Eventually, the laundry went broke and Oscar decided to go to New Orleans on the Southern Pacific. But instead of boarding the train, he stepped in front of the lead engine as it approached the depot.

The Federal government film producer did not last long with our Blondie. She left the creep in Los Angeles after he introduced her to his third wife. Blondie was supposed to live with them in some weird mom and dad arrangement. Tía Yolanda was detailing the reason for Blondie's absence from Sandra's quinceañera when Blondie walked down the stairs and, without crying one single tear, sat next to Jesús, the young savior, Vargas. Chuey smiled and offered her a taste of la Perla. She swallowed loudly.

The summer before my second year of high school I changed my clothing style. I started wearing Tony Lama boots, Levis, and let my hair grow long. Wearing boots made me feel taller. And tough for the first time in my life. The hair down to the tops of my ears made me feel wild. On the first day of school I wore my shiny, burgundy-colored, ostrich leather boots, new, washed and shrunk, Levis, and my revolutionary hair. I was not allowed to enter the Jesuit-controlled building. My hair was "too long." I would not be allowed access to school until I went to a barbershop for a proper haircut. I walked away from the religion of my youth, never again to turn back in that direction.

The first two months of my second year of high school were spent following Jesús "Chuey" Vargas everywhere he went. On our first "school" day together, we stood on the middle of the Sante Fe bridge and "J.C." pointed toward the Franklin Mountains. Chuey and I had backtracked from his cousin's restaurant in Juarez.

Ciro's was our favorite place to eat whenever we crossed the border. Ciro never changed us. He told his crew to serve us anything we wanted. Jesús, in turn, helped his cousin learn more English words. We even got free beer because Ciro said Chuey was destined to become a great poet and teacher. He swore that someday Jesús, his primo a todo dar, would be a saint.

With our bellies full of Juarense food and Juarense beer we stood together under the bright sky. I felt contempt for El Paso. For the Tejas skyline. For the border guards that would not allow Juarez whores to cross arm in arm with me. I wanted to feel the same, but I did not understand the separation of skin by invisible lines protected with lethal weapons.

Jesús shouted at me, "Buzzy, look at those old rocky dirty mountains and then look to your right. Los gavachos have filled us with their right-handed history. When we look to the north, their homelands are always to the right. Right-handed history gave us anglo poets like T. S. Eliot who suffered to become something other than American. This vato Eliot was born in los Estados, but he spent his entire adult life trying to become an Englishman. His point of origin is not ours. He wrote all this shit and nobody knows what he is talking about, but the universities declare him a great poet."

I remembered having read the poem. "Chuey, the only fucking Jesuit at that school who was worth the sweat off my balls, Brother 'Honorary,' as we used to call him, made us read 'Wasteland.' Shit it took me a week to figure it out . . . but it made me feel so good inside about something that I didn't understand what that something was . . . so, does that make a poem good? What about Don Pablo? How did he react to this lost Americano, English poet?"

"Neruda could not stand for that. Don Pablo was more tuned in to Whitman and Walt's absolute love for humanity. T. S. was a liar. You're right though, his poem, "Wasteland" was great. After I read that, it was impossible for me to read anything else of his because I expected the same understanding. We never connected again." Chuey lit a joint.

"And some guy named Pound suffered because his philosophers led him back to the Nazis. Buzzy, we are not that way. Listen to Neruda. His heart lives in Chile. He will die in Chile not wanting to be anything other than a poet from the Americas. There are no schools in this town that teach us about Don Pablo."

I dropped out of high school when I was sixteen years old. And then every day seemed like a new summer. I did not return to Nana Kika's house. Granny had always said that all of her nietos were welcome in her house as long as they were going to school. "If you think you don't belong in school, then get a job and find out what it is really like to be out in the world on your own. And if you don't stay in school, mi'jo, that Army will take you and send you into war."

The sun was sartorial on the day I first went to work during a time when I should've been in school. My faded Levi's were stained with old paint. This old pair of pants and I had gone through a thousand-day nights. Yet, they still clothed me. The muggy room cradled us. I had moved into an unnamed colonia across from Sunland Park. To the south of us the border was now desert. The rio took a turn north toward New Mexico and from this dusty poor colonia it was very simple to get in and out of Juarez.

The roar of dust assaulted me and I breathed in a desert air coated with the eternal footstep cough of migrants. Freddie, the boy with no mother, saw me first and ran to warn the barrio that el borracho poeta has arisen. The truck that came to get me was loaded with bricks and a dented keg of beer. There was no ice and I asked what happened. Jesús (Chuey was attempting to abandon "Chuey" and go back to being Jesús) was driving, so he said, "Just get the fuck on and let's get the fuck going." I told him I was not jumping onto a truck full of bricks and warm beer with two idiots in the cab who don't know how to find ice for the beer. The laughter circled the desert rocks.

Jesús/Chuey had contracted us to work for his uncle as day laborers at construction sites. The old Chuey had also decided that he was no longer a poet. He had become a poetry teacher. He told me I had a talent and gave me some books on poor writers who had spent entire lifetimes trying to write, barely surviving poverty. But my life as a day laborer was brief.

Abuelita was right. I had dropped out of high school at the wrong time. The government had started a lottery for the draft and the first numbers picked came my way. I was not really eligible, because when I started first grade, Nana Kika had lied and said I was six when I was really only four. It was the fastest way for her to get me out of that home where some government agency had placed me. When the military called my number, I revealed that I was not eighteen yet. That my birthday was a lie. I explained I couldn't be eighteen because I had just left my sophomore year of high school. They said they would look into it. I called Nana Kika and she could not remember if there were ever any real papers on me. She said she would check it out. "Do not sign your name to anything right now. Don't accept anything they tell you. It will be a lie," she demanded. But I never listened.

Six months later I was spending my last day at Fort Bliss. I was at the designated turnout spot in McKelligan Canyon waiting to meet my connection. Instead, I met two women on the verge of a kiss which got me wild and high. I watched the two of them sitting in their car. I saw the driver's face. She was dark-haired. Beautiful from a distance. She moved like she was much older than her friend, a redhead. I stared into the soft desert air, impatiently watching them while they smiled at each other too much. I wanted to drown in the mystery of this mid-afternoon encounter while searching for some smooth "brown sugar." Mexican heroin is almost always brown and not very potent, but it gets the chivo done.

This was better than Scenic Drive, where all you can see is boys and girls kissing. Women embracing and touching each other between their legs is different. More powerful. Even after they spotted me watching them they didn't stop. They ignored me and I ignored the world around me. My only focus was on them. Only the three of us were there, sitting in our parked cars in a desolate canyon. I was convinced they would invite me to join them. But they didn't. When their desert fling was over, they drove away and glanced back at me with wide eyes and soft smiles. The car had California license plates. 444 is all I remember of the license number.

First Sergeant Ortiz called out two names. "Verbrosky." "Diss-a-shit." He was mean as ever and waved a signed requisition form in front of us. The form canceled the original request for thirteen more bodies to the Nam. Only eleven were needed. Sarge said it fast and hard. "This fuckin' gook war was not made for punks with colored toenails. You two have been omitted from the lucky list of those who get to go to the Nam!"

I wanted to hear the rejection again. Ortiz snickered that Verbrosky and I were now cousins. Overnight, the magic of rewritten requests had shifted a small numb numeral from 13 to 11 . . . Ortiz, my temporary god, said we were spared the trip to Viet Nam because the commander needed to choose the bones of white bodies for the end of the war. "Hell, all I did was close my eyes and point at two names on the list. The fuckin' war is ending. This kinda shit always happens. I been dropping guys names off the list alphabetically, but today I decided to change things around. You two little shits will remember my pretty fucking face as long as you fucking live. This shit gets me all excited. Saving the lives of little punks gives me a goddamn hard-on. You can give me a blow job now. I'm ready." Everyone, except Verbrosky and me, laughed. "Dismissed. Hey, don't worry, little sissies. I wouldn't let your ugly lips touch my dick."

Verbrosky and I stayed at Fort Bliss for seven days of Army limbo. We thought we would be sent to Germany. But counting bodies during wartime is a fickle game. Our new orders arrived on a Tuesday morning. Verbrosky was sent to Germany. After reading my new orders, I had left for the canyon in search of some brown chivo. I had been ordered into southeast Asia.

Inside this box, I am afraid those hauling me might not like sending bodies to be burned. Specific instructions on my next-of-kin paperwork detail that, should anything like this happen, my remains must be burned. A few of the many jokes on how to cook me bounce in and out. There is much to fear now. If they do not toss me into the oven, this memory will be stuck underground forever. I wanted to learn about Alaska. That estrella de oro in the north always pulled me. Golden star . . . no recollection that I have been there . . . except for a slight, insufficient suggestion twisting within. Did I meet a girl who once lived there? Nothing is certain.

The southeast Asian highlands rage with a crawling infection of gloom . . . A dark red nightmare. A junkie jungle exposing the litter of so many sleepless motions of growth. I want to hush the green silence of terror. A big rain drop slaps an erratic brilliance against a small colored dot. The heavy red crosses the green. O. O map my exploration . . . the last thing I see is a small colored dot and then a rain of brown and red across the green.

XIII

Travelling

with

a

Woman

Once the Army took me overseas, it was la Red who corresponded with me. Mostly, she could not bear the heartbreak of this sissy she loved being taken away from her. I answered Red's long letters with even longer ones. I sent her all my memories. And when I told her about my secret desires, she would write a story in response. I told her I didn't know the difference between porno and eroticism and that I was stupid with horniness. I wanted her to send me a smutty story with cunts and cocks and sloppy kisses and warm, wet bodies and the great smell of an orgasm.

Before the mercado got invaded by la Migra and FBI, I used to sneak into Red's room and slurp through her notebooks to where I found the beginning of another of her "silly little romantic novels." At first it was hard to read because her left-handed writing was so erratic. But after reading the first paragraph, it was impossible to stop reading. When I heard a door slam downstairs, I escaped by climbing out the window of la

Red's room. I walked quickly through the alley, trying to do something with my erection.

Cousin Red had written so much weird stuff and I was the only one in the family who admitted to having read any of it. I especially liked reading passages she was working on. She had recently been selling "novels" to a company that paid her in money orders. She never kept copies of the books around the house. Once she finished with a manuscript, it would get tossed in the garbage. She told Nana Kika that they were not worth saving because they were "silly romantic stories." They were written in English. Her pen name was "Lilly Crista." No one else knew this but me. It was another one of her rooftop revelations. The passages she left lying around the house were nothing like the ones she kept hidden. Around the house, Red would leave a lot of poetry and assorted beginnings of new stories. Hidden in her room were the real treasures.

Red was writing about a girl named Yolanda, and I told her that the story reminded me of the Yolanda who had kissed me before I got attacked by the Nazi mongrel. Red laughed and said, "I use anybody I can, Buzzy." Then she walked into her room and locked the door. She slipped some papers under her door so that I could read them.

I finished reading one of his stories about a woman wearing a pirate's eye patch and her sissy boyfriend and yelled at Red. "How come all your stories sound like I'm in them?"

Red responded by shoving another paper under her door. I picked it up and walked outside.

On the day the FBI invaded the mercado, everything inside came to a halt. Nana Kika was facing ten thousand soldiers. She looked grim. Her place was under siege. Maybe it was ten soldiers ... it doesn't matter, they were all aiming large-caliber weapons at her. The first thing I did was kick one of the soldiers. He moved his elbow directly into my nose and left eye. I saw stars and a white light was wrapped around my whispers. I didn't hear Nana Kika's screams because I was listening to little birds who had voices of steel. Their sound was scratching my ears. The stars were moving in and away and my vision was blurred. I noticed that my hand was soaked with blood and that it was stuck to my left eye. I was afraid to let go because it felt like my eye would drop out of its socket if I stopped holding on to it. I heard la Red screaming. She had never screamed like that before. She kept telling the soldiers that they were all jotos. I heard a terrible noise. It sounded like a little girl's face falling on a concrete sidewalk. My good eye could see that la Red had just been shoved into the ground. A big anglo, breathing with rage, stood over her.

A week after the bust at Doña Kika's stall in the mercado, la Red and I boarded the Southern Pacific headed for Tucson. Nana Kika sent her to stay with our older cousin Socorro and I was her twelve-year-old protector. The rails were passing us fast and Red cried that she wanted to die. I begged her not to do it on the train because I was having too much fun on my first passenger train ride.

La Red, depending on which guy she was talking to, said she was somewhere between seventeen and twenty-six. Her hair was half carrot-red and half red-robin-red. Her face was gavacha pink and sprayed with fifty-two freckles. I know, because after the riot in the mercado, we both got out of the hospital together and she made me count them. I also know that she has 237 freckles on her breasts. That was fun. I lost count on her arms and legs and toes. She even had some on her butt. She didn't have any on her belly or around her pussy.

The day Nana Kika told me to go with Red on the train to Tucson, the brilliant girl la Red took me home in the middle of the day and took off all her clothes and told me to start counting freckles. She kept score until I got tired. She said that when she died, she was going to haunt that guy who got the raid started at the mercado. She was going to come back as a red-haired ghost spotted with the hundreds of freckles on her body.

The lounge car on the train was full, but when two marines noticed la Red walk in, they zoomed in to give up their seats. She whispered a fine "thank you" and we sat down. Suddenly, she was twenty-one and the marines were buying her drinks and buying me Cokes. One guy was from New York. He acted like that was important. The other one was nice. His hometown was

Green Bay, Wisconsin. I wanted to talk to him about the Packers. But he wanted to talk to Red. Both marines started talking at once and la Red just sat back, looking real relaxed, as if she had found some guys who would not get tired of counting her freckles.

The rails rolled by until my cousin got bored with me and told me to go back to my seat. I refused because abuelita ordered me not to separate from la Red. Then the marines turned on their "extra nice," offering me ice cream and candy. The one from New York even took out a dollar bill. I got so angry that I threatened to spill the story. "Do you guys want to really know why she is on this train?"

In unison, "Yeah, why kid?"

"Because she almost sent my grandmother to prison."

Red wiggled and smiled. "You guys, Buzzy has always been lleno de chistes. He just likes being a clown ... Buzzy!"

The nice one was determined. "So kid, what did she do?"

Red would not let me answer. Her entire body transformed. From eyeballs full of flames, to fingernails embedded in my arm. Still, she was polite with the marines. "Thank you, guys, for the drinks. It really was very sweet of you to let us sit down. Maybe we'll see each other later. We have to go now."

In unison, "Are you sure? Can't the kid find his seat on his own?"

New York offered his condolences. "Hey kid, I hope you survive."

The nice one invited la Red back, "once things get settled."

The movement of the steel wheels on steel rails was smooth. The movement of la Red and I walking back to our seats was nice. "God, Buzzy, after all this time I thought I could trust you. How could you be so pendejo as to try to tell complete strangers what is going on in our familia?

"What do you mean?"

"Don't act so stupid. And listen, I wanted to get away from those guys anyway, and so did you. O.K.?"

"I know. Oye, Red, do you think Nana Kika will ever talk to you again?" I sat down in my seat.

Red started to answer, but she quickly threw a blanket over us, saying we should go to sleep. The rails turned into a lullaby as la Red put her arms around me and moved me to lay my head on her lap. She was wearing a short, dark-brown skirt. I rested my chin on her left thigh and she fondled my head around so I was facing the inside of her thighs. As she stared out the window, I stared into her skirt. The train whistled as it passed a small crossing in the night and la Red pushed my face closer into her center. I smelled the smell between her legs. The creation of desire. Slowly, she pushed my face against her V and rubbed her hands through my hair. She hummed a small song. Rails kept rolling. I stayed exactly where she had put me. She kept humming. La Red moved her legs farther apart and hummed me into her V. Her legs tightened. She sounded like she was trying to stop from screaming. I smelled her again. She was fresh and full of something I had never smelled before. I did not want this to end. The night rolled faster than I had ever known. Full of her gentle legs and her gentle brown skirt and her fingers in my hair.

In Tucson, Red demanded that I keep quiet about everything at the mercado. But I didn't have to. Cousin Socorro could hardly contain her disbelief when she picked us up. She was ecstatic. "So, crazy niña roja, what did you do to your pobre nana¿

La Red was even more beautiful when she was embarrassed. "O, Sochita, nada más, but I will tell you it was not my fault."

Socorro, when she lived in El Paso, was known as the family newspaper. Anything that happened con la familia never got past her. She would find out everything there was to know about anybody. Now that she was in Tucson nothing had changed. She even knew about my involvement. "So, Red, y también you were using the Buzzy to do your dirty work¿ You were also using Buzzy¿ Wow, girl."

"Socorro, it's not the way you think. This guy I liked was using me and I didn't know it. Nana Kika hated the guy from the beginning and kept telling me not to do anything with him. She said que el era muy viejo para mi. He was from Chihuahua and a little bit older."

"How old¿"

"Forty-one."

"Forty-one! Mi'ja, are you toda loca? How old did he think you were?"

"Twenty-seven."

Big, brown, tiny Socorro, with tits the size of Tejas and legs the size of tall pines, and la Red, who was everything in perfect proportion, walked into the ladies bathroom together to continue their conversation.

I knew the girls would be in there long enough for me to take a small nap. I sat down on a bench and watched the people moving around as if they were walking into their own part of our tragedy.

"Buzzy, do me a favor, huh?" La Red is holding a large box wrapped in old newspaper. I have just come back from an especially busy day of transporting supplies for Nana Kika's stall. Abuelita yells at Red that she can't send me too far because I will have to go back again to Don Martín's pretty soon. Red is the only girl Nana Kika allows to smoke. Red has a cigarette in one hand, the package in the other, and a promise from both. If I don't help her, she will strangle me. And besides, if I do this right I will earn some extra money. Fifty cents per delivery. Nana Kika pays fifty cents per day. But I'm not comparing, just thinking about how much money it is.

"O.K. But how far do I have to go? I have to be back pretty soon. Look how busy it is today."

"Listen. Go to Alfaro's pharmacy. On the side next to the pool hall, you will see a taxi. Number 4678. Can you remem-

ber that? Should I write it down? 4678." Red gets a marker and writes the number on an old rag. She throws it into the wagon along with the box. "When you see him, just give the box to the driver. That's all. Then come back."

The taxi driver in cab number 4678 looks like a girl but he is really a guy. 4678 takes the package and drives away. Red reveals to Nana Kika that she and the viejo have arranged to buy clothes for guys who want to dress like girls but are too embarrassed to shop on their own. She buys them everything on their lists and the viejo charges them double what they cost. They are willing to pay. Many of them are married, and still joto, but they hide it from their wives. Nana Kika tells la Red, "It is all right to pretend." And with one of her sneaky smiles, she says, "Not all of them are jotos." So Red better watch out because one of them will want her to help him dress up. La Señora Soldano, during various periods in her youth, studied with artists, theater people, writers, and gypsy magicians. She has never been afraid of illusion. "Reality is what scares us all, niños."

The girls exit their warroom with enough laughter to fill all of Tucson. Socorro, at thirty, has a college degree and worked at the University. She used to say the more she dressed up, the more those gavacho professors would chase her around. She would proclaim boldly that half of them were in love with her. Sochita never married. The longest time she ever spent with a boyfriend was three years. That was in college at the Texas Western. They graduated together and the gavacho left town with a million promises. He never even wrote her a letter. After that, we never met any of her boyfriends.

Cousin Socorro had a brand new car and lived in her own air-conditioned apartment. It had two bedrooms and a swimming pool. I walked inside and wished I could live there, too. But Nana Kika had her plan. La Red would be trained by our successful, college-educated cousin on how to make it in los Estados. Red said she never liked to read and she never liked to write and she never liked to study. We both knew this was a lie.

"This is not the remedy." Red was reading from a book of poems. I couldn't even understand the title. When she read poetry she always mumbled. "This fine concern invites all into madness . . ."

"Red, what the hell are you saying?" I woke up having to listen to her mumbling from a poetry book.

"Buzzy, child of no one, master of none, this is not the remedy." Red smiled and told me to go back to sleep.

Socorro walked in and laughed. Red was reading from a book a friend of hers had written. Sochie had three full boxes of his books. "You know, Red, you would have liked this guy. Pretty wild, but he was real smart in a way you don't find from those professors at school."

"So where is he?" La Red sounded destitute.

"I don't know. Rumor is that he went to either

Cuba or Bolivia. He disappeared about five months ago. The chota came to my house to ask if I knew where he was. Then after the local cops, the FBI came by and asked the same questions. They wanted to know if I was hiding anything of his. I told them that he had nothing. I don't even think he owned a watch. I told them all I had was three boxes of his books. About four hours later, los federales were back at my door with a search warrant. Esos pinches desgraciados tore my house apart. They looked through each box of his books and went through every page of each book. I know one of those gavacho queers took some of my things. Can you believe they went through all my things? Even my clothes. One guy wanted to know where I kept my dirty clothes. Cabrón! Anyway, I am missing one girdle, two bras, one I just bought the day before, and four panties. Can you believe those guys? The mean one kept asking about the title. 'Just what the hell does that mean? *This fine concern invites all into madness'.*"

"Sochie, did they come back again?"

"No. Once was enough for me. One of the law profs at the school heard what I had gone through and contacted the FBI in my behalf. He's one of the ones who wants me badly. He said he would represent me and promised to threaten them with a lawsuit. The only thing he said to forget about was my clothes. Whoever took them would never give them back."

La Red laughed and coughed and lit a cigarette.

"Do you think he would trade them for some bloody ones from your period?"

"Aye, Red, sometimes I think you are nastier than me. But you're still so young. Probably, huh?"

Sochita finally gave us the name of her poeta friend. Pablo something. She said he kept changing his last name. Part of him was gavacho, but most of him was Chicano. His dad's last name was something anglo and he started digging into his mother's territory for a new last name. Hers was Ruiz, but he didn't think it was poetic enough. He was trying variations on Neruda. Pablo Dura. Pablo Rude. Rude Pablo. Pablo Daneru. Pablo Aduren. She was not certain which name he took with him.

Red asked Socorro, "How good was he in bed?"

"I mean I never really did it with the guy. We would just go out together and drink beers and listen to crazy music and weird poets. He was great, but he never even made his moves on me. And then the first time I heard him read his poetry at one of those weird bars, I wanted to real bad. His words were beautiful and they made me feel so indecent. I just never knew when to make my movida. When I finally decided to make my movidas on him, he was very polite and agreed to get nasty, but he also told me that he would be leaving soon and probably wouldn't be coming back. So I chickened out. Now I wish I had done it. You would have liked him, Red."

"Yeah. At least he didn't fuck you over like that

viejo did to me. I wondered why the boxes were always so big for so little clothes. He would give me a list of different undies to buy. Always two or three nighties. Sometimes a skirt or a dress. But mostly panties and bras and stockings. I would give him the bags and then he would come back later with a wrapped box and instructions on who to give it to. It was always a cabby and one time Buzzy got lost for more than an hour and the veijo was all over me at Nana Kika's asking if I gave Digit the right instructions. What had happened was that Buzzy was standing a block away. Finally, he realized he was at the wrong street. The guy saw Digit running toward his corner in the rear-view mirror and made a fast turnaround. He grabbed the box from Buzzy and didn't say a word. But Buzzy got scared of the look in his eyes. This was the first cabby who didn't even try to look like a girl. He was fat with a greasy mustache and mean looking. If Buzzy had been one minute later, something bad could have happened to all of us. I never saw Buzzy so white."

"Red, I would have been whiter if I had known I was a drug smuggler. How much mota did I deliver anyway?"

"O. Shut up, Mr. little Digit."

Sochie joins in on the curiosity. "Yeah, Red, really, how much yerba buena did the Buzzy deliver? Boy, you guys were doing it for over a year . . . what, almost two years, no?"

Socorro and la Red left me alone on the sofa and

walked into the kitchen. I could hear them talking. It soothed me. They smoked cigarettes and drank coffee. I put my hands between my legs.

The next morning the phone rang. Nana Kika said I could stay over for two more trains, but that I must be back soon for baseball practice. This was the first time she had allowed me to play baseball during the summer. I told her that I could hop a freight that night. "No, Buzzy. You can wait. Little League practice doesn't start until next week."

Red stayed on the phone with abuelita for a long time and when she hung up, her crying got uncontrollable. "Buzzy, I am so sorry. Please understand me. I liked the attention that viejo gave me. He was always sweet with me when we were alone. Always. Buzzy, I am so sorry you got beat up by those soldiers because of me. At least Nana Kika didn't get hit. I got it pretty bad, too, but I guess I deserved it."

I embraced my most beautiful cousin and told her that no one deserved it. Then she cried even louder. Sochie came running into the room, demanding to know what had happened. Obviously, she didn't have all the details about how Red and I got beat up. The Feds eventually called an ambulance for us. When it came, I thought I was already dead and that I was just watching everybody for one last time. So did la Red.

"Goodbye, Buzzy. Tell Nana Kika that things will be all right now. Have fun with that baseball. O.K.? And thanks for taking care of me. When I go to Hollywood, will you come with me? Well, you have to, because

Nana Kika would never let me go without you." Red embraced me with all her fear and it felt like joy. She kept kissing me all around my head until the conductor laughed and said to either get on board or get loved to death. He grinned and stared at la Red.

And Your Eyes, Vague and Wonderful

you enter me

with fever

and high frail notes

of

desire.

the red

ribbon

from

a holiday

gift.

ominous

lights

form

a tunnel.

your

yes

penetrates

me.

we promise

to fly

like

angels

and

laugh hard.

a sad boy

trying

to be

worthy of

a warm girl.

mad and

noble.

—la Red

XIV

They Came Home Before I Did

I never suffered as much in my entire life as I did during the two years I went to church regularly and tried to be one of God's children. The priests confused me. Three of the men in robes at our parish not only listened to your confession, but if you were a Little Leaguer, you also got privately blessed by them in their office. Because I played Little League baseball on a Catholic team, regular attendance at church was a must for starters. Attend church on Sundays or warm the bench on game days.

Johnny Renterría was a mediocre outfielder but he had an older sister who made me lose sight of fly balls when she was sitting in the stands. After Little League ended I did not see her again until a week after I had dropped out of high school. It was early in the morning and she knocked softly on my door. I opened the door into a darkness that held Elena's whisper. It was so harsh it sounded like the kiss of a priest. When you get a public kissing from a priest, it is always after he has made a lot of noise to announce it. He wants everyone to know his intentions are pure. So the racket usually has his bad breath mixed in with a speech about the beauty of God's children and the need to regain one's sense of eternal life in heaven by being kind to the children, especially the boys.

Elena's whisper carried the news that her brother Johnny was coming home dead. She touched my nose and I repeated what she had said. *Johnny Renterría is coming home dead.* A year and a half earlier, he had his birth certificate changed to make him look like he was old enough to enter the Marines. They made a medic out of a boy who was just one week over his sixteenth year. In those days, when this country was just learning about southeast Asia, Johnny was in the midst of its jungles tossing pieces of people into dark, thick bags.

Johnny was the first vato to teach me how to steal hubcaps. When I really got good at it, he was already over there. I would do my night work, thinking about how badly I wanted to let Johnny know that I was ultimately good at it. When he first showed me how to lift them and when I was the most afraid, Johnny whispered to me, "Just don't be too clumsy and too loud. You're supposed to be afraid. If you're not, then you'll get caught. Whisper through the fear that nothing can touch you. Whisper before stealing anything. Whisper to yourself that you will get away." I'm sure he was whispering to himself when the explosion in the Nam made his body look like a truck tire blowing up on the highway.

His mother would not allow an open casket because she had seen her oldest son's remains. His father broke wide open, screaming in the street. It was a scream that rang in my ears for a thousand hours. Finally, my abuelita took Mr. Renterría by the hand and walked him to the hospital. After that day, when I saw Don Pablo Renterría crumble into the arms of my grandmother as she guided him to a place she thought could fix him, I never again saw Elena, but in my mind I can still hear her whisper.

Manny Santiago reads the telegram to us. It states that his primo, Fernie Acosta, has been killed in action. We do a group sign of the cross. Then we make brave promises to get even. We decide to steal a keg from Acosta's warehouse, knowing Fernie will not be drinking with us at his coming-home party. The theft will be easy, because Manny is a delivery driver for his boozeman uncle, and he has keys to the warehouse. We walk inside the old freight-yard warehouse to find old man Acosta sitting there with the tapper ready. His crying sounds like a flooded river breaking a dam. He pours beer for everyone. "I'll pour the first one. After this, you guys are on your own. The first one is from Fernie." None of us talk for about the first hour, and then Turhan decides to thank the beer man, but Acosta tells him, "We all should be thanking Fernie."

Just before the sun rises, during the coldest part of the night, the bells of St. Andy's church rang. It is the choir song of sad angels leaping from destitution. Their angry notes fall into my drunk ears. In the desert of El Paso, these bells signal the return of another boy whose box will be covered with the flag. He will be given glory for his teen-aged death, for having fought jungle commies. It is early in the morning by the time we kill the keg. The big puzzle for us is old man Acosta. No one wanted to leave him. "We will stay borracho with you forever if you need us."

He ordered everyone home. "Hit the sack. A lot is going to happen in the next two days." On our way home, we stumbled through the cemetery where the veteranos were buried. No one remembered the first time he met Fernie, but each of us had a story of our last talk with him. The last time, in this time of grace, was all we had. My last time with Fernie was when we both went to Yolanda's house on Montana Street in Zaragoza. We had to take three damn buses to get there. The transfer at Plaza park took so long we had time to eat at Pinky's hot dog joint. I kept bugging Fernie, asking him why we had to go through all that shit when we could easily sneak into the Plaza theater and watch movies all day. But he insisted on saying goodbye to his Yoli and he didn't want to say it on the phone.

The bells stopped and I was full with the sickness of death. Abuelita heard me in the bathroom. My granny had always been a wise and soft wizard. She said, "More bad happens after the bad than before. And if you do not count your blessings during this nightmare, then your life could remain broken, wounded, and desolate." I did not answer. I heard, but did not hear her warning about Viet Nam.

Fernie came home dressed in colors, carried by

strong, sharp, colorful men. I could not speak about the ceremony because these things are private. Death is a very private thing. Especially for kids. The bad vibrated in my bones and I believed my abuelita was right.

Beto Garcia, my cousin Pulgas' fiancé was the first flag over the coffin. I still remembered the taste of her tears when I hugged her while she screamed. Then, Johnny Renterría. Then, Fernie. After that, they came back in rows and rows. So many that I lost count. Mando, my dad's best friend, and an old fucker who went back to their Guadalcanal days, came back just short of retirement as the casualty of a secret mission. Mando's nephew, whom we used to call, "Stoofo the scholar," was going to teach college. He came back the day after he got there. The young scholar's flag was bleeding during the ceremony. Flaco Leasure, my neighbor who said he was French, and the first vato to teach me how to kiss a girl, got it three hours before boarding the plane to come home.

Everywhere I turned, one of us was dying. Becoming a hero for my dead "compas" didn't take shape in the Nam. After my junkie, Crista days in Deutschland, I was returned to the Nam to finish my tour of duty. I was there exactly three weeks, three days, and three hours. Well, I made up the three hours. Ain't nothing that perfect in the army.

I will come home perfectly dressed in my dress greens. My medals for wartime heroics will shine like stars across a February winter in El Paso.

XV

Everywhere I Turned, One of Us Was Dying

According to the United States government, I am supposed to be celebrating my eighteenth birthday today. The system had been lied to. But in El Paso, if you are Mejicano, they don't care about underage liars. They gobble us up like candy. My military career as a hero didn't take shape quite like I figured it would. If it hadn't been for Johnny Santiago's funeral, I don't think I would have gone. I allowed the U.S. Army to draft me knowing I was underage. Not that Johnny was the first. He was the one who finally tossed me off the bridge of despair. After his death I started to believe that I could go to war and return home as a war hero. Their families would welcome me back as a survivor. A survivor in a box.

XVI

Sky Come Get Me

On my true sixteenth birthday, terror between my knees as I kissed Angie for the first time. Her boyfriend ran the druggiest gang in southwest Tejas. Not just mota, but real chivo. White China heroin. Belligerence runs through soft veins. Or, on discount, brown dirty baja, or brown sugar from Zacatecas. Chivo that would make you suck your dick. I wanted to suck Angie from her toes to her buttocks. She moved about like the movie queens move when their first film kiss is shown to an audience. She was more concerned with how it looked than how it felt. She was Red's best friend and scored some of his chivo for us. "Buzzy, if you do this shit, they can't take you in that army."

"Angie, who the hell said they were taking me? Are you doing this for Red? Did she tell you I'm going in?" I resisted her offer to get stabbed in my crotch vein. She called it that. It is the vein on the inside of the elbow. Angie hit it six times with her fingers.

"Stop. It's not working. Stop damnit. I want to go home."

"Buzzy, you are such a puke sissy. Listen. If those fuckers in the draft center see all these needles and marks all over you, they won't take you." Angie looked like she needed to sell something to someone. Otherwise she was going to lose her house, car, dry cleaning, status at restaurants, and her ability to protect the right from the wrong. Angie was worn out.

Sixteen months later I was in Germany with my army pal, Sammy. He was in a hurry and yelled for sugar. The water faucet was broken, so he cut the brown heroin with standing dish water. The sink was full of day-old stinks. He mixed the dirty water with the sugar, saying, "It will sweeten even the rats." This new stuff had an unknown potency. "If it works," he mumbled, "it will be cheap and sufficient bounty for the three of us."

Crista, his girlfriend and our steady connection, provided the crummy apartment. This was our postwar Germany. All of us in the 62d AD Hawk missile battalion had been shifted from the green steamy jungle surrounding Plieku to the cold snowy Nazi mountains surrounding a town called St. Wendal. Some of us were going back to the Nam but we did not accept that with each other. Sammy and I were in the first group of useless missile units to get evacuated from the Nam. Since the dollar bought almost four Deutsche marks, junk was cheap in this colorful world.

Crista had a soft voice and dark eyes. She had family from the Alsace and fucked for dope. Sammy told me of the many times they were going through a bad jones and she would go get stuff from Bargarder. Bargarder was the shit sergeant in charge of the NCO club. Sammy made so much money from selling dope to the troops, he bought a house for his mother in Brownsville, Tejas. He paid cash. But when Sammy stopped selling, he got pure into fixing. Sarge made sure of that. And Sammy always insisted that it was Bargarder who knew all the tricks. Sammy said that buying a house for cash was nothing compared to what the sergeant had done.

The stuff falling out of the tin foil was so brown it looked like dried blood on dirt. I watched Sammy fix. Crista was a sixteen-year-old junkie. She had been a junkie for three years and her favorite expression was that she would die young and high. I had seen her naked and it felt like a treasure. Sammy always said that if the dope got too strong, he could still get hard, but that he couldn't come quick and the women loved it. If they could get him up, he would go forever.

I peeped at Crista once when I wanted to score after coming down from the missile mountain. It had been three weeks. Sammy was on a temporary duty reassignment. He was sent pushing to the south of Spain from Bargarder. I walked in and heard Bargarder telling Crista, "You look like everything beautiful I have ever seen." They were in bed in her room. It was the finest and goofiest room I had ever seen. The outside windows opened onto the main street, but there was no logical way to walk into her room from the inside of the house. The door to her room was a false window in the stairway. One had to know this. The deception was that good. In one of Crista's many panics for supply, she told me about it.

Crista's mother had abandoned house, children, dead father, memory, and love, and was living in Munchen with no desire to return. She left behind a daughter destined to frogs and foreplay for drugs. Crista said the false window was installed when her mother was a baby. She told Crista that not even the Gestapo could figure out where she hid and to make sure to stay guilt-free and quiet when the time came to hide.

Crista was doing Bargarder with her lips and he had his uniform on. Bargarder was the ugliest, stinkiest shithead with power I had ever known. I was too young to understand this beauty and beast shit. I stood still at her false window and watched him protrude into her face. He kept telling her how beautiful she was and to keep her fingers deep into him. As ugly as the fucker was, from behind, he had the nalgas of a woman. Curved and molded like the curves of a mother who has given birth to twins. She had her fingers sunk into his crack and I heard the explosion. His knees buckled and she smiled and wiped herself on his uniform. He stood with a limp cock over her face as she begged him to finger her so she could come. Ugly Bargarder stuck his tongue at her and told her he wanted to spank her with his belt. Crista asked him for some dope and he shot her up. Then he undid his belt and began to hurt her until she cried. She came with her knees shaking like a misfire and he walked out of the room laughing and commanding that she must obey him. "That is if you know what can be good for you, bitch."

The ugly finger fucker didn't know me. I walked out of the house before him. On the street, I watched him scratch his balls and give some dope to Crista's aunt. I heard him tell Crista's aunt that he was going to butt fuck young Crista next time she begged for dope. Her aunt said she would lick her for him so that he could slide in easily. His junk was heavy in her hand.

The rain felt like mud. The black German sky was spotted with the broken lights of dead stars. I walked fifteen kilometers back to base looking across their Nazi sky for my bearings home.

From:
APO NY, NY
    32d ADA 2/62nd D-Batt
    PFC Dsysia(Digit)

June 17, 1969¿

Dear Red,

Hell, I even forgot how to spell my name and I no longer believe that we are really timing our lives by the number of the year. What goddamn year is it anyway¿ Feels like the dark ages to me. This old Nazi country is full of willing blondes and good dope. Don't know yet if I get to stay here and finish my duty or if I have to go back. Every fucking thing with this unit seems to happen overnight. Listen, over the past few months, I've had some tough dreams.

I haven't dreamed for a long time, but now that I am leaving Deutschland to return to the jungle, I want to know more about these dreams that I don't understand.

                love,

                Buzzy (Major Digit)

From: APO NY, NY
      32d ADA 2/62d Delta
      PFC Digit

Aug. 6, 196?

Dear Red,

This is the second letter but I am mailing them both at the same time. I am waiting for the fkn plane which will be another boring ride across the water . . . lots of hours and then I just touch back down in our country and go back to that sad, red, and green spotted country. My APO address will be the San Francisco one again, so write to me there.

When I get home, when I get home, we will sing songs of being gone, and when I get home we will dance. We will embrace the sun, in pink, small drops, into our red hearts, walking with the destiny of grace from a grandmother who left all of us a trail marked with the common goodness of a woman letting her children feed themselves upon her breast.

It is so hard writing to you because I have to keep trying to correct myself so that you get a letter without too many mistakes . . . but then with you that would be impossible . . . you know Red, it is very difficult to write to a writer because then all I worry about is if the grammar and shit is correct and how you will be disappointed with my poor writing skills . . . but at least I am getting the fucking story down on paper so that if something happens to me . . . Red, I keep having these memories and wondering if they are real. Do you know? My sisters are dressed up. I want to hold their hands and walk with them. They laugh because I am naked. Someone took me to their house. I'm alone with a man who looks like that viejo lover of yours who got us into all that trouble at the mercado, but it's my mother's lover. I hold his soft flesh on my rough fingers. I'm alone with him and he fingers my crotch. The girls laugh. My sisters are always laughing. I lifted him off of me when he was spent. My sisters shushed me to sleep so that I would not hurt. Lifting my shoulders and laughing at my long hair. Longer than theirs . . . I am dead so long from the day I walked away from nana and never said one word about her funeral, to anybody. Never left her either. She woke me up the first time I fell asleep in this southeastern Asian jungle. She helped me wipe off flesh from my uniform the first time I saw a land mine take away a buddy. She always kept something cooking on the kitchen stove, waiting for me to come through the door.

My mother letting me softly kiss her nipples, rubbing me to sleep . . . my mother touches me there in my most unknown center while telling my sisters that if I go with her I won't ever be happy. But maybe if we leave you with your grandmother . . . And I was weeping in the purple clothes of a widow . . . my mother tells me being widowed so young from your father . . . and I was weeping in the quilted night when I sinned with thousands of sinners, breaking our flesh against the stars.

Red you pull me from another memory but I am still remembering. Mail call Sarge announces your words on my letter to everyone in the unit. We are actually breathing salt ocean air for the first time in what seems like years. Those of us who still have all of our body parts attached act like it is the first day of grade school. Shy and excited. Memory ends.

Fear can so quickly turn to happiness. We respect happiness now, like it is the only thing worth moving another muscle for. Like it is the stop and end of our marching through green beautiful buzzing vegetation alongside hills and alongside mountains, and alongside villages. Everywhere villages with great-grandmothers speaking a tongue that was always theirs, and many times, lazy fingers dangling across the sky. Many times, as the others trembled and trampled across an ordinary village with no witness, with no one left alive to be healed by their ancestors. It or we or this or something that I will never see happen again is happening now. We trade agonies with small children wearing large caliber weapons. All the world includes me and all the world uses me, and all the world curves into my gentle moods when I knew I could be anything and when I knew I could fight for peace. But I could never fight. I would so much rather have kissed, held, wrapped around the sulky embrace of a welcoming smile, around the seductive shadow of my mother tossing her nightmares into the sky.

>love,
>
>Buzzy

XVII

Return to Sender

I can see Red. She is talking to Uncle Martín.

Uncle Martín, sitting inside his MG, tries to cheer her. "Maybe now we can have a party for Buzzy when he gets home. I just talked to that Red Cross woman and she said that the Army promised her that as soon as they found his unit, he would be sent home. Beside that, his time is up real soon, so they got to find him."

"Can I get a ride downtown¿" La Red is watering my tree. She is wearing a short dark skirt and very light blouse.

"Mi'ja are you going to go like that¿"

"Oye, tío, how come you only worry about my clothes when I'm outside¿" She moves her hands across the front of her breasts and then sticks a finger into her mouth. She wants him to shut off the engine, call the bakery to say he will be late, and to take her downstairs like they used to before he started seeing his latest puta de Juarez. For Red, every Juarense was either a pig or a whore. Her vision toward her ancestors had been clouded by the white heat desire for her uncle. She did not want him to be a bachelor anymore. O. To be his bride. Especialmente, now that his mother had died. Red felt it was her duty to take care of him.

I was thirteen when Red and I celebrated a new year of hiding in the attic. We climbed up there at two o'clock in the morning and Red told me that she was sixteen and not a virgin when Uncle first took her. She said he always answered her questions with his erection plunging through thin white sheets. That bed and those see-through sheets seemed to first define his territory for her. She needed to touch him and so often after he had penetrated her he would so gently fall asleep inside of her. She had never known that sleep could be so kind. She said she wanted to be his baby, wanted to baby him, wanted to be his mother, wanted to be everything and every kind of a woman he would want. She said Uncle kissed her there and she suddenly knew that history was just starting and suddenly death would never be and suddenly the pushing of herself onto his big erection hurt it hurt Uncle but ... even after he came we still kissed.

I see that Uncle Martín is impatient. "I have to take care of you, baby. If you walk around downtown looking like that, only God knows what will happen. When do you want to go back to work at the panadería? You know you can cashier whenever you want. Mi'ja, it might do you some good to do that again, and it could help take your mind off so many things that aren't going right right now." Tío Martín turns the engine off and jumps out of his tiny car.

Red wants him to pick her up and carry her downstairs, but he gets out of the car to see if there is room for him to start parking it under the tree. She gives up. "Well, if there is room enough for the Southern Pacific back here there is enough room for your tiny little carrito."

"Yeah, huh, the MG will fit okay underneath next to the pond. I can keep it in the shade when it gets too hot." He jumps back in and tells her he will wait for her to change clothes.

Red wants to cry but doesn't. "No, go on, I've changed my mind."

Tío Martín drives away and la Red begins to feel more uncomfortable than horny. She screams to herself. "He didn't even ask me why I wanted to go downtown. After all he did to me, he could at least care about what I am going to do." She goes back to her room to finish writing a letter to me. But I am dead.

The radio disturbed Red in the morning. She was yelling at me from her room. "Buzzy, if you loved me you wouldn't be playing that stupid Wolf Man radio so early in the morning." Red stopped yelling and asked me to go into her room. She was crying.

It was the November of my sophomore year at the Jesuit high school. I still worked my paper route and had just finished another warm and voyeuristic entry into Mrs. Triana'a bathroom. On this particular morning her hair needed combing for a long time. I stood outside helping her with each and every stroke. I helped her with her makeup. With her towel. With her nails. I massaged her feet while she sat on the toilet. I kissed her breasts. She pushed my head onto her lap and she let me feel the pulse in her thighs. Her soft flesh was softer than mine. Her lips were softer than mine. Her hair was softer than mine. The flesh between her legs was wet. Mine was hard. I left her combing her hair again.

I walked into Red's room and asked her, "Which boyfriend is making you cry now?" She laughed at me and ordered me to sit on the bed next to her. She was under the sheets wearing one of uncle Martin's white v-neck t-shirts. Her eyes were bright green from the tears and her hair was a strawberry red with the sun shaking loose the misery from her face. "Buzzy, go close the door and lock it. I want to talk with you about that viejo. That old guy that I've been seeing told me last night that he wants me to live with him."

I rushed back to the door and bolted it shut and told Red she didn't have to whisper because we were the only ones at home. Nana Kika had left early to visit with Don Martín and Uncle was not yet back from the weekend trip he took to Chihuahua. "Red, why do you even like that guy? Qué feo. He is ugly. Kinda like the viejo that always stays at Mrs. Triana's."

"Buzzy, you better stop peeking into her room. If that fucker catches you, you won't have any huevos left after he finishes with you. Besides, I thought I was the one you loved."

"Red, I love you in all the ways of love. What's it like⸮"

"Qué⸮ What is what like⸮ What are you talking about, Buzzy."

"What's it like to be with you⸮" I was sitting on the edge of the bed.

Her eyes said, "Move over here."

I moved closer and touched her face with my fingers. Newsprint was still on my fingertips and it smudged some on her freckles. She put both arms around my shoulders and pulled me into her mouth. We kissed. We did not stop. We stayed in our mouths for more than five minutes and breathing was shared between us, as the first small flowers of the morning sang to us.

When we stopped, Red told me to take off her shirt. I did. I had seen her breasts before but never like this. I put my newsprint stained fingers on her nipples. They grew taut and she pushed my face onto the center of her breasts and told me to lick either one. I started with the right one, went to the left, stayed on the left as she unbuttoned my levis and stuck her hand inside my pants searching to touch my pinga. I had never felt fingers so soft and so full of love ever touch me anywhere like she was touching me. And as soon as she touched me, it went soft. Disappeared. The excitement scared it away.

Red was not a puta from Zaragoza where you would get a rubber put on you by the "nurse" and then just run over to the bed with a dangling erection and stick it inside an old woman's twat and push and hump and listen to her tell you lies about how big you are and how good you are and to hurry up and why does it all take so long when guys have been drinking . . . "and listen, why don't you come by in the afternoon someday? Before you go drinking. Get your pussy first and fresh before all those other pendejos have filled my twat with their purchased love."

Red was the first real girl I touched and kissed this way. So I told her. I also told her that my pinga was conditioned to having a nurse check it for disease first. Red used one of her miracle laughs. It was a laughter she had borrowed from heaven. "O.K. Buzzy, stand up and pull your pants down and let me check that thing."

I was silent as I stood and dropped my levis to the ground. I stepped out of them and then Red noticed that I was wearing a pair of her old panties. "Red, I hope you don't mind but when you throw away your panties, I keep them. I love wearing you on me all the time."

Red shook her hair and flowers surrounded the room. "Don't worry, baby, I'll just give them to you from now on. Looks like we're both the same size. Come here, let me take them off you." I stood in front of the most beautiful girl in the world and she pressed her lips against her old discarded panties and made my small man become a giant again. She circled my erection with her mouth and the panties were crushing me with desire. She started to suck on my pinga through the panties and I started to explode. She stopped. "Buzzy, you're getting your panties all wet, take them off now."

We were both naked in her bed and kissing again and she tasted like the earth on the day it was born. Red directed my face between her thighs and told me to start licking her legs on her knees and then to lick behind her knees and then her legs behind her thighs and then on the front of her thighs, and then to lick between her thighs and to then reach deep between her thighs and to taste her wetness that was flowing out of her center and onto her thighs and I tasted the love that love was made with. She orgasmed with my mouth on her twat and she dripped into my mouth the cum from the old man. We were kissing when I first entered her and we were kissing when I finally got out, which was late in the afternoon. We made an imprint of this morning. We did it again three more times.

O. Green from forever. Snakebites and dancers with children in their arms. Green from forever. A Texas Sunday was invented for dancers whose frontier snakebites have receded. My daddy said that girls who waited for ships to come to port were the isolation that makes men dream. Girls. Think of it son. Fine girls in the Sunday afternoon waiting for a ship to dock. Not waiting for a priest to tell them that they have to keep from sinning. Not listening to anything. Men not listening to anything walking off their ship. Women, waiting for the first whistle. Waiting for the captain. A girl first listening to her lover undressing her. A soft cloud that fights with the sky. A rose in her early thorns. A velvet star. Cross my heart. Cross my country in your absolute desire. I returned from the war wanting all these things.